LULU'S CHRISTMAS STORY

Ludmilla Bollow

Title Town
PUBLISHING

Library of Congress Cataloging-in-Publication Data

Bollow, Ludmilla.
 Lulu's Christmas story! / by Ludmilla Bollow.
   pages cm
 Audience: Ages 10-12.
 ISBN 978-0-9911938-5-1 (paperback : alkaline paper)
 1. Bollow, Ludmilla--Childhood and youth--Juvenile literature. 2. Manitowoc (Wis.)--Social life and customs--20th century--Juvenile literature. 3. Manitowoc (Wis.)--Biography--Juvenile literature. 4. Christmas--Wisconsin--Manitowoc--History--20th century--Juvenile literature. 5. Depressions--1929--Wisconsin--Manitowoc--Juvenile literature. I. Title.
   F589.M2B65 2014
   977.5'67--dc23
                          2014016475

For information, or to order additional copies, please contact:

TitleTown Publishing, LLC
P.O. Box 12093 Green Bay, WI 54307-12093
920.737.8051 | titletownpublishing.com

Published in the United States

Distributed by Midpoint Trade Books
www.midpointtrade.com

Printed in the United States of America

For Mama:
Wherever you are, we know
you celebrate Christmas with us every year
"to make up for the Christmases you never
had..."

LULU'S
CHRISTMAS
STORY

JANUARY 1935

There's this loud banging on our back storm door, as if someone's trying to break into our house. It scares me every time, because that dreaded pounding means another tramp's waiting outside. I quickly run to my watching post behind the bedroom curtains, my curiosity stronger than my fear of strangers. Mama's footsteps click across the linoleum floor and the door creaks open.

"Ma'am, do you have any food you could spare?"

They always look the same. Raggedy clothes, shaggy hair, and oh, such sad eyes. "Just wait a minute, please," Mama says, and goes to the kitchen to fix him an extra thick sandwich from leftovers, wrapping it up in newspaper. She never turns anyone away.

"Thank you kindly, ma'am," the tramp murmurs, grabbing the package. He tears it open right away and begins hungrily chomping off big bites.

"Maybe times will get better," Mama tells him.

"Let's hope so," he mumbles, still chewing as he shuffles away. Only, tramps don't have homes, so where does he go to live?

Last week, Mama bought the popular record, "Hallelujah I'm A Bum." Right away, we wound up the tabletop phonograph, laughing and singing together as the comical song spun round and round. But watching this tramp right now, I know being a bum isn't funny at all.

I'm nearly eight years old and know many things, because reading is my favorite thing to do. I read the newspaper every day, skipping mostly to the funnies in back. Only sometimes I get stopped by stories on the front page, about people looking for work. There are photos of sad-looking families who don't have any money, or even a house; of men waiting in long lines for food from big kettles. I hurry past these stories. It's better reading comics, because they're not true. Mama says newspaper stories have to be true.

I hear Mama talking to other grown-ups about things printed in the *Herald Times*. "Paper says the future of our country doesn't look very good."

"Never been this bad ever before."

Radio announcers broadcast every day, "No good news today. America is still in a great depression, and it won't be ending any time soon."

I'm not sure what "Great Depression" means. It must be about other people, not us. We have a house. We have food. I know we don't have much money, but neither do most of my friends. I think it means everybody's having a sad time because there's no way for them to get food, or find jobs to earn money.

The whole world feels different lately. Daddy doesn't go to

work anymore. He used to work at the Mirro Aluminum Goods Company, a giant building that's shut down now.

We used to run down the block yelling, "Daddy! Daddy!" the minute we'd see him in the distance, carrying his black metal lunch box. Quickly, we'd grab his other hand and walk the rest of the way home with him, jabbering the whole time.

We don't do that anymore.

Some days, Daddy cuts wood at nearby farms, hauling it home in his small car trailer, piling it up against our garage for "the long winter ahead." Other days, he helps the junk man, Krause, at his over-cluttered second-hand store. He brings home different pieces of odd junk, telling Mama, "Well, I just might use that stuff some day, you never know."

And Mama tells him, "Someday, you'll be having your own junk shop right here."

A few times, Daddy even brings the junk man home to eat dinner with us at our large kitchen table, making us squash together tighter to fit Krause in. We try to keep as far away from him as possible, because he scares us—his greasy clothes, dark grizzly beard, and thick foreign accent. He even smells different.

Mama works hard too, every day, but she works at home. Well, except on Fridays, the day Mama works as a cleaning lady.

I hate that Mama has to be away, cleaning for a rich doctor and his wife, when she has children of her own to cook and clean for. It never seems fair.

There's six children in our family. Catherine, Betty Jane, and Buddy are older than me. Sonny and Mitzy are younger. We live in a two-story painted white house on the corner of Columbus Street in

Manitowoc, a small town in Wisconsin. There's a large front porch, dark scary attic, and roomy damp basement. The giant elm tree in front, so big it pushes up cracks in the sidewalk, is our goal post for neighborhood games. I really like that house, except not on Fridays.

That's the only day I come home from school to an empty house. No cooking smells greet me when I open the door. The wood-burning kitchen stove is icy cold. There's nothing simmering on its blackened lids. It just doesn't seem like the same house when nobody's there, especially without Mama.

Because I get home first, it's my job to begin supper. I quickly change my school clothes to play clothes and start shaking out the gritty ashes in the frigid stove, wishing Friday was already over.

Besides having to be meatless, because church rules say "no meat on Friday," food never tastes good when I make it. Pancakes are what I do best. Milk, flour, eggs from our few chickens. I can even make homemade brown-sugar syrup, only mine mostly turns out too watery.

Catherine, my big sister, picks up Sonny and little Mitzy on her way home from school. Grandpa and Grandma take care of them on Fridays.

It's Buddy's job to help me start the fire and dump out the ash basket, because it's too heavy for me. He grumbles about missing his favorite Jack Armstrong radio program as he lugs ashes back and forth from house to ash pile in back of the garage, clomping his knee-high leather boots, with his scary penknife in the boot's side pocket.

Pancakes soon pile up on the plate in the stove-top warmer, and I soon hear voices all over. Catherine tells Mitzy, "Hold still!" while she takes off her outside clothes. Little Sonny races to the play room, making zooming noises with his toy cars. Betty Jane, who's sickly and walks real slow, comes home last, and begins coughing soon as she's in the door. Voices fill most every room. But it's Mama's voice I'm waiting to hear—her voice I miss the most.

Night is already darkening as the outside door opens and Mama walks in. She pauses for a moment in the kitchen doorway, looking like a picture inside a wooden frame.

Her faded blue felt hat's pulled down over her brownish hair. She's wearing her old green plaid coat with the scraggly fox fur collar, which used to belong to the doctor's wife. Her tan cotton stockings have holes worn in the knees from scrubbing floors all day, and her torn rubber galoshes are wet with snow.

"Mama, Mama!" we call, stopping whatever we're doing and running to her.

In one hand, she carries her shabby black purse, in the other, the bulging brown paper shopping bag filled with things from her work.

"I'm home," she says, nothing more, and begins taking off her hat and coat.

As soon as she sets the shopping bag down on the floor, we begin searching through it. First, we look for the Sunday funnies, which don't come with our daily paper. We hastily spread them on the kitchen floor to read, sometimes even before eating.

Within that overflowing bag, besides Mama's used dust cloths and oily cleaning rags, are giveaways from the doctor's house—old fancy Christmas cards, shirt cardboards to draw on, half-finished boxes of cookies, and containers of leftover food, which we kids usually don't like, but Daddy eats anything.

Friday mealtimes are different, too. We have to wait till then to tell Mama all the things we've saved up to tell her. Daddy has first say at the table, and Mama's busy telling him about her day at Doctor Mack's. We've learned not to interrupt. "Children should be seen and not heard!" is what we'll hear if we try to interrupt Mama and Daddy when they're talking.

Even if Mama never complains about going to work at that big fancy house, I notice an extra tiredness about her on Friday nights. It seems all she wants to do is sit, as though she hasn't quite returned to our world yet.

Why does she go away from us every Friday if it does this to her? We don't like this different Mama coming back to us.

One time I asked her, "Why do you have to work at someone else's house?"

"Because we need the money."

I kind of guessed that, but I still want to know more. "But what do you do with the money?"

"I save it for special things."

Only, we never have special things. Never. Well, except at Christmas time.

All year we wear hand-me-downs and discards from rummage sales, play with broken and homemade toys, and divide pieces of candy. But at Christmas, it's as if a magic door opens up and we step through into a never-never land where dreams and wishes do come true. It's always such a spectacular day that the twinkling lights keep glowing in our heads for a long time after.

It's January now, and Christmas has been closed down, packed away. Only, for me, it never leaves; it's always there waiting, deep down inside. Already, I'm thinking about next Christmas. So are my friends.

My Catholic friends all have saints' names, picked out for them when they were baptized as babies. My baptized saint's name is "Ludmilla." Mama named me after a rich lady she worked for who didn't have any children and Mama thought she might will me some money. She didn't. Ludmilla is not a well-known saint's name, and it's hard for most to say, or even spell, so everyone just calls me "Lulu," which I like better anyway.

On the outside I'm plain and quiet, but inside there's so much burbling.

My imagination works continuously—no way to stop it. It's a whole other world I can enter at will, a magical one. And I believe in magical things like fairy tales, dreams, and angels. Most of all, I believe in Santa Claus. Everybody does.

Mama is Irish. Daddy is Polish. At school, we have to fill in blanks that ask what our nationality is. When I ask Mama, "Do I put down that I'm Polish or Irish?" she answers right away.

"You put down you're American. That's the nationality you are and that's what you tell anyone who asks."

On the second floor of our house are three small rooms with slanted ceilings—a kitchen, bedroom, and sitting room where our renters live, a couple without children. Ida works at the tinsel factory, where they make all kinds of Christmas decorations. She gives us discarded tinsel ornaments, and we like to go upstairs and visit with her, but not when Frank's there. Frank doesn't work, he just walks around town lots, smokes a corncob pipe, listens to baseball games or whatever else is on his radio. His radio plays late into the night.

Mama says we can't complain about the noise because, "We need that rent money."

Ida goes to bed early, since she has to get up early, and walks down the stairs real quiet when she goes off to her job. The radio starts playing soon after.

We have lots of relatives. Uncles, aunts, cousins. Some live in the city, others on farms in the country. All are from Daddy's side of the family.

Mama doesn't have any family. That's because Mama is an orphan, always has been, ever since she was little and lived in New York City in an orphanage asylum run by nuns.

When she was six years old, Mama and other orphans were packed onto a train, called The Orphan Train, that went across the country, stopping in small cities, and people could pick out any of the orphans they wanted and adopt them. When the train stopped in Wisconsin, Mama was adopted by some really mean farm people.

Mama doesn't like to talk about those days, but I listen carefully whenever she does, especially when she tells us her Christmas story. It makes me cry inside every time.

"You're my family now. That's all I need," Mama says, and we stop asking questions.

We need her too, because we don't ever want to be orphans. None of the stories I've heard about orphans are very happy ones, especially Mama's. It's scary to even think about it. What would it be like to live without Mama or Daddy?

The other week, my best friend Geraldine and I went to the movies and saw Shirley Temple in *Bright Eyes*. Even before we're out the lobby door of the Strand Theater, my mind's made up.

That's it! That's what I want for next Christmas—a Shirley Temple doll!

I'm so happy with the thought that I start twirling about in the fresh snow, stopping in front of Shirley's giant face papered on the brick wall outside the theater.

"Isn't Shirley the prettiest girl you've ever seen?"

"She's okay." Geraldine begins throwing wet snowballs at Shirley's eyes. "But I still like Jane Withers better. Especially when she plays a spoiled brat, like she just did."

How can Geraldine say such things? All the girls in second grade at St. Boniface School idolize Shirley. She's the model of goodness and beauty in days filled with bad things happening in our city and in the world.

I save my pennies so I can go to these Saturday matinees as many times as I can. My heart gets jiggly as I watch Shirley dance across the big screen, her shiny curls bouncing, ruffled dresses twirling, and her dimpled smile meant just for me.

We know all her songs by heart. "On The Good Ship Lollipop" is a favorite sing-along at birthday parties. Shirley just sang it in the movie, so Geraldine and I warble the words in giddy fun as we walk home together.

Since that afternoon at the movies, my wish for a Shirley Temple doll for next Christmas is topmost. I don't care if I don't get anything else. I'll be so good. I'll come when called, finish my oatmeal, and mind my little brother without whining.

Shirley's bright face appears on the front of the cereal box we begged Mama to buy. We watch excitedly as Catherine opens the box and digs through the flakes. There it is, the blue glass mug with faint white outlines of Shirley's dimpled face etched on the front. Even in all blue, she's beautiful. I can't wait till it's my turn to use the mug.

Sure, there's other dolls on the shelves at the stores, many wrapped in bright cellophane boxes. But for me, Shirley Temple is the doll! She'll be my first grown-up one, too. Betsy Wetsy, my baby doll that drinks water and wets in a diaper—who wants a doll like that anymore?

I can't wait for the new Sears Roebuck Christmas catalog, which comes by mail in the fall, announcing that it's nearing that special time of year. "The Wish Book," we call it. "I wish I had this. I wish I had that."

After Mama and Daddy get to look at it, it's our turn. We spread the huge catalog open on the worn linoleum floor in the sitting room, turning the pages quickly, right to the toy section. Three or four of us crowd around the catalog, each exclaiming, "I want this!" "I want that!" As if pointing and staking out our gift claim will make the wishing doubly sure to come true.

"What's the price of that big truck?" Sonny asks. He can't read yet.

"Prices don't matter," Buddy explains, "Because Santa brings all our presents."

"Then I can ask for anything I want?" Sonny seems surprised.

"You can ask, but it doesn't mean you'll get them all. And you have to be very very good too," Catherine pipes in. She's kinda' the boss in our family.

"And you have to write a letter to Santa," Betty Jane tells him. "But I'll write it for you." She does lots of writing and reading when she stays sick in her bed with asthma.

"Write it in big print, so Santa can read it good, cause he's really old," Sonny tells her with his big sunny grin. Mama always sings "Sonny Boy" to him when it plays on the radio.

Each of us has one big gift wish, so we don't sound too greedy, and usually we get it. Still, wishes also have "what ifs." So we try to wish deeper, stronger, maybe even writing an extra letter to Santa. He reads letters sent to him aloud over the radio, and if ours is read—well, that's an even surer sign he knows what we want.

Last year, my big wish was for a dollhouse. Only I couldn't find the kind I liked in the Sears catalog, so I wrote down what I really wanted, as best I could, in my letter to Santa.

When I saw that dollhouse Christmas morning, my heart leaped in somersaults. It was even better than I asked for. Teensy crocheted rugs, lacey curtains, rooms filled with fancy hand-carved and painted furniture. Even tiny doll people. No store had such a beautiful dollhouse. Santa's so magical he knew exactly what I wanted.

We always keep the old Christmas catalog till the new one arrives. I still go to the worn-out toy pages and gaze longingly at Shirley Temple, sometimes even kissing her picture. I'll be so excited when I get her next Christmas and can touch her for real.

I'm already writing down what I want for next Christmas. I write down lots of things so I won't forget them. I never throw away anything I write, keeping the papers in a big cardboard box under my bed.

I always think about writing down Mama's Christmas story. Only, each time she tells it, her words change, but it's still always sad.

SPRING

There's a 1935 calendar from the local funeral parlor hanging on the kitchen wall. There's a pocket attached for letters and bills, and it's slowly filling up. The January and February pages are already torn off.

"SPRING" is printed on one square of the March page of the calendar. But I can tell when that day arrives without even looking at the calendar. Some inner dance begins soon as I open the outside door, and warm breezes lift me upward into a soaring ballet that waves goodbye to winter.

As if on cue, beckoning sounds of spring resound throughout our neighborhood. I hear the whirr of roller skates, thumping of balls, clicks of bats, and a coaster wagon rumbling by. Coatless girls chant singsong verses while twirling their jump ropes, as if they are pipers calling me outside.

"One, two, buckle my shoe..."

I don't want to watch, I want to join in as soon as I can. "Daddy, take the wagon down!" we clamor, badgering him to get the coaster wagon off the wall hook in the basement, and hang the abandoned sled in its place.

"Daddy, wipe away those icky cobwebs," I say, pointing while standing far away.

"I get the first ride," Buddy announces. He likes to be first in most things. "Boys rule" is his motto if we question him.

Daddy wipes away the cobwebs and oils the wheels for us, and soon the wagon is rumbling along on the sidewalks. That echoing sound means spring is really here and we no longer have to stay inside the house, as we did most of the cold winter.

We have several fun-filled days of nothing but coaster riding from the time we change our school clothes till we're called in for supper, with the sun still shining.

Up and down the block we go, zigzagging crazily to the bottom, then halting quickly so we don't go over the concrete curb. Kids with clamp-on roller skates sometimes hitch rides, holding onto the wagon. The double vibrations of skates and coaster sing through the leafless trees, clunking over and over, hitting sidewalk cracks, all of us squealing with laughter. Our wagon, an old wooden one purchased at some farm auction, rumbles horribly, especially when empty, but for our clan it's a magic carpet that carries us to far-away places, if only a few blocks from home.

We do have a family car, but it's only used for visiting country relatives, or Sunday picnics. Daddy puts the old Ford up on wooden blocks during winter. "To keep the tires from getting flat on the bottom," he says with a laugh. And to save gas, Daddy turns off the ignition at the top of steep hills and coasts as far as he can. We never expect to be driven anywhere, and we never are.

Two wheeled bikes? You don't even ask for one till you're in eighth grade. When we ask Mama for things, she usually has two answers. "Wait till you're in eighth grade," or "Wait till you're married." So the coaster wagon's our wheels.

On Saturday morning, we quickly do our chores so we can go on our favorite outing, which is to the local high school, a castle-like building on a high hill overlooking Lake Michigan. For grade-schoolers like us, it's a mysterious, forbidding place, where the "big kids" go to school, looking so important as they walk by in chattering groups, holding stacks of books. We go to the high school when they aren't there.

"You get the blankets, I'll make the sandwiches," Catherine tells us, and we quickly gather things. We throw the itchy army blanket and package of thick homemade bread and jelly sandwiches into the wagon. Buddy calls out "Everybody on board!" and we begin our wagon train to the high school, picking up friends along the way.

We take turns pushing or pulling, switching places at each corner. The little ones usually get to ride all the way on someone's lap.

Once there, we go right to our favorite picnic spot, which is the bandstand area, circled by a wall of flat stones, perfect for sitting on. It's grand for after lunch speeches, because there's such a resounding echo when we talk loud.

Other times, we eat lunch under the football field bleachers, an army blanket draped over them, forming a perfect tent area underneath. It's especially good during rain, which happens quite often on spring days. But we don't mind. Being outside on our own, away from home, is all that matters.

We're anxious for the highlight of our Saturday trip, the wild ride down the grassy high school hill in our speeding wagon. It's even more fun than winter sledding on the same hill, for whatever spills occur now are onto soft new grass.

While waiting for our turns, we watchers find our own thrills, lying down on the grass sideways, rolling from the top of the hill down, gaining momentum as we turn faster and faster, over and over, till the last halting rotation. When we open our eyes and try to stand up, the whole world's still spinning crazily, and we're ready to do it all over again.

Our wagon isn't only for play. We've gotta' haul things in it, too. About once a week, two of us are reminded, "It's your turn to go for dried bakery." Getting dried bakery is the trip we hate most. Fresh bakery is sold to people with money. Returned bakery, which dries out pretty quickly, is for the down-and-outers. These days, everyone's scrimping. Still, there's a certain stigma attached to some things, and going for dried bakery with our noisy coaster wagon is one of them.

We leave early to make sure our friends aren't out yet to see us going on this trip which we feel ashamed to make. The empty wagon sounds like rumbling thunder as we try to walk quietly, certain we're waking up everyone along the way, that people are watching from behind their sheer curtains.

Returned bakery, brought back from grocery stores by truck because it didn't sell, is sold at the rear entrance of the store. In the early morning, there's always lines of mostly silent people, white aproned bakers, and yeasty smells at the back of the bakery. There are always more customers in back than in the front of the store. Being kids, we have to push and shove extra hard just to hang onto our place in line, juggling the coaster between us.

Finally, it's our turn to go inside. We try to fill our box quickly with the stickiest buns, frosted or filled doughnuts, and the fewest hard rolls. For 25 cents you get a large cardboard box of hardening, finger-poked bakery. We don't care how they look; it's the enticing smells that make our mouths water.

The trek back is miserable, with evidence of our mission in plain view in the open box. Sometimes we go blocks out of our way to avoid familiar streets. But once home, we hungrily dig in with the rest, taking our allotted two choices, the rest saved for later. Even days later, those last remaining hard rolls are still tasty, especially when dipped in hot Postum.

Mama says getting dried bakery is nothing to be ashamed of, and she doesn't know why people on Relief can get oranges, and lots of other things we can't afford, for free.

I hear her complain to friends, "Just because we own our house, which we're still paying for, they won't give us Relief, no matter how many kids we have!"

I also hear her say, "Auntie Rose is too dang lazy to go out and scrub floors, because she'd rather be sitting around, munching on her Relief oranges."

Only she never says such things to Auntie Rose when we visit her, even when we get to eat the good food Auntie sets out on the table for us. There are always fat pieces of oranges in her fancy Jell-O molds, too. Mama just says, "No, thank you," when the plate of wobbly Jell-O is passed around and never even tries any.

I don't know what Relief is, but if it would give us oranges and other delicious things like Auntie Rose has, it can't be as bad as Mama says.

~ GYPSIES ~

Some of our greatest family fun times are when we do dishes together. We play guessing games and tell stories. When we sing together, mostly cowboy songs, Mama joins in and harmonizes with us, even if she's in another room.

Today, we're singing "When it's springtime in the Rockies," because it's springtime in Wisconsin. Tiny green shoots are peeking up in our small garden next to the chicken coop.

Because Daddy was a farmer, he still likes to do some farming. He rents a plowed lot outside the city, where we grow rows and rows of vegetables. We kids go there in Daddy's car to pull weeds, pick bugs, and other work. Mama keeps reminding us, "Extra work means extra food." Mama thinks about food a lot. We kids do, too, but not in the same way.

Each spring, our school launches the annual seed-selling program, sponsored by a local seed company. Prizes are given for selling certain amounts of seeds: Mickey Mouse watches, fancy yo-yos, fountain pen sets. We're each handed 25 seed packets. It's up to us to sell them, return the right amount of money to the nuns, pick out our prizes, then sell more if we wish. But 25 always seems like more than enough for me to sell. And a yo-yo's a good enough prize.

Contests are everywhere these days—newspapers, magazines, over the radio—all promising grand prizes, attainable dreams for the lucky, lucky winners.

Geraldine always wants to enter every contest, not caring if she wins or not.

"It's always possible to win," Geraldine claims. "And we can have so much fun just trying to win." She gets excited about each contest she sees. "Just look at all the possibilities for winning!" she exclaims, reading them off to me. Her excitement is catching, convincing me to enter, too.

"Here's a new contest!" she says, pointing to a large cartoon square in the newspaper. "All you have to do is find all the mistakes in each of these pictures."

"Looks too hard," is my ready reply.

"So what! We can figure out the answers together. We're both smart," she prods me. "And the winner gets a new car, a brand new sedan!"

A new car—that's unbelievable. No one we know has a new car.

Different squares are printed every day. We work on them diligently, over and over, positive we've found all the mistakes, sending in the carefully cut out answers all together at the end of the week.

Anxiously, we await our letter telling us we've won. It takes a while.

"We are winners!" Geraldine screams as soon as she sees me at school one morning. "I told you we'd win." She's waving the letter.

"We'll open it together at my house after school." We race to her house and go to her small bedroom. Excitedly, she tears open the envelope. I hold my breath, waiting to hear what it says.

Geraldine begins reading. "Congratulations—you are a winner!" She starts jumping up and down, reads further, stops, then goes on hesitatingly. "Because so many others have found all the mistakes too, there will be another play-off contest for those who tied in the first one. In order to break the tie, new winners will be chosen from those who sell the most jars of Rosaline Salve." What? We have to sell salve!

"The top one hundred salve sellers will have their names drawn randomly for that big, big prize—the new sedan." Geraldine is quiet, nothing to say. That's unusual for her. I'm ready to give up right then and there. I never expected to win anyway.

"We can't quit now. We have just as much chance as those others," Geraldine says after a moment, with renewed enthusiasm. "Together, we can sell lots of salve."

"I don't know. Selling seeds is hard enough," I say. I really don't like selling anything. I'm very shy about making requests in person, especially to adults. But I also have a hard time saying no to Geraldine.

The jars of Rosaline Salve come by mail, 25 of them, to Geraldine's house. The company letter says that when we sell all of these and send in the money, we can order even more to sell. More?

Geraldine tries to get me excited about selling more salve.

"We could pretend we are traveling gypsies selling our magic salve. That'll make it more fun." Geraldine knows I'm always interested in anything to do with Gypsies.

It began when Geraldine and I saw the movie *The Hunchback Of Notre Dame*. Quasimodo looked so scary and pitiful on that big movie screen, with his scrunched face and twisted body. My eyes would tear up when he'd cry out "Watah, watah!" over and over as he was turned round and round, tied up on that heavy wheel.

But Esmeralda, the beautiful Gypsy girl who gave him water—she fascinated both of us.

"I wish I looked like her, have long dark wavy hair, wear lots of spangly necklaces and jingly bracelets," I say to Geraldine after the show.

"Me, I'd rather dance around in bare feet like she does, and shake a tambourine as wildly as she does," Geraldine adds. "Such mysterious eyes—Let's stay and see this movie twice." We did, and talked about it so many times.

From that day on, I wanted to know more about Gypsies. I'd search in the school and public library for books that told about Gypsies, captivated by the colorful pictures of them, riding in decorated wagons, playing violins, dancing about in bright colors and gaudy jewelry, capturing me in the mystique foreign people always conjured up in me. Their carefree lifestyle and vagabond ways—what fun to live like that.

Sometimes, I'd hear talk about Gypsies on the front porch steps. I always listened avidly. Warm nights are an open invitation for renters and neighbors to gather on our front porch. They sit on the steps, spinning never-ending tales, relating stories from bygone days. I never tire of listening. They're like talking books, many times telling stories without endings. It's nice to hear stories in different voices in the near dark.

Once a subject is brought up, each person on the porch has to relate their own personal experiences. The grown-ups use hushed tones when speaking about "the Gypsies." Everybody has a different story to tell about them. It's upsetting, hearing some Gypsy tales about chicken thefts, phony fortune tellers, and things hidden in their huge skirts.

What they said on the porch can't be true, can it? These are a fairy tale kind of people for me.

"You be careful when those Gypsies are around," Jake, the old neighbor who's always teasing, warns in a threatening tone, looking right at me. "They like little blonde girls, and try to kidnap them."

"Jake, stop scaring the kids all the time," Mama tells him.

"Kids need to be told about such things," he retorts, waving his finger at me in the dusky twilight. "You just stay away from those Gypsies! Run, fast as you can, if one even comes near you."

He must know, since he's an adult. So I decide I'll stay away from Gypsies, even if I still enjoy reading about them.

Just outside of Manitowoc is a semi-wooded area where bands of Gypsies sometimes camp. Mama always remarks, "That's where the Gypsies gather," whenever we drive by the spot on our way to visit our country cousins. Black poles stand like skeletons over darkened fire sites. A wagon without wheels is partially buried. I always imagine Gypsies dancing about, shaking their tambourines.

Sometimes, they really are there. For several weeks each summer, the Gypsies come back to the camp. I scrunch down in our old car, packed between the other kids, as we drive past, listening to Mama's comments. I'm afraid to look, yet fascinated when I do give a quick peek. It's like watching a movie that goes by quickly. When the Gypsies are there, the site takes on a carnival air. Huge black kettles now hang on the poles, makeshift tents and battered old cars crowd the area, and even a few horses. Screaming, laughing children scurry around, dancing about in bare feet.

What fun to live like they do. But I don't see any blonde children.

"Well, the Gypsies have finally gone," Mama says, driving by the next time. "Vanished like the moon. But they'll return when we least expect them. Seems they just can't stay put."

Some Gypsies did stay put, settling in town in an abandoned grocery store. They hung colorful shawls over the soaped-up windows. "After a while, wanderlust beckons," Mama remarks. "And most move on."

Still, one old Gypsy stayed, living alone upstairs over that same store. I would hear neighbors gossip about her.

"You know, that one, she reads tea leaves and tells fortunes to make her living."

"Well, course, there's no sign over da outside door, or on her vindow," Mrs. Schultz, our neighbor who talks with a thick German accent, comments. "But evryvun knows da Gypsy lives there. Yah."

"Oh, lots of people go to see her secretly," neighbor Jessie adds in a lowered voice. "To learn their fortunes."

"Throwing money away on such trash. Sinful."

"I don't know why they allow her to stay in this town."

The women usually meander into our backyard if they see someone out there, an excuse for a break in their housework.

"I hear she even casts spells—for a price," Mrs. Kolancheck, our know-it-all neighbor, adds.

"You can't believe every story you hear," is Mama's usual answer to Mrs. Kolancheck and others.

But I believe. They're grown-ups.

Sometimes they talk over wash lines on Monday morning. In the summer, I'm out there handing Mama wooden clothespins, making sure to listen, not letting on that I am. You can learn lots by listening—about childbirth, sicknesses different people have, and family fights. Sometimes they make sure I don't hear about certain subjects, pointing to me, then continuing to talk in whispers, faces turned away.

Children are never told about certain subjects by parents or the nuns in school. Only the allusion to "sin" makes us aware that some topics are to be kept hidden from us.

How and when will I ever find out if no one ever talks about those things we aren't supposed to know about?

I figure out many things on my own. I conclude that music from the phonograph comes from little bands that play inside the wooden box. The record you put on top tells them what song to play. It's the only explanation I could think of. It makes perfect sense to me, till my big sister tells me how foolish I am. But even she doesn't know exactly how music comes out of that wooden box we call a talking machine.

I don't know why the Great Depression and stock market crashes make people jump out of high windows, or live in tents down by the railroad tracks, either. When I ask, Mama just says, "You kids don't need to know about such things." But I feel I do need to know.

Sometimes I give up trying to figure things out. It makes it easier, just believing, like I do when I read story books. I never bother figuring out stories, just let them tell me whatever they want, without any questions.

After the Rosaline Salve arrives, Geraldine calls a two-person meeting, making me agree to her pact to go door-to-door every evening after school.

"We have to go to every single house." Geraldine makes it sound like both a threat and a promise.

"Every single one?"

"Yes," she says firmly. "You said you would do whatever I decided so we can win that sedan."

Winning the sedan and keeping Geraldine happy move my trudging feet from house to house, when I'd rather be home playing jacks or with my Shirley Temple paper dolls. I didn't even tell Mama about selling salve, as the jars are kept at Geraldine's house. I just say, "I'm going over to Geraldine's." Mama usually lets us kids do what we want after our chores, as long as we're home for supper.

The selling business is bad. When Geraldine asks, "Would you like to buy some Rosaline Salve?" doors shut almost as fast as they're opened.

We've been knocking on doors all week and are pretty discouraged. It's already Saturday, the day we scheduled to go up and down both sides of 11th Street. The last building on the block is the abandoned store with soaped up windows.

"Okay, time to go home," I say, turning around.

"You can't go home, not yet. We have to go upstairs here." Geraldine stands firmly in front of me, the shopping bag full of salve on the sidewalk beside her.

"But that's where the Gypsy lives."

"We said we'd go to every house, no matter what," reminds Geraldine.

"This isn't a house. This is a store." I don't want to go anywhere near the Gypsy, much less try to sell her some salve. Once we go up those stairs, no one will ever know what happened to us. Even Mama doesn't know I'm out selling salve today.

Looking up, I see a wavering lace-curtained window above the ghostly empty store. I'm positive I see a face peering out, someone holding a crystal ball—a kerchiefed head with golden earrings. The setting sun shines brightly against the bleary window, causing all sorts of distorted patterns.

"You don't even want to win this car!" Geraldine chides.

We had such grand illusions about the car, taking turns driving, maybe even letting our parents use it sometimes. We never even consider that we aren't old enough to drive. If you have a car, you just drive it.

We walk up to the paint-chipped outside door. I'm hoping it will be tightly locked. It isn't, and Geraldine easily yanks it open. Reluctantly, I follow Geraldine up the shadowy dark stairway, floorboards creaking extra loud. Maybe the Gypsy won't even be home, I think, my heart thumping faster with each step. If we knock softly and leave quickly—

But Geraldine is already knocking loudly. Why isn't she afraid of Gypsies?

Maybe because she has thick black hair—mine is blonde. Jake said Gypsies only kidnapped blonde-haired children. I hear his gravelly voice and see his grim face as we wait in the small dark hallway at the top of the stairs.

Peculiar smells fill the tiny area, wrinkling my nose. What are they? Where are they coming from? Nothing seems right about this trip today.

I hear noises stirring, then the shuffling of footsteps behind the door. The click of a lock. The doorknob rattles. *Squeak. Creak.*

Slowly, the door begins to open. The smells become stronger. I'm all set to run. "What do you want?" a raspy voice asks.

I can't look up. I don't even want to peek, and have her put the "evil eye" on me.

"Would you like to buy some Rosaline Salve?" Geraldine asks matter-of-factly in her practiced manner.

"Come in, come in, children," the voice invites.

I panic. We can't go in. We never go inside homes—Mama has strictly forbidden it. But Geraldine is already over the threshold, so I follow, whether in fear of being left alone in that dark hall or to protect Geraldine, I'm not sure. But suddenly, I'm inside, the door slamming shut behind me.

"What do you want?" the voice asks. "Why have you come to see me?"

I expect the witch from *Hansel and Gretel* to materialize. I have to see what she looks like. Slowly, I lift my head, and take a quick peek at the person with the strange voice.

Why, she just looks plain, like any other old woman. She has crinkly skin and wears a wrinkled, soiled blouse with a tattered lace collar, an ornate pin at her neckline, and a long dark skirt. A black fringed shawl covers her stooped shoulders. Her graying hair is tied back into a knot. She isn't even wearing any earrings or beads. "Sit down, girls," she orders.

Geraldine sits primly on the rickety wooden settee. I remain standing, stiff with fright, my eyes wandering everywhere, making plans for a quick escape.

The feeling of being in a very strange place overtakes me. The room is small, cluttered with so many foreign-looking items. There is a mixture of old and odd furniture crowded together and piled up, with wild plants intertwining everywhere. Walls and tabletops are covered with once-bright shawls, framed pictures of people and places, and curious knickknacks. The floor is covered by a worn carpet with huge faded roses, and scatterings of smaller rugs on top. Everywhere I look, something unusual holds my attention. This is better than a book beginning; I'm standing right in the description.

All of a sudden, a strange noise startles me. There, sitting on a perch nearby, is the most brilliantly colored parrot I have ever seen. He's huge, and he's not even in a cage, just sitting there, out in the open, on a wooden perch. I'm afraid he'll fly at me and bite me with his huge beak. I'm ready to run, but stay frozen, not wanting to turn my back on this giant bird.

Geraldine is busy pitching her salve. "Rosaline Salve is a wonderful, one-of-a-kind ointment, and it can only be bought from us."

She opens the sample jar, rubs a bit on her index finger, and waves it in the air with a flourish. The sweet smell of Rosaline Salve obscures the other unsavory scents for a moment, then blends back into the mixture.

Geraldine is talking faster than usual, almost as if she too wants to get out of here. "We only have a few more jars left—"

The old Gypsy sits in a moss-green worn velvet armchair, with a dirty frayed rug under her slippered feet. She listens, chewing on her thick lips, breathing heavily through her half-opened mouth. She doesn't say anything.

Quite suddenly, Geraldine stops talking and begins packing up her things. Why is she giving up already? Usually she tries harder.

Something about this place must affect those who enter—maybe a spell? I'm not sure, but I know I feel different since entering, and I also know I don't want to leave anymore.

"All right, all right, I'll take a jar of your salve," the Gypsy says, then gets up with great effort and disappears into another room behind a fringe-curtained doorway.

I'm stunned. She's really going to buy a jar of salve from us? Why would a Gypsy need salve, when she has so many magic potions of her own to use for cures?

We wait in silence. Geraldine gives me a smug smile as she digs out a jar of salve from her rattling paper bag. After what seems like an extra-long time, the Gypsy shuffles back in and sits down once more in the big armchair, sinking into the dented pillows, exhaling a huge sigh, followed by a snorting grunt and wrinkling of her nose. I don't take my eyes off her.

With great precision, she opens a black drawstring leather pouch. I notice her long fingers have sparkly jeweled rings on them. So she does wear jewelry. Maybe she wears her beads and earrings only when she goes out. Maybe she looks prettier then too, I think, imagining her in a colorful Gypsy costume. But I could never picture her with a tambourine, or dancing about in bare feet.

"Here you are, girls," she says, carefully counting out the right amount of coins, then she closes the pouch tightly. She places the salve and pouch on the nearby table next to a lamp with beaded fringe dangling from its crooked shade.

Geraldine takes the coins, thanks her, and hastily gets up to depart. But I'm reluctant to leave at this point. I want something more to happen. Here I am, in a real Gypsy's home, and nothing unusual has occurred. I'm in the heart of an adventure—I can't step out of it so quickly. Something more has to happen. I don't want this special chapter to end just yet; there's no skipping to the back of the book this time.

All of a sudden, the parrot lets out a loud, frightening squawk. Even Geraldine jumps at the sound.

I rein in my fright and, with a big gulp, ask, "What's the parrot's name?" Those are the first words I've spoken since we arrived. If I make small talk, maybe I can prolong our visit.

"Persa," the Gypsy answers, walking over to the bird. She squawks again.

"Persa?" I repeat and walk closer. "Persa! Persa!" I call, but not too loud, fascinated that the bird recognizes its name.

"Oh, that one's a hundred years old," the Gypsy cackles.

"Really?" A hundred years seems like forever.

"Oh yes. She's been in the family for many generations. Traveled all across Europe with us." She pauses, "That's when we had the wagons yet..."

She gently pets the bird with her bent, ringed fingers. Persa ruffles her feathers and begins talking. It seems like she's saying words, but they aren't like regular sounding words. Maybe it's special parrot talk.

"What is she saying?" I really want to know.

"Oh, Persa, she only talks in Roumanian," the Gypsy sighs, then sits down. Her eyes look into the distance, squinting in the fading sunlight, the lace curtains making wiggly patterns on her wrinkled skin.

"The tales that one could tell. . . ." The Gypsy shakes her head from side to side. She sounds sad, yet gives me a mysterious, toothless smile.

That smile erases my remaining fears. I want to stay and hear more about Persa—the stories that bird could tell, and whatever else the Gypsy might tell me.

"Would you girls like some tea and cookies?" the Gypsy asks, getting up from her chair.

Tea and cookies with a Gypsy? That surely would make this an extra exciting adventure. Already, I'm wondering what kind of cookies she would serve and on what kind of dishes.

"No, thank you," Geraldine says, quickly moving toward the door.

"I don't drink tea, but I might like a cookie—" I try to say as Geraldine grabs my arm and drags me through the doorway.

"We have to leave now, but thank you for your purchase," Geraldine utters in a voice I've never heard her use before, almost scared.

"I enjoyed meeting you," I quickly blurt, "and your bird, Persa."

I never hear what the Gypsy replies. Was it, "Come back and see me again"? I'm not sure, because Geraldine is hurriedly shutting the door.

I half turn around to go back in, but Geraldine is already halfway down the dark stairway. What to do? Stay alone, or—

I follow dejectedly, my heart still lingering in that memorable room.

The joy of selling a jar of salve doesn't override the feeling that I lost out on a rare opportunity to connect with a real live Gypsy, an opening into another world that might never come my way again.

My steps downward are slow, reluctant.

Back on the sidewalk, I turn around and look up at the window above. I'm sure I see the Gypsy waving her ringed hand at me. I even hear Persa squawking in the distance, or is it only remembered sounds spinning in my jumbled head? Geraldine mutters, "Who knows what might have happened to us if we ate or drank something in that weird place."

Who knows indeed? I know I never will.

~ GOING TO WORK WITH MAMA ~

My birthday's circled on the calendar: Wednesday, April 24.

Mama promised I could invite eight girls to my birthday party, because I'll be eight years old. Only, there's not going to be a party because one week before my birthday, I came down with chicken pox and I'm quarantined for two whole weeks. That means no party at home or at school.

I still have a family celebration. Mama makes macaroni and cheese and angel food cake with pink frosting, my favorites. I wear my Sunday dress all day, and don't have to do dishes. There are cards piled on my plate at supper time. We don't give gifts for birthdays. Gift giving is saved for Christmas.

Eight candles are lit on the cake. My family sings "Happy Birthday" to me. With all the breath I can gather, I blow out all the candles, making my silent wish: "A Shirley Temple doll, for next Christmas."

Finally, the itchy blisters have gone away, and just a few red spots are left. Tomorrow, Mama goes to her cleaning job and I don't want to be home alone again like last Friday. It's my only chance.

"Mama? Can I go with you tomorrow?" She's sitting down, mending holes in socks. "No one will be at the doctor's house; no one can catch my chicken pox. See, they're all gone."

Mama doesn't even look up, just says, "I'm much too busy to keep watch on you while I'm there cleaning."

"But I can help you clean. I'm good at it," I blurt out.

"Well," Mama hesitates. I hold my breath as she jabs the needle in the sock hole. "Maaybee—Well, maybe you could help dust under the beds. My bad knee still bothers me."

I'm so happy I want to jump up and down, but try to stay calm.

"Thank you, thank you! I've always wanted to go to the doctor's house, see all the rich things he has, and—"

Mama cuts me off quick. "I don't want you snooping around while we're there. I need to work fast, and get things done quick as I can."

"I'll work real hard," I promise. "And I can learn all about cleaning from you too. Maybe I can clean houses, same as you do, when I get bigger."

Mama stops darning. "I hope you'll find something better to do than cleaning houses. Besides, you'll be married, have a house of your own to clean."

I never think about being married, it's much too far away.

The next morning, I get up early. I don't even tell the others I'm going, because who knows what they might say. Mama doesn't talk about it either. I just hope she hasn't forgotten. Catherine has to take Mitzy and Sonny to Grandma's and I help get them ready. Daddy's already gone cutting wood, and Mama's doing things around the house before she leaves.

"Don't get too lonely all by yourself," Buddy warns me in his scary voice. "And make sure you stay out of my stuff," he adds, closing the door with a bang.

Finally, everyone's gone. I have old clothes on for cleaning, and a tablet and pencil in a paper bag, in case I want to write down anything while I'm there. I can hardly wait for my new adventure to begin.

Mama's ready, her shopping bag filled with cleaning things, purse in hand. "All right Lulu, let's get going. It's a long walk and I don't want you complaining along the way."

We close the door, but don't lock it. "Nothing worth stealing in this house, and surely no money." Mama's favorite words.

We walk fast, all the way to the other side of town, the houses getting bigger and richer each block.

"That's it," Mama says, pointing to a grand house with tan stucco siding, an orange tiled roof, and lots of plants and trees in a yard big enough to be a park.

I start going up the front walk.

"Not that way," Mama interrupts. "We go in the back door."

So we walk up the double driveway to the back of the house. Mama has a key to let herself in. As the door opens, I can already smell a different kind of place—like it has lots of unused air, ritzy things, gigantic spaces. I keep close to Mama so I don't get lost right away.

"We'll start upstairs," Mama says, taking off her coat and hat and setting out her cleaning things.

I want to stay downstairs and look around a bit, find out where all the doors go, and what's inside each room. Instead, I follow Mama up the giant winding staircase, away from the huge downstairs hall that has pretty stained glass windows and flat colored stones on the floor.

On the second floor, there are four bedrooms. Even though no one uses most of them, or the three bathrooms, they still have to be cleaned and dusted every week.

"How come you have to clean rooms when they're not even dirty?"

"Because that's what they want, and that's what I'm paid to do," Mama answers.

We go into a room that's all different shades of green. Flowers and vines are painted on the walls, outlining the doors and windows, as if they were really growing there. I feel like I've walked right into a lovely picture.

Mama gives me a big dust rag and tells me to wipe the floors carefully under each bed, leaving no speck of dust, and then wipe all the windowsills in each of the upstairs rooms.

"Whose room is this, Mama?" I'm still entranced at how it's decorated.

"It's the guest room."

"A guest room?"

"Yes, people who come to visit, they use this room."

"But, don't they use the parlor for company?"

"This is where guests stay overnight."

"You mean they have a whole empty room, just waiting, in case people sleep overnight?" Nobody I know has such fancy rooms that are just "extra."

"I can't spend all day talking." She goes back to polishing things. "When you're done here, do the room next door."

I'm in the peach room now, where the doctor and his wife sleep, but not together—in twin beds. The unwrinkled silky taffeta bedspreads look like they've never been slept in. The tall windows have long drapes of peach taffeta over lace curtains. There's a big dressing table with a skirt of puffy peach and turquoise ribbons, and a huge round mirror above. On its glass tabletop are all kinds of fancy perfume bottles, lotion jars, and matching ivory comb and brush sets. I'm so tempted to smell each of the perfumes and try some lotion on, but know Mama would certainly catch me. She has eyes in the back of her head—we all know that. I pick up the blue perfume bottle and sniff the outside. It's sweet and spicy. Quickly, I put it down and wipe off my hands, but the scent remains.

What if it stays on me?

I stare at myself in the mirror with ruffled gold edging. I look small, far away, as if I don't belong in this picture at all. Maybe it's a mirror you can walk through, into a different world. I've read about them, but wouldn't know how to make one work.

Mama uses furniture polish on all the furniture, and soon the whole upstairs smells like lemon furniture polish. Luckily, it covers the perfume smell. Next, Mama washes the windows till they're all sparkling.

The doctor and his wife are away in Florida and won't be home till next week. "So we have to make sure everything is ready for them," Mama informs me. *Ready for what?* I think, but don't ask.

I'm really tired. Mama must be more tired, because she works harder and faster than I do.

"Well, we're through up here; next we'll tackle the downstairs," she says, which means I won't get back up here again.

"I have to go to the bathroom," I say, and I really do. "Which one can I use?"

"The small one, end of the hall, and don't you dare get it dirty."

I was hoping I might use the fancy one with the pink bathtub and gold swan faucets and pink toilet. I have never sat on a pink toilet before and just wanted to be alone in that room for a bit, with the door closed, so I could check out everything and walk on the soft fluffy bath mat.

"Can't I use the pink bathroom?" I plead, "It has a stool I might need—"

Mama looks at me, then says, "Oh, all right, but don't be in there too long. I'll be wiping down the stair rails."

I close the heavy door and I'm all alone in this bathroom that's even bigger than my bedroom. The gold wallpaper has white swans on it, and the shower curtains too.

What must it be like to take a bath in this deep tub? I can see myself repeated in the mirrors hanging everywhere.

What's in that decorated medicine cabinet? Does a doctor have more medicine than most people?

There's a big scale like one we have at school. I want to weigh myself, but don't know how to work the lever on the top.

I sit on the curved bench by the window that has criss-crosses of wood on its panes and opens outward. Quickly, I write down things in my tablet so I won't forget them later.

I look at the garden below. There's the pond where Mama says they keep big goldfish in the summer. Where do they go in winter?

There's white metal garden furniture, and some big statues. It would be fun to play down there and explore everything. Maybe another time? Better do what I came to do.

I carefully use the toilet and one piece of pink toilet paper, then flush, making sure there's no paper or anything left behind. Then I dance around on the fluffy rug and make a final bow in front of the big mirror, watching myself as I do it. Time to leave.

I open the door, making sure I don't leave finger marks on the polished knob. I'm on my way downstairs, sticking that whole upstairs in the "special memories" section of my head. I'll write more about it too, so I won't forget how everything looked and felt.

Mama's already in another room, pushing the upright vacuum cleaner, buzzing it over the thick purple and black oriental rug. The room appears shadowy, with brown wood paneling and darkish furniture, and no bright colors at all. The outside trees and bushes crowd the windows, blocking out the sunshine. Even though it's a rich place, it seems so downcast, lifeless, and gloomy.

One whole wall, floor to ceiling, is filled with books, heavy and dark-looking ones. I wish I could peek at a few, but don't want Mama catching me. Besides, there doesn't seem to be any books for children. They're probably all about medicine. I never like looking through medicine books full of eeky pictures, sick body parts, and ugly skin things.

On the table, by the curved-out window, there's a photo in a silver frame. I tiptoe over and see it's the face of a little boy. I stand there, staring at his picture. I need to know more about him. Mama turns off the vacuum and comes over. I'm afraid she's going to holler at me, but I have to ask.

"Who's this picture of, Mama?"

"It's—" She takes a deep breath. "That's Danny, their son."

"Their son? Where is he now? Why isn't he living here?"

"Because—he died, that's why. Many years ago. From pneumonia."

"You mean doctors' children get sick and die too?"

"Nobody escapes troubles, nobody." She looks away. "That's all I'm going to say about it. You can dust in here, windows, bookshelves, furniture, and all the corners too. And no more snooping."

I work hard and fast, thinking about Danny all the time.

What he was like? Which room was his in this large house? Where did he go to school? What kind of toys did he have?

His face and eyes follow me all around, but they're not scary, almost as if he wants to tell me things. I know he can't, and know Mama won't tell me any more. No wonder this house seems sad—all that money, and no children. No children at all, except one that's dead.

Finally, Mama says, "Okay, Lulu, we can rest a little while we eat our lunch." I didn't know we got lunch here, or could even take a rest.

I follow Mama into a sunny room that's all yellow and white. It's a kitchen that's big enough to dance in, with black and white squares on the floor.

"We'll sit in the breakfast nook," she says, pointing to a part of the kitchen that sticks out into the backyard. There's a yellow wooden table with attached yellow benches, and windows on three sides. So, this is what a breakfast nook looks like, and I'm going to eat in one. I'm happy now; sunny yellow does that for me.

Mama opens the door of the big white Frigidaire. Cool air rushes out. "Where do they keep the ice?" I ask, peeking in at everything.

"It doesn't need ice, it runs by electricity," she answers. "It even makes ice."

She shows me a tray with little cubes of ice in it, and a shelf with icy frozen food. "Let's see what's in here. Would you like a bottle of soda?"

I'm still thinking about how hot electricity can keep an icebox cold, but the word "soda" stops those thoughts.

"A bottle of soda—a whole bottle?" I want to make sure I heard right.

"Yes, a whole bottle. You've earned it. What about an orange, too?"

"They have oranges, even when it's not Christmas time?"

"An orange a day is Dr. Mack's motto."

Our school health books always say children should have oranges and milk and other things. But our family doesn't have them. Those health books seem to be more like make-believe stories, not about real children or real families. People in them look different too, not at all like Mama and Daddy.

"I'll make some tea for myself," Mama says, putting on the copper teakettle, then looking through the cupboards. "Here's some crackers, and a little cheese left."

I'm already drinking my red cherry soda through a long straw as I kneel on the nook bench. It's delicious, and I sip it slowly so it lasts longer.

"For being so rich, they sure don't have much food, do they?" I comment. This surprises me.

"They don't eat at home as much anymore, not since they let Marie go."

"Who's Marie?"

"Their cook."

"A cook? For just two people?"

"Yes. Marie was with them for a long time. But they had to let her go, even though they didn't want to. Times are bad for everyone. So now they eat at the club most days."

"What's the club?" I'm eating cookies now from the shiny tin Mama got down from the high cupboard.

"The Country Club—"

"Is that in the country? Like where Uncle Steven and Auntie Ellen live?"

"No, it's at the golf course."

"Oh." I don't know much about golf courses, or the kinds of clubs they might have. "Cindy and I had a club once. A secret club and nobody else could join. Do you belong to a club, Mama? Maybe a secret one?"

"I don't have time for clubs," she says. Then, after thinking a bit, "Well, I do belong to the Christmas Club. It's not secret, but—well, maybe it is."

"What kind of club is the Christmas Club?" I'm really curious. Just then, the teakettle starts whistling and Mama jumps up.

"Time for tea," she says, and I know the subject is closed. And if it's a secret, Mama wouldn't tell anyway.

I'm carefully peeling my orange, enjoying the sweet smell, savoring each juicy piece. "What else do we have to clean here?" I ask, hoping there's not too much more. What if we have to clean the basement and garage too?

"Lots more to clean. We have the kitchen to scrub and wax, and the sunroom to clean—"

"But you still have some rest time, don't you, Mama?" I'm looking at the big round clock on the shiny white tile wall. It's almost one o'clock.

"A little, while I drink my tea, and eat my cheese and crackers. Maybe that last orange, too."

I've been waiting for this opportunity for so long, a time alone with just Mama and me. Every day when I was home sick, I tried to ask her, but could never find the right moment, and Mama was always too busy. I have to do it now, here, with no others interrupting. I want Mama to tell me her story just one more time, in this different and remarkable place.

"Mama, can you tell me your Christmas story again? Please. About when you were a little orphan girl?"

"You kids have heard that story so many times."

"But, I never hear it alone. Others are always butting in."

"It's not an easy story to tell." She sips her tea. "No happy ending, either."

"I don't care. I like listening to your stories, Mama. They're even better than those in books, and I can watch your eyes as you speak... Only, tell it right from the beginning. Don't skip any parts."

Mama is quiet for a bit, then begins telling me her Christmas story.

~ MAMA'S CHRISTMAS STORY ~

"I was an orphan, you know. I never knew who my real parents were, only that they died, and that my baptized name was Elizabeth McCann.

"The relatives took all the money, then put me in an orphanage— St. Ann's, in New York City. It wasn't a bad place. It was clean and warm, and we ate together and dressed alike. The nuns were good to us, from what I remember, and taught us to read, pray, and work hard.

"Then the Welfare Department decided orphans needed real homes and that it would be better for us if we went to live with regular families. So they put us on the Orphan Train, a long black train filled with orphans, which traveled across the country, stopping at small cities along the way. People would come and check us over, picking out the ones they wanted. They'd look in our mouths, pinch our cheeks, and ask us to talk.

"It seemed nobody wanted me, because I was small and scrawny, never smiled, and wouldn't talk. Most people wanted someone big and strong, who could work hard, because even if they said different, that's what most were really looking for.

"When the train stopped in Wisconsin, this mean-looking couple decided they would take me—mostly because there weren't that many orphans left to choose from.

"I cried so, because I didn't want to leave my friends and go off with this strange man and lady, who kept telling me gruffly, 'Keep quiet. Stop crying.'

"They took me to this farm where they lived in an old, unpainted gray house. They put me in a tiny attic room where it was hot in summer, cold in winter, with only a peek hole window which didn't open. But I'd still look out of it a lot, always wishing I were someplace else.

"I had to work very hard in the house and the barns, so I was glad to climb those stairs at night and escape into sleep and dreams. There were no other farms or children nearby. I had no toys, no dolls, only raggedy clothes and bad-tasting food.

"One time, the hired man, who lived someplace else but talked to me every once in a while, made me a corncob doll with husks for the skirt and a painted-on face. I called her Jennie and kept her hidden in my room. I'd sneak Jennie out at night to play with and talk to. One day, my step-ma found Jennie under my mattress and asked me what kind of buggy piece of trash I was hiding in my room. She shredded it all up, right in front of me.

"'Now, throw this junk on the manure pile, where it belongs,' she yelled.

"Step-ma and Step-pa were always screaming and hollering at me. They called me 'Lazy Lizzie' and hit me hard for any little thing.

Sometimes I even got whippings with the leather strap. I hated living there, and wished every day I was back at the orphanage. I kept praying, prayers the nuns taught me, asking God to take me away and make my life better.

"Step-ma and Step-pa had to send me to school; it was part of the agreement they signed. They also had to write letters to the orphanage about how I was getting along, but I never got to see the letters, so I don't know what they wrote. But no one ever came to take me back, which they had promised they would do if the place wasn't right for me.

"I had one dress, an itchy stiff black one that was never washed. I also had black stockings and high top black shoes to wear to school, which was miles away. I had to walk there and back, even in bad weather. But being at school was still better than staying home with them.

"The kids at school were mean, too, and made fun of me because of my clothes and because they knew I was an orphan. No one played with me. The teacher was nice, and said I was a good reader, which is what I liked doing best. My step parents had no books and didn't like it that I learned to read and write. I was 'wasting my time,' they said. I hid throw-away books the teacher gave me in my room, reading them over and over, till the print wore off.

"At the orphanage, we had always had a special Christmas celebration. People sent gifts; we'd get a new dress, new shoes. Santa always visited and gave us toys and candy. Christmases there were quite wonderful. We'd sing songs, and open presents around a big, candle-lit tree.

"One time, President Teddy Roosevelt even visited the orphanage and I got to sit on his lap and sing a little song for him. He gave me such a big kiss, making me feel so special. Everyone talked about it for a long time after..."

Mama closes her eyes, and pauses. I don't want her to stop, not now.

"That first year on the farm, I knew Christmas was coming, but didn't know how they celebrated, so I asked.

"'Christmas! I don't believe in it and never did,' Step-ma said, looking meaner than ever. 'There'll be no celebration here, so don't even ask about it.'

"They didn't go to church either, so I knew I wouldn't even get to see the manger. I still thought about Christmas and got very excited when I found out the school would have a nice Christmas program. I was chosen to sing a song by myself, "Away in the Manger," for the afternoon program. It was easier for me to sing than talk, and I practiced that song for weeks on the way to and from school.

"The big day arrived. All the girls came in wearing fancy dresses, with big bows in their hair. I had on my raggedy dark dress and black stockings, my hair tied with a string.

"There was a small fir tree we all helped decorate. After lunch, we did our program, sang songs, and told stories. I hadn't felt so happy since coming to the farm, and sang my heart out. 'I love thee, Lord Jesus, look down from the skies—'

"After, Teacher said, 'Children, Santa left a gift for each of you,' and called out our names one by one, handing each of us a small sack of candy. I clutched my bag so tightly, knowing it would be my only gift, then stood off in the corner by myself while the rest were giggling and talking with each other.

"'I can hardly wait till Christmas morning to see if I get my French doll—'

"'I'm getting brand new ice skates—'

"One of the girls pointed to me and asked in a mocking voice, 'Lizzie, what are you getting for Christmas?'

"Before I could answer, Polly interrupted, 'Lizzie's not getting anything. Orphans don't get presents for Christmas, because Santa never comes to children who don't have parents.'

"I had been counting on Santa.

"'Is that really true?' I had to ask. 'He'll never come, long as I live?'

"'That's true, Orphan Lizzie! Santa never comes to children unless they have real live parents.'

"They giggled, while I cried, that day and for days after. What they said was true. Santa didn't come that year.

"Maybe by next year, I kept hoping, Santa would forget I was an orphan and stop at the farmhouse anyway.

"I waited that whole year, and never gave up hope. The day before Christmas, I sneaked into the woods, cut down a small pine tree, and put it up in my attic room. Step-ma and Step-pa didn't come up there so much anymore. I trimmed it with paper decorations from school and strings of dried berries from the woods. So, just in case Santa did come, he could see that this house celebrated Christmas, even if an orphan lived there.

"That night, I prayed harder than I had ever prayed before.

"'Please, dear God, let Santa come tonight, just this once. Let him bring me a doll. Any kind of doll. I've written him so many times. Step-pa Harry, he promised he'd mail my letters. I never told Santa I was an orphan. How does he know?'

"That night, I had the most wonderful dream. I was showered with all kinds of presents. There was even a lit Christmas tree.

"Next morning, the sun shone brightly, and there was frost on my peep hole window, and snow on the ground outside. It was Christmas morning!

"I got up quickly to look under my decorated tree. Maybe, just maybe—

"I couldn't believe it! There, on the table next to the tree, was a big cellophane-wrapped box, and inside was a doll! A beautiful doll with golden curls and a ruffly pink dress.

"It was a miracle, or else I was still dreaming. Quickly, I tore off the cellophane and took out the doll, hugging her over and over. Santa did get my letter!

"I was the happiest girl in the whole world.

"Right away, I named her Mary, and played with that doll for what seemed hours, lost in another world.

"Then I heard Step-pa stirring below. He'd been drinking the night before and always slept late after. Soon, I could hear Step-ma screeching at him. I didn't want to hear, but could never shut out their voices downstairs.

"'What do you mean, you went out and bought Lizzie a doll!'

"Suddenly, I became frightened, clutching Mary tighter as I heard more.

"'We put out for her room and board. That's enough! There's no money left over for any such kind of foolishness! Sale or no sale, that doll goes back to the store!'

"I wanted to run, hide, or jump out the window, but there was nowhere to go.

"'I'm going up there right now and taking that doll away, before she gets it all dirtied up and we can't get our money back.'

"Footsteps were on the stairway, voices coming closer. 'Emma, don't—'

"'That doll's going back, first thing tomorrow. If you won't take it back, I'll do it myself. You and your drunken spending!'

"I quickly hid Mary under the covers and pretended I was asleep.

"Step-ma came stomping in. Right away, she picked up the empty box by the tree, her angry voice echoing, 'Empty!'

"She came to the bed and began shaking me, screaming, 'Lizzie! Lizzie! Where's that doll?'

"'What doll?' I said, eyes still closed.

"'You know what doll, you little brat!' She pulled back the covers. 'Give me that doll, Lizzie.'

"'Santa brought it. He brought me this doll for Christmas.'

"'Santa never brought you that doll! Your boozing Step-pa, in one of his drunken splurges, went out and bought you that doll, with money we don't have—and it has to go back!'

"'No,' I screamed, 'Santa came—'

"'Emma, not today,' Step-pa started saying.

"'Shut your beastly mouth,' she screamed in rage. 'Do you think we're made of money? To throw away on booze—and dolls!'

"She was really mad now, yanking my hair and yelling, 'Give me that doll, Lizzie!'

"I jumped out of bed, clutching Mary, and quickly crawled under the bed far as I could, cowering next to the cold wall.

"Step-ma bent down, yelling, 'You come out from under that bed!'

"'No, I'm never coming out!' I didn't care how much I'd be punished.

"'You come out or I'll give you the worst whipping you've ever had!'

With one big jerk, she pulled the small metal bed away from the wall and there she was, standing right over me.

"'Give me that doll!' She grabbed for it, but I wouldn't let go, hanging on as tight as I could.

"'You'll pull her arm off, you little witch!' she bellowed. 'You're ripping her dress!'

I had to let Mary go or she'd be torn into pieces. I was left holding a tiny bit of her golden hair.

"'You'll pay for this, you ungrateful brat! You're going to get the worst whipping of your life.' She grabbed me roughly. I was crying my eyes out, unable to talk.

"Step-pa moved closer to her. 'Emma—'

"'She's going to learn to obey!' A new rage overtook her.

"Then Step-pa said, in a voice I never heard him use before, almost like a growl. 'Take the doll back, if you must. You probably wouldn't let her play with it anyway.'

"Forcefully, he pulled Step-ma away from me. 'But you're not going to whip her! Not on Christmas day!'

"Then he pushed Step-ma out the door, yelling, 'Now take the doll, and get out of here!'

"They were both gone, screaming at each other for a long time after.

"I cried the rest of the day, that night, and for weeks after, for the doll I almost had. The most beautiful doll in the whole wide world."

Mama's crying now. I'm crying too.

I wait for her to go on and tell me more about the rest of her life on that farm. Instead, she looks away and says something she's never said when she told the story before.

"I made up my mind then, if ever I had children, I'd make sure they had wonderful Christmases, no matter what. To make up for the ones I never had."

She looks away for a minute, then goes back to drinking her tea.

It's quiet for a while. I have to ask. "But, Santa brings our toys, doesn't he, Mama? Even if you help with the other things, it's him—"

"I've said more than I should. Time for us both to be getting back to work." Mama wipes her eyes with her apron and starts clearing off the table.

I never asked to hear Mama's Christmas story again. I didn't need to. Every word was now printed in my head.

~ GUITARS and FLOWERS ~

It's pure magic how our yard changes almost overnight. Golden dandelions sprinkle our grass with bursting circles of sunshine. Lilies of the valley quiver under the bridal wreath bushes. Lilacs and honeysuckles paint our backyard in splashes of lavender and yellow.

It's also picture-taking time. Mama brings out her Kodak camera and poses us in front of the flowers. Sonny gets dressed up in his sailor suit. I wear the white Sunday dress Mama made me, with rows of embroidered flowers. We stand motionless in front of the flowering almond bush. *Click.*

"Okay, now another one," Mama says, stepping back. *Click.*

Mama enters the best snapshots in picture contests. Sonny won an Honorable Mention once and received a shiny goldy medal. I haven't won anything yet. Pretty soon, Mama says, I'll be too old for the Children's Class. That's okay with me. I never like how I look in pictures anyway.

The flowering almond bush under our bedroom window near the sidewalk blooms early. It's such a shower of pink beauty that people walking by break off tiny branches so they can take a bit of spring with them. I never rap on the window like Mama does when they do this. I just watch from behind the curtain, happy to share something from our house.

I love flowers of all kinds. One time, I even became a flower, a big orange poppy. You see, Mama thinks I'm extra bright. I hear her tell others, "I don't know where she gets her brains from, but she has them. Maybe she got mixed up at the hospital." Mama doesn't know I heard, but I did. My ears perk up when people talk about me.

But I never think I'm smart, not when I have an older brother and sisters who know so much more than I do, and tell me so.

Anyway, Mama is excited about this Hawaiian music, which is very popular now on the radio and in the movies. She thinks that if I could learn to play the Hawaiian guitar, she could hear this melodic music any time she wants. Or maybe I would be fulfilling some dream Mama once had for herself.

Mama has lots of dreams. Sometimes, when she's in a certain mood, she shares them with us—dreams about what kind of house she'd really like to live in, if she ever had lots of money. I think she'd really like to live in one of those big fancy houses I see in the movies, that's always clean, with acres of rooms and fancy furniture.

Maybe that's why Mama writes shorts for the movies and sends them away to the movie people. It's an extra special day when she gets a letter saying they're buying two of them!

"We're all going to the movies tomorrow night, and buying buttered popcorn too!" She waves the check around. "I sold two shorts,

54

and here's the proof." She's so happy about it. So is Daddy.

Of course, she's always hoping to sell more, but never does. We want her to be happy, but sure don't want her moving away to Hollywood.

Another time, Mama took some mail order course on how to make belts out of bits of celluloid and colored paper, braiding and twisting them into odd long shapes. I don't think she ever sold any. There's this flat cardboard box filled with unfinished and unsold belts that moves from closet to closet.

Auntie Stacia took a course on how to make tin cans into bouquets of metal flowers, snipping down the sides of cans to make the stems, cutting the tops into odd shapes of tinny flower petals, which she paints in bright colors. I think the only people she ever sold them to were Mama and the other aunts, because all the aunts have them displayed on tables somewhere in their houses.

Catherine, my older sister, received a Spanish guitar one Christmas, but never played it. It just stood silently in the corner of the sitting room. One day, nuns from the conservatory behind our school sent a flyer home announcing special spring rates for new music lessons they're offering. One is a class for Hawaiian guitar.

Mama goes into action. She visits the music store and finds out she can buy a steel nut to put under the guitar strings to raise them, making the Spanish guitar sound like a Hawaiian one. You also need a steel bar to hold in your left hand and a finger pick and thumb pick for the right hand. "The music store man said that's all you need, except you have to sit and play the guitar instead of standing up," Mama tells me.

"So now you can take Hawaiian guitar lessons without my having to buy a new guitar." Mama figures she can sacrifice a small sum each week for me to take lessons. Besides expanding my many talents, she'll also be helping support the nuns. The final reward will be this unique Hawaiian music playing in our house, anytime we want. It also means my having to play for visiting relatives. I hate doing that. But it's ritual, a normal part of company visits to our house—displaying any new talent we kids have achieved.

I don't protest too much about the lessons. I usually do what I'm told. Adults are in charge and we have to follow their rules whether we like them or not. I just hope I don't have to learn to do the hula. When I mention I'm going to learn to play the Hawaiian guitar, kids ask, "Really? Are you going to be doing that hula dance too, in a grass skirt?" That possibility scares me more than learning the guitar.

So every Wednesday after school, I have to go home, then lug this huge guitar in its new heavy black case for three long blocks to the conservatory, an odd, forbidding-looking red brick building.

Going by myself to this strange new place frightens me. I'm not sure where to go or what to do when I get there. Mama says the nuns will tell me what to do, and to just show them my signed slip that says, "For Hawaiian Guitar Lessons."

"It won't matter if the guitar has a painted picture of a Spanish lady doing a Flamenco dance on its topside. You tell the nun it's a Spanish guitar made into a Hawaiian guitar." These are Mama's parting words to me as I try to somehow get out of leaving. It doesn't work. Never does.

So I trudge to my first lesson, with no way to hide from onlookers where I'm going, or why.

Once inside the conservatory, it takes lots of questions, many wrong turns, and numerous doors before I finally find out where I'm to go for my lesson. I keep hoping I'll remember the way next time I come, as all the rooms and doors look the same.

So here I am, just me and this older nun, whom I've never met before, in this large room with a big stage, lots of instruments, and music sounds coming from all sides. It's a real jumble of noises. She tells me her name, but I can't figure out what she said and I'm too afraid to ask her to repeat it. So I just call her "Sister." But I don't speak too often, mostly, I just listen.

She gives me a guitar book. *Hawaiian Guitar Lessons #1.* There, right on the cover, is a Hawaiian girl dancing in a grass skirt, and a straw-hatted man sitting under a palm tree, playing a guitar on his lap. I could never wear something like that or dance around with flowers around my neck and feet.

What if I left now? Would they come after me? What would they do if they caught me?

The nun says to take very good care of the book, even if it's mine and already paid for. "You will use this book every day for your practice. And remember to bring it along with you each time."

Something more I have to carry back and forth.

I quickly turn the cover page over so I don't have to look at the grass-skirted girl anymore. Inside, it all looks like a foreign language. There are lines running across the pages, with big dots scattered everywhere on the lines. I know nothing about guitars, notes, or clefs. The nun says to look the book over, and leaves the room.

I'm all alone. It seems like such a long time since I first came.

This certain urge happens whenever I'm scared, only I don't know what to do about it here. If I go out of the room to look for a bathroom, I'll just get lost, which makes me more scared.

I rise up from my chair, not sure what to do.

It's already too late. A puddle is forming on the floor beneath me. I just stand there, looking down at the floor.

The nun returns. I'm so afraid of what she'll say. All she does is take my hand, whispering, "Follow me."

Where is she taking me? What kind of punishment do they give for doing something like this? I bite my quivering lips and follow.

The nun stops at a door, opens it and points inside. "You must use this room if you feel the need the next time," she says and walks away.

I don't have to use the room now, so I just stand inside there and begin to cry. I'm afraid to come out, afraid I'll get lost again.

After a while, the nun comes in and tells me the lesson is over and that I can leave now. "And don't worry about what happened. We all have accidents."

I walk back to the music room close to her. I really don't know this nun that well, but I love her already. I pack up my guitar and new lesson book and follow her.

"We'll see you next week at the same time, Ludmilla," she says as she opens the outside door for me. "Ludmilla" never sounded nicer.

I take the longer way home, hoping everything will dry up on the way.

Still, I don't really want to go back anymore. I don't remember anything I learned, only that shameful thing that happened.

I tell Mama the minute I get in the door, "I don't want to go to lessons anymore." Mama doesn't even ask why, just tells me, "I paid for eight weeks of guitar lessons for you. You're going to go there every week whether you like it or not. And you're going to practice every night too, whether you want to or not."

"But, I can't go back—"

"Well, you are. I don't know why you don't appreciate being given an opportunity no one else in this family has had."

I can't tell her the real reason, knowing that would make her even madder. In addition, I sure don't want her walking me there, as she sometimes has for other things, which is never any fun.

So I go back to lessons the next week, and make sure to excuse myself if I feel like I'm going to have another accident. I know where that room is now and a fast way to get there.

But I never do get the hang of playing the guitar, though I try as hard as I can, and Sister Josef tries as hard as she can. My brain never connects to those strings. There's a big gap there somewhere. I'm just not musically inclined. I think I heard someone else say that when they heard me practicing. My brother says even worse things, like "Can't you practice in the basement, so I don't have to hear those awful sounds?"

Any music I finally manage to ping out on those strings does not sound at all like the Hawaiian music heard in the movies or on the radio. Even Mama agrees, and says she's not going to pay for any more lessons after these are done. Catherine says she wants her guitar back, too, since it's hers, and "It was not meant to be a Hawaiian guitar, anyway."

She has taken to learning the ukulele, maybe thinking Mama might like her kind of Hawaiian music better, but gives it up pretty quick like she does most things. Mama doesn't seem to like Hawaiian music that much anymore anyway.

At the end of the music sessions, there's to be a spring concert featuring students from each musical section. After hours of extra practice onstage and at home, the big talked about night arrives. I'm too nervous to eat, hoping I'll remember all the notes and when to play them.

I have to go early, by myself, but that's better because I don't have to talk to anybody on the way there, just say extra prayers to lots of saints for help. Mama and the rest will come later. Daddy never goes to our school stuff, but Mama always does.

The concert is free for family and friends, but you still need tickets, as lots of people always want to come. Everyone dresses up, making it a special event. I just hope they don't sit too close to the front because I don't want to look out and see anybody I know, or Buddy making faces at me.

I wait backstage while the others do their pieces. Then it's my turn. I walk slowly onto the huge stage as practiced, place my music book on the stand, then sit on this wobbly tin folding chair, trying to balance my guitar on my lap. A twisted gold rope around my neck is connected to the guitar to keep it from slipping, but it still does sometimes.

Luckily, I don't have to play alone, because they paired me off with another guitar student. He covers up lots of my mistakes. Only the really good students get to play by themselves.

We sit, stiff and silent. Then the nun off at the side nods her head, our signal to begin. With the steel bar gripped tightly in my left hand, I try to glide it across the strings with a slight tremolo, to make it sound like what I had practiced for so many days before. My fingers, with picks on them, pluck out the notes.

I keep my eyes glued to the book on the music stand in front of me, not daring to look up or out into that audience, knowing they're watching me.

As I'm sitting and playing, I keep thinking how lucky I am, knowing where the bathroom is, because now I feel I have to go and don't think I can wait. Sitting on that chair, it seems like forever, and it does no good trying to cross my legs, not with this big guitar on my lap.

After the last tremulous note, the bathroom agony magically disappears as I hear the audience clapping. What a joyous sound! Right then, I decide that being onstage and getting applause is worth the previous days of misery, and the agony I just suffered plastered to that tinny chair. I'm ready to do it all over again. It would all be so much easier the next time.

But that's not going to happen, since I know there'll be no more guitar lessons. "You learned all you're going to." Mama's words echo as I leave the stage, knowing I'll have to walk home with my family. When I do, they make silly remarks about my playing, my appearance, and other unwanted comments. "You're just lucky you had some guy playing with you, so you didn't have to squeak by yourself," Buddy teases.

But the previous applause drowns him out, along with the other shaming words.

Maybe playing music on the radio, and not being seen, might be better than sitting on a stage. But I know for sure I'll never get to play on the radio, not me, so I cross that thought from my head. The guitar goes back in the corner, minus the steel bar.

During recital practices, I heard music students talk about the Spring Operetta that would be happening next month. They made it sound like a really wonderful event. "You don't even have to play an instrument to be in it," they told me.

Oh, how I wish I could be part of something like that, be on that stage again, and not have to play an instrument.

For days, I rub the magic stone I carry in my green leatherette purse. It works. My wish comes true when someone tells me that, because I was a conservatory student, I'm eligible to be in the Spring Operetta. There's even a note from the music nuns saying the same thing.

I bring that note home to Mama right away so she'll believe me.

She has to let me be in the operetta and not say "no" just because the guitar lessons didn't work out.

"It says it doesn't cost any money to be in the operetta," I blurt out even before handing her the note, holding my breath for her answer.

"Well," Mama muses, "maybe you'll have more success being in that operetta than playing the guitar."

She signs the slip and reminds me on the day I have to go to try-outs. I don't even know what "try-outs" are, but I go anyway.

Other frightened children from the music classes are there also. We have to sing, dance, and talk some, while the nuns write stuff down in a yellow tablet each time we do anything.

I know I can't sing. I tried singing along with the guitar till Sister Josef finally said, "Just play the music. One thing at a time is enough for you to learn."

We wait anxiously as names are called for speaking parts and singing parts. The chosen girls prance up on the stage like such smarties. There's a big group left over. I'm one of them, all set to go home, even glad about it. New stuff is sometimes too hard to figure out.

"Stay put," the nun announces. "All you girls who weren't picked for special roles will also be in our operetta. You will each be a poppy. We are going to have a whole field of them."

What? I am going to be a poppy? How could that happen?

I run home to tell everyone. "I'm going to be in the operetta—I'm going to be a poppy!" No one in the family understands how learning the Hawaiian guitar could turn me into a poppy. I don't either.

Rehearsal time begins the next week, but it's not like the guitar recital when we practiced alone. There are lots of kids, boys and girls. After school and on weekends, squealing children and screaming nuns fill the room, with pianos plinking, songs to memorize, and dances to learn. The nuns tell us where to stand, what to do. Everything happens all at once.

We have to rehearse for six long weeks. Still, it's fun, after I figure out what I'm supposed to do. I just follow what everyone else is doing. Easy. If I don't know the dance steps, I just watch the feet next to me. I watch lips too, for words to songs. Since I don't have to do anything by myself, I become one of the group quite easily and happily.

First, we practice Act One. This is the part where we're all poppies, standing in a huge field, swaying back and forth, heads reaching up for the sun. We sing our songs, do our dances. Near the end of the act, this fairy princess comes wandering through our field, touching each one of us with her magic wand. As the sparkling wand taps our heads, we have to wilt, and slowly slump to the ground.

Oh, how we practice wilting, over and over.

"Make it real," the nun repeats, tapping her pointer on the floor. "Let your body go limp. And loose. I don't want to hear a sound when you wilt."

I practice wilting at home, too. Finally, nobody thinks I'm sick and fainting like they did the first time. I get so good at wilting; I can wilt any time, any place. Acting is easy.

Since we have to sing songs and dance as a group, I'm no longer just me; I'm part of something bigger—a field of swaying poppies. Surprisingly, I do feel like a poppy. Somehow, I even become one when I'm on that stage.

Is this how flowers really feel, swirling in the breezes? Light and airy and never wanting to stop flowering. No chores. No rules. Just glowing in the sunlight. It's so much better than playing guitar.

Geraldine doesn't like it that I spend so much time rehearsing.

"Who wants to be in a dumb operetta," she says when I tell her I will be too busy to play with her for a while. "Making believe you're a fake poppy—just singing and dancing around, not even getting to say anything."

"I like being a poppy!" I tell her, but she's already walking away, not wanting to hear any more. I don't care; I have new friends from the operetta group. They ask me to come to their houses to rehearse songs, and I even get invited to one of their birthday parties. So it doesn't matter so much that Geraldine stops asking me to do things.

Next, we practice Act Two, and we're no longer poppies.

At the very beginning, the fairy princess sprinkles magic dust on us, and we all rise up from our wilting positions and magically turn into dancing fairies, wearing ballerina skirts, wings, and pink ballet slippers. We're told this is what we'll be wearing, as we don't have any costumes yet, but I really feel like I'm a dancing fairy, costume or not.

I'm in such awe as I listen to the fairy queen practice her lovely songs. She's only in eighth grade, but her voice is so good she could even be in a big opera. And she looks so beautiful wearing just her school clothes. She even talks to me sometimes.

Two weeks before the operetta, we have to get fitted for our costumes, but we can't wear them till two days before the show, or they might get dirty or torn.

A group of older ladies comes into the downstairs hall with hangers full of costumes, and tape measures, scissors and stickpins. First, they have us try on these round flat hats that cover our head with large floppy orange petals. The big hats flip around a lot, but are held on by black elastic stretched snugly under our chins.

"These bands must be kept tight at all times so the hats stay on!" the nun warns as red marks appear on our necks.

Next, we have to take off all our clothes, except our underwear. I've never done this before in front of other children outside of our family, and hesitate a long time, but I know if I want to be a poppy, I have to do it. I close my eyes during most of the process, not looking at anyone, hoping they're not looking at me either.

"You're next," the lady says.

Now what? I wonder as I stand there in my underwear, hoping I don't have to take anything else off. She slips a long shiny green sleeveless dress over my head. Attached to the skirt are pointy jaggedy leaves, layers and layers of them, that move as I twirl. I also get long green stockings, but no shoes.

Just for the few minutes that I have the whole costume on, I really feel like a flower, and lift my head to the sun, even though the nun always says, "Girls, don't look up too high, or your hats will fall off. Just look straight ahead, so we can see your flowery faces. And smile. Remember, these are happy poppies, not drooping ones."

The hat makes me smile automatically, and I don't even notice the tight band anymore.

The next day, in come the fairy costumes. It's as if it's snowing pink cotton candy all over the basement room. I've only seen such airy dresses in fairy tale books, never thinking I would ever get to wear one. I'm not dreaming either. One of those floating dresses is for me.

My clothes come off much quicker this time. Soon I'm in this fancy dress with a pink satiny top and a net skirt that poufs out like a ballerina outfit. There are sparkles all over the dress, and some fall on me, making me sparkle, too. There are also pink ballet slippers that are oh so soft. Then we have gauzy wings attached to our shoulders and carry a tiny wand with a silver star at the tip.

"One more thing—" The lady halts me, then puts a crown of flowers atop my hair. They're not real, but almost smell as if they are. I've drifted into a far-off land, where everything is floating about and sparkling. I begin to twirl till a stern voice tells me to "stand still." I do, but inside I'm still twirling.

Each piece of our costume gets a tag with our name pinned on it before it's put on a wooden clothes hanger. Then the costumes get hung on long poles hanging from the ceiling pipes of the basement rehearsal hall, waiting for the big day. The room is now dancing in colors—green, orange, and glittery pink.

Every time before I go on stage to rehearse now, I stop, linger, and touch my outfits, to make sure they're still there. I can't wait to really put them on.

There are ads in the church bulletin, and even tacked on trees, about the Spring Operetta. The price isn't too much, so Mama says the whole family will come to see me.

Geraldine says, "Well, I'll come, but I still think the whole thing is pretty silly."

Dress rehearsal night. There's such excitement as thirty girls are helped into poppy costumes and told to wait at the side of the stage.

It's so hard just waiting, not saying a word. Giggles keep exploding, hats flopping off. The music starts and we tiptoe quietly to take our places on stage.

The big velvet curtain opens slowly. The lights that are supposed to be the sun begin shining and we all become a field of swaying poppies. We sing. We dance. It's pure magic. All that we have practiced turns out even better than I imagined. I can feel myself wilting as my pile of green sinks to the floor and my poppy hat droops and covers me up. I even feel like crying, because I'm dying like this. But there isn't time to be sad, because as soon as the curtain closes, we have to rise up, quick as we can, and rush to the costume room.

I hurry to get into my fairy costume, though part of me is still a poppy. These outfits are harder to put on, and we need help with our wings and the flower crowns. "Next, who's next?" "Who else needs help?" "Hurry! Over here." Everyone is rushing about. "Only two minutes to get back on stage."

These stiff skirts itch, and my pink ballet shoes are too big, or I have someone else's, and they have to be stuffed with toilet paper. Our hair is combed back, held with hairpins by some big girls who have come over to help. They even dab rouge on my cheeks. I've never had any on before.

Oh, I feel magical now, and look like a real fairy princess. The smile on my face stays put, as if glued there.

And this isn't even the real show, they tell us, only a dress rehearsal. But we must still act like there are people in the audience. We know the nuns are out there, and can hear them talking and clapping every once in a while.

There's even a photographer from the newspaper.

The next day, the picture he took is on the front page of the paper. I'm not in the picture, just the fairy princess. But I don't care. I'm in the show and I'm a small part of something big that's on the front page. Mama even reads the story aloud to Daddy.

It's a beautiful spring night. I have to go early. I want to go early. I can hardly eat anyway. My brother teases, "Lulu's going to be a poppy—a big, big poppy seed!" I don't care what he says—I'm just happy about everything.

I put on my poppy costume as soon as I get there, without any help. Right away, I know I have to go to the bathroom. It's not easy lifting all the long leaves up without getting them into the toilet. But we've been told that once we're in the stiff ballet costume, there will be no going to the bathroom.

We wait in the dark. My stomach is quivering. But once the curtain opens and the music starts, I immerse myself in the stage world, a world I don't ever want to leave. I just want to keep doing this show over and over and over.

We do three performances—Friday, Saturday, and Sunday.

After final curtain of each, we can come out in our fairy costumes and talk to people.

I know I sparkle. I've never sparkled before; I've always been in the background, satisfied to stay there. Now I want everyone to notice me in this beautiful costume. I realize I can become someone else—someone different from my plain, everyday self. All I need is a costume.

The nuns have told us that if we wanted to, we could buy our costumes. Then we'd get to keep them always.

Mama says, "No, we just can't afford to buy any kind of costumes."

"Only the poppy one. Couldn't I just get the poppy one to keep?" I beg. "That outfit doesn't cost as much as the fairy one does."

"No," Mama repeats, "We can't even afford the poppy one. We bought tickets for the whole family to see you as a poppy—we'll remember how you looked."

I know it's no use to ask again. I also know I can't change into a fairy princess unless I'm on that stage. But I'm so sure I could become a poppy anywhere, if I could just put on that green costume, sing the poppy song, and wilt over and over. I want that leafy dress and poppy hat more than anything else—well, unless it's the Shirley Temple doll for Christmas.

The show is over; the curtain closes, never to open again. I linger as long as I can with the audience afterwards, giving me more time to be in my fairy costume.

I go into the costume room, slowly take off my fairy dress and hang it up for the last time. Most of the girls have paid for their dresses and are wrapping them up in crinkling tissue paper, putting them into big brown dress boxes, so anxious to take them home. Some can hardly manage to carry their two boxes out the door at the same time.

They call to one another that they'll be putting on their own show this summer. "And we can wear our special costumes. Won't that be fun?" Which means I won't be seeing them anymore. I won't have any special costume, so I can't be in their shows.

Only a few of us are still lingering. Nobody's talking anymore.

I don't want to leave. Both of my dresses look so sad and lonely on their hangers, as if waiting for me to put them back on and bring them to life once more. I try to stop the tears, but they come anyway.

We were told we could keep the wand with the shiny star. I decide I don't want that wand anymore. It would mean nothing without the rest of the clothes. I throw the wand on the floor. I want to smash it, break it up, but can only stomp down over and over, hard as I can with my soft tie shoes, till all that's left is a pile of smashed crunch.

I walk out, not even turning around for one last look. Best to leave everything behind.

Still, there's this aching pain, as if pieces of my heart have been broken off and remain attached to those costumes left hanging alone in that room.

The door slams shut. I'm on the other side now, where everything is newly dark.

~ SPECIAL DRESSES ~

Every morning, I carefully pick out which dress I'm going to wear, one which will make me feel a certain way. I don't have too many. Catherine and Betty Jane's dresses are also in the same jam-packed closet. I like looking at their fancy dresses, and sometimes even try them on secretly. Catherine's red silky dress that she wears to parties is my favorite. Most of my dresses are hand-me-downs from Catherine. Their colors are faded, and the hems taken up or down. But I like wearing her clothes, and sometimes I think I can feel her in the material. Betty Jane's clothes still have a medicine smell and I always tell Mama, "Don't give me any dresses from Betty Jane."

Mama only has one good dress, which she wears on Sundays and for company. It's a soft dark blue material, with small flower pictures all over. It always smells of Blue Waltz perfume. Most days, she wears plain cotton dresses with an apron over them.

I can't wait till the day I'll be wearing that longed-for First Communion dress. Or the dazzling prom attire. Then the magical

71

one, which means I've reached my fairy tale ending—the flowing white wedding gown.

On certain days, girls in special occasion dresses grandly parade around our neighborhood. Friends and strangers gather around the glowing girl as if she were some movie star. I stand in awe, picturing myself in that same gown, wanting my body to grow bigger quicker.

I attend Catholic school, so religion is part of my daily life. I go to Mass each morning before class and learn about the Sacraments in my religion class.

The first Sacrament we get ready for is Confession. I don't look forward to going to confession, having to tell a priest behind a screen things I've done wrong—sinful things.

Sister Regina tries to explain "sin" to us. It sounds like the same things Mama tells us not to do.

First, we do a make-believe confession and can make up sins. But it's hard to even make up any. I never do anything really bad, but finally come up with a few. "I disobeyed my mother and father. I hit my brother or sister. I thought bad thoughts." I'm never quite sure what that covers, but our nun says we shouldn't have them.

My one ambition is to be a saint.

Sister Regina reads us stories about holy saints who never do anything bad and are willing to give up their lives for the love of Jesus. Some of the stories about how they died are pretty gruesome. I don't know if I could ever be a martyr and have such terrible things done to me without crying out or giving up. But I like to think I could.

I would just close my eyes and wait for it to be over—let it happen real quick, knowing I would go straight to heaven right after. I'd just need to go through that short minute of pain, that's all.

I think I could do it. But I hope that minute never happens to find out for sure. I also know that if I want to be a saint, I have to go to Confession so no sins will be left on my soul, making it pure and white as a saint's should be.

We learn about the soul, too. It's something you can't see, the part of us that goes to Heaven after our body dies. Having a soul is what makes us different from animals. We ask Sister Regina questions about our souls and she tells us, "You will be learning more about souls next year. Right now, you know enough for Confession."

I still wonder where the soul stays. Just inside the body? Or can it go in and out? What if it couldn't get back in?

I'm dreading that first Confession after hearing stories from others, especially my brother.

"Be careful when you get behind that curtain," Buddy warns. When I ask why, he says, "I can't tell you what happens when you get in there. It's a secret we're sworn not to tell." Since he's an altar boy, he knows more about church things than I do. He also gets to go places in church where girls are never allowed.

Rehearsing a confession in the classroom is not the same as when I go alone into the curtained church confessional the first time. It's very dark in there.

I talk through a window with a covered screen to someone I can't even see. I know it's a priest and can tell by his voice which one, too. I hope he can't tell by my voice who I am, so I talk very softly, which makes him ask me to repeat what I said.

My hands are folded tightly, and I squeeze my eyes shut until I hear him say, "Your penance will be three Hail Marys and two Our Fathers. Go in peace, my child. Your sins are forgiven."

It's over. I can unclench my hands and breathe normally.

I push aside the curtain and leave the confessional with a much lighter heart and a pure white soul. But I will never tell my brother what went on in there. You can't. What happens in the confessional is never to be revealed to anyone. Priests can't tell, either. They would rather die than give out Confession secrets, Sister Regina tells us.

I always wonder about those other sinners, who stay in the box for such a long time. My imagination thinks up all kinds of things they might be telling. Are there really such bad people going to our church? But we've been told that Confession is to make bad people good, so it's a good idea that they do go.

I go to Confession about once a week after the first time, usually repeating the same list of sins and getting the same penance. It gets easier each time.

During religious instructions, the priest tells us that we have reached the age of reason, which is the age for Confession. So now I'm responsible for everything I do, good and bad. God does not punish babies or really small children, because they haven't yet reached the age of reason.

I'm not sure if I'm glad I've reached that reason age or not, it just seems to come with everything else that happens along the way of growing up. The bigger kids always get blamed for things anyway, because they should know better, and the little ones are generally excused, because they don't know any better.

After our first Confession, we prepare for our First Communion. This Sacrament is easy, and I look forward to it. I just have to be sure I don't have any sins left on my soul before I go up to take the host. I also can't eat anything twelve hours before the big event. Another big reason I'm looking forward to that day is getting to wear the white First Communion dress, with a crown and a short veil. I can hardly wait.

"Make it pretty," I tell Mama as I watch her cut up an old white dress she's making over for me. "And put lots of lace on it." Rows and rows of lace make anything prettier.

"Don't be worrying about how you'll look, that's not what the day is for." Mama keeps cutting.

I don't see how those junky white scraps can be made into a pretty dress. But when I try it on, it's beautiful, and it makes me look beautiful, too. It has lots of lace, and a full skirt that stands out over a stiff petticoat. I also have new white stockings and brand-new Mary Jane shoes. I feel like an angel, even without having wings.

I also get a new First Communion prayer book and a sparkling blue crystal rosary. "Religious things are worth spending money on," Mama says when I ask.

I think the rosary is a used one. Even though the beads still sparkle, the chain and cross look pretty dull. Worn out by prayers, I guess. Still, better than my old broken one that has beads missing. Though it did make the Hail Marys go faster.

Finally, Communion Sunday arrives. I have to make sure not eat or drink. The whole family keeps reminding me.

What if I did eat? Would I be left out? Would I have to sit in the pew alone?

Mama helps me put on my dress, then the crown with the short veil. We go outside to take pictures. Afterwards, Mama walks with me to church, making sure nothing gets dirty along the way. I step very carefully in my new shoes, feeling like I'm a one-person parade.

Our whole second grade class is gathered in a church side room where we are given extra instructions. We say our Communion prayer together, then march saintly outside and into the church, all the way to the front pews with big white ribbons marking them off, so no one else sits there. After carefully genuflecting in our fancy dresses, we sit in the spot saved for us.

I can tell everyone's looking at us.

I feel so holy, so special, even pretty, but Sister Regina said that we should not be thinking about how we look, just about the host we will be receiving—the body of Jesus.

I sit very carefully, as the big skirt on my dress flounces about the pew. My head is held high with the crowning veil. We listen to the sermon telling us, "Your lives will be changed forever once you receive your First Holy Communion."

After the small bell rings, the priest lifts the host up high, then the chalice. We walk up to the Communion rail, as practiced. The altar cloth is spread over the rail. We hold our hands solemnly underneath, so if the host falls, it will be onto the cloth, not the floor. We've been warned never to bite on the wafer, just soften it with our tongue and then swallow. Biting would be sacrilegious. If the host should drop, we mustn't touch it. Only the priest is allowed to touch the host.

The priest and altar boy move along the rail with the gold chalice, saying a short prayer as they put the host onto each communicant's outstretched tongue.

It's my turn. I lift my head solemnly, not even worrying whether my veil will fall off or not, and stretch out my tongue. Soon, the wafer's on my tongue. I swallow it without my teeth touching.

I am now a Child of God. A Bride of Heaven. I have Jesus inside me—a holy feeling. I really do feel different, like Sister said we would. I glow within and without. I am surely on my way to sainthood.

I wear that dress, without the veil, all day long, in the house, outside, wanting the neighbors to see me in it too. The relatives come for food and drink. Today, I'm the star of the show and in all the photographs. Everyone says something nice to me. Even if I'm not sure what they're saying. I just smile and try to look holy.

All too soon, it's over. The dress is carefully hung back in the closet for the next occasion. The snapshots we get back from the drug store only show how the dress looks on me, not how I felt wearing it. But I do think I look more saintly than in any other picture I've ever had taken.

The next time I get to wear the Communion dress is for the May Procession, honoring Mary. It's held every year, the first week of May, at night, in our old St. Boniface church, which looks like the churches on holy cards. It has lots of statues, curlicue gold borders that twist along the walls and ceilings, and saintly pictures painted all over.

In previous years, as I watched the girls wearing their First Communion dresses in the May procession, I could hardly wait till I would be walking down the same aisle. Now, it's finally my turn.

Mama curls my hair the night before. Sometimes she uses the hot curling iron, but this time she puts in rag curls. When they're taken out the next morning, I shake my head, and the bouncing curls make me look like Shirley Temple. If only I had dimples, too. Pressing eraser tips into my cheeks has not worked.

After supper, I carefully put on my Communion dress and newly-polished white Mary Jane shoes.

"I'm ready, Mama," I call out. We're going early, before the others.

Mama puts on her brown sweater and takes my hand as we walk the three blocks to St. Boniface in the quiet twilight. I know everyone is watching as we pass by. I try to walk as slowly as I can, so they can see my whole outfit, even though I want to get there as fast as possible.

"I'll be watching for you, but don't you turn around to look at me when you go down that aisle," Mama says when we get to the church. She gives me a quick kiss then leaves to get a good seat on the aisle.

The girls from the First Communion class congregate in the vestibule where each is given a bouquet of real flowers tied with a blue ribbon. Mine are multi-colored sweet peas. They smell like heavenly perfume.

We wait outside till the big church bell in the tower peals loudly. Hand bells begin ringing and the priest and altar boys, carrying the huge cross, swinging the smoking incense burner, begin the slow procession into the church and up the center aisle. Tonight, there's a white silky runner rolled out on it. We girls follow slowly, picking off flower parts from our bouquets and dropping them along the runner. Streams of fragrant flower bits trail us as rainbow patterns are crushed into the glowing white footpath.

The whole church feels different, and even smells different this evening. Candles cast flickering shadows across the dark walls. The hanging ceiling lights make the gold fixtures glitter in mysterious wavering reflections. The holy paintings appear more alive, and the entire church emits a miraculous glow.

I feel as if I'm floating down the aisle alone, not part of the procession. I gather in the whole event, each particle of celebration that surrounds me. I want to save it, and keep it alive as long as I can.

We march slowly, singing memorized May songs: "Tis the month of our Mother. The blessed and beautiful May—"

We file to the side altar with the big statue of Mary, her arms outstretched to us. We place the remainders of our bouquets at the hem of her blue garment, then go sit in the reserved front pews.

It's a glorious, miracle kind of night. I can only be in it once, but this once is truly worth the holy feeling it brings.

I linger a bit, and I'm the last one out the huge church door. Mama is waiting outside the church, smiling.

"You looked like a little angel," she says. Then adds, "Let's hope you stay that way." We stroll home on the still-warm sidewalks. The air is filled with soft breezes.

Mingled aromas of spring flowers gather from all the yards. People are sitting outside on their porches. They stop talking as we walk by. I can feel eyes watching us through the dimness.

My white dress glows and shimmers in the moonlight. I feel transformed, as if I have visited another land and am now returning, but having been there, I am a changed person. I have walked where flowers were strewn beneath my feet and candles glowed like polished stars, and Mother Mary welcomed me lovingly into her new group of Holy Communicants.

Just for a while, I felt maybe I was walking somewhere in heaven.

~ CHICKENS and EASTER ~

One sure sign of spring is the arrival of the large flat cardboard box with round holes punched all over, and tiny peeps coming from inside. It's the baby chicks Mama ordered! I'm not sure where they come from, but there's much excitement around our house the day the mailman brings them.

We stand close by as Mama carefully opens the box with a sharp knife. Packed inside are these tiny fluffy yellow balls—baby chicks, cheeping and moving about. Mama already has a place laid out for them—a pen made with chicken wire, set up in the spare room. It has upside down watering bottles, where water gurgles down into a circular tray. There's also a tin feeding trough with holes to peck in. On the bottom are newspapers to catch droppings, which we'll have to change daily.

Each of us helps lift these quivering balls into their new home. They must be so glad to get out after their long trip. Sometimes, one or two don't make it, lying stiff and cold in the box.

Mama counts each as we take them out, otherwise it would be too hard to keep track of how many there are. We're supposed to get thirty.

"One chick, two chicks, three chicks—" we all repeat after Mama.

Mama used to keep eggs in a warm metal incubator in the basement and get new chicks to hatch from the eggs, but she says having them sent by mail is easier and faster.

You can order so much stuff from the catalog, even Christmas presents. You want it, you order it. I think all you need is stamps. But you might need money, too. Course, I don't worry too much about it, as we kids never order stuff, or pay for our Christmas presents, just those we buy for each other. Mama orders quite a few things by mail. But not too many boxes come from the catalog these days.

The chicks are soon cheeping in their new play yard.

From then on, we each have our chores with the chicks—watering, feeding, and cleaning. I love to just sit by the pen and watch their antics. There are twenty-eight pets to play with, not just one. They're also pets we can keep inside our house. We hear their voices all day and sometimes at night. They cuddle together in clumps at night to sleep, then they're up real early, peeping for food.

We watch as they begin to grow bigger each day. Their feathers, no longer fuzzy, start turning whitish and scraggly. Pretty soon, Mama says, "I think it's time for the chicks to go out to the chicken coop."

By then, we're mostly ready for them to leave too.

In our backyard, we have this chicken coop with a high wire-fenced yard. Here they can roam all day, scratch in the dirt, and cluck to each other. They lay their eggs in nest boxes nailed on the walls inside the coop where they sleep at night.

Eventually, the time comes when one of the chickens has to be killed for a Sunday dinner. I try never to watch, or be near the dreadful deed. However, whenever I see the chopping block next to the coop, with dark red stains, or the sharp hatchet hanging on the garage wall, I imagine—*Chop*—a chicken's head being cut off. Sometimes I really hear a chicken squawking loudly, then dead silence. I know what's happening, even if I try to block it out.

I don't stay around to see Mama do the rest either, pulling off feathers, cleaning the insides out, all before putting it in the oven. So I feel somewhat sad when these little chicks leave the protection of our home, not knowing how they'll end up.

Mama says, "Chickens have a good life. They don't have to work, get their food free, and don't even pay rent for their housing."

Still, I don't like the way they end up. Even if I love the taste of roast chicken, I try not to remember how it got on the platter. I wonder if a chicken can wish on its own wishbone.

What would it wish for?

I do like gathering eggs when they're still warm. If there's lots, that means an angel food or sponge cake with the roast chicken dinner. Mmm. Just thinking about them, I can almost taste those sweet cakes with their sticky gooey frosting.

So chickens add some nice things to our lives without too much fuss. Our country cousins have cows, horses, and pigs, and they have to work much harder. When they visit, they always have to leave "to get home to milk the cows and feed the pigs." I'm happy to just have chickens in our lives and house once a year.

Springtime is when Easter arrives, too. It's always on a different Sunday because it has to do with Passover. I do look forward to that Sunday, but it doesn't hold the same looked-forward-to feeling Christmas does. Nothing tops that.

We do anticipate the Easter Bunny's visit. Easter morning, I'm excited to get up and go into the kitchen. There it all is. Such a wonderful sight. The kitchen table has an ironed white tablecloth over the cracked oilcloth. The Easter Bunny came secretly during the night, filling the colored straw baskets at each of our places with chocolate eggs, marshmallow chicks, and colored jelly beans.

In the center is the sparkling carnival glass bowl, piled high with brightly colored boiled Easter eggs. The floor is scrubbed and waxed. It's the prettiest our kitchen ever looks. I stand there and look at it all for the longest time. But pretty soon the other kids are there, hungry for the candy, but we're not allowed to eat any till Mama says it's okay. Pretty soon, she's there too.

"Well, look at all the Easter presents the bunny has brought you children. I guess candy fasting for Lent is over." Before her last word is out, we're all digging in our baskets.

"That's enough now. No eating anything till after church!"

Mama starts boiling different eggs for Daddy on Easter, using onion skins to give them a burnt orange color. "An old Polish tradition," she says.

I'm glad we have our own colored eggs, because Daddy's always have soft insides. "Because he likes them that way," Mama answers if we ask about it. Luckily, Easter rabbits don't bring us his kind of soft eggs. Magic rabbits don't need onion skins for their colors, either.

Where do they get their colors? Flowers, maybe?

Of course, Easter is a religious holiday too. It begins with Ash Wednesday, when the priest puts ashes on our foreheads, followed by forty days of Lent. We all do penance, saying extra prayers, walking the stations, making sacrifices, which mostly means not eating candy. We don't have to fast and abstain as the adults do. They can only eat one full meal a day and not eat meat on some days. But as most meals are prepared for adults, we observe some of their food rules by default. We do many things by default.

On Palm Sunday, we get blessed palms in church and put them up in our house, usually sticking them behind picture frames on the wall.

The last week of Lent is Holy Week, one of the holiest weeks of the year. We go to special church services with our classmates on Holy Thursday, Good Friday, and Holy Saturday. Even though we don't have regular school these days, we're still expected to show up at church. Mama makes sure we do.

Good Friday has a solemn grimness to it. Special Tre Ore church services are held from noon till three o'clock. All the statues are covered in purple cloths. The sacristy light is out, a sign that no hosts are in the church today. There's no organ music either. Even though we hear the story about Jesus dying so many times, it still makes me sad to hear it over again, especially on Good Friday. It's even painful to see Him still suffering on that big crucifix hanging above the front altar.

We all march up to the altar in a line after the Tre Ore service. We kneel and kiss the relic of the real cross, then quietly leave the church.

Many times, the sky is dark that day too. Sometimes there's huge thunderstorms. Mama says it's a reminder of what a sad day it is. The whole earth is crying. She reminds us that there were storms and earthquakes when the day really happened. I've seen pictures in holy books of the earth opening up the day Jesus died. They're kind of scary pictures. Bad things can be in holy books, too.

Nothing in town is open from noon till three. All the movie theaters close down that night, too. "Remember, keep the radio off, and no music from twelve to three today. No talking either. You just keep praying during that time," Mama tells us. So we keep mostly silent, and point our fingers instead of talking. We're supposed to be praying, but it's hard to keep prayers going for such a long time. I try, but other thoughts keep coming into my head. I don't think I'm going to make it to being a saint. It's not as easy as I thought it might be.

There's always lots to do at home to prepare for Easter. All week, Mama's busy baking and cleaning, and we all help her. The day before, we lay out our Sunday clothes, make sure our shoes are polished, and try on new or old Easter bonnets. The night before, we have our hair washed, and take a longer bath. Once in our beds, we talk about the Easter Rabbit and what he might bring us before happily falling asleep...

Then lo, it's the glorious Easter morning. Church bells are ringing all around town. We can smell the ham already baking as we get ready to go to Mass in our Sunday clothes, not eating anything before because we'll be going to Communion. But what we're really looking forward to is getting home, eating our candies from the baskets, as well as frosted rolls and colored Easter eggs.

Later, we'll be having a delicious Easter ham dinner and the white iced Lady Baltimore cake with creamy filling that's already waiting on the fancy cake stand.

It's a day filled with so many good things. Plus, there's usually no school the week after, so the sadness of the preceding week doesn't stay around for too long. But Holy Week does make life different. It's a time that makes us think more about death and suffering. Only you can't think about it too much, Mama says, because there's so much to live for.

I do want to keep living. Of course, it's mostly old people that die, so I don't have to worry about dying right now. I will though, some day, when I'm really old. I wonder when that day will be, and what I will look like by then.

~ HOUSE CLEANING ~

House cleaning turns everything upside down. It's as if a big wind has blown in and swirls the insides of our house all about.

We never know which day it'll happen. But it has to be a sunny day, because we always hear Mama say, "Next sunny day, I'm going to begin the spring house cleaning." So, we're never really prepared.

I come home from school one day and, surprise! Our whole bedroom's cleared out. The bed's taken apart, and most everything has been placed in the back yard.

I quickly look through all that's spread out there, even before changing out of my school clothes. Mama has old clothes on and a kerchief tied around her hair, and is busy, busy, busy, moving this, shaking that. My box of saved pictures I drew during the school year, the stories I wrote, all kept hidden in a special box under the bed—it's gone.

"Where's my box of pictures and stories?" I ask Mama, trying to keep up with her.

"Thrown out."

"But I wanted to save them."

"I have to clean stuff out once a year, or we wouldn't have any place left to live in." Words I've heard many times before. She keeps moving about, adding, "Now quick, change your clothes. I need you kids to help me."

I don't want to help, not if it means getting rid of things I want to save. It's no use to look further. I'll never see those pictures or stories again. My older sister's box of movie star pictures clipped from movie magazines, plus photos movie stars sent her, even autographed ones—that's all gone, too. In secret, Catherine tells me she keeps some things in places where Mama will never find them. I don't think there is such a place, not in our house, anyway.

Our closets are bare. All the clothes are hanging on the wash line to air out, then they'll be put in the attic for next winter, or given to country cousins, or put in the ragbag. I see my green satin dress with creamy lace trim on the line. I know it's too small, too tight, but I don't want it given away or thrown out. It's my favorite dress, even if it has spots that won't wash out. I hate to part with anything, but haven't yet figured out a way to keep all I want, or where I can keep it.

Some day, I'm going to have a big house of my own and never have to throw anything away.

Sometimes our bare bedroom gets repainted during house cleaning time. When it's empty, there's nice echoing sounds if you sing or holler in it. This is the only time we can do that. This year, Mama's giving the room a coat of pale green paint that was on sale. I like this new color—spring green. I watch Mama brush paint over the old faded rose, recoloring the whole room.

I don't do coloring books anymore, but I'd sure like to try using paints, if I had any. Only paints in tubes are too expensive, so I'll to have to stick to the stubby broken colors and pencils for my artwork.

Mama has paint left over and decides to paint our old bedroom furniture, making everything match, pasting bright rose decals on all the pieces. Now everything looks brand new. It's a whole different place, but it smells of paint for a long time after.

If rooms don't get painted, they get washed. Mama gets up on the stepladder with her scrub pail and washes the ceilings and scrubs down the walls. We learn to keep out of the way of dripping water and a tired Mama. Windows and curtains get washed, too. Nothing gets skipped during house cleaning time, except cooking and baking.

The bedding all hangs over the clothesline, being aired out. One of our few small rugs hangs there too. It's fun being out in the fresh air, beating the dirt out of that rug with the flat wire beater, hard as we can, making whacking sounds that echo throughout the neighborhood, answered by other neighbors whacking back.

It makes me think of tom-tom messages—before telephones were invented, when tribes sent out secret messages to one another. I don't think they were about housecleaning, though.

Mama says it's important to do this cleaning of beds and mattresses to make sure there's no bugs living in the places where we sleep.

Sometimes, when we've been sick, she fumigates the whole room. This happens after there's a sign on the front door that reads: "QUARANTINE," which means someone inside has a contagious disease and nobody can come visit us, like when I had chicken pox. Sicknesses go from one kid to another, so the sign stays on the door a long time.

Fumigation takes place after the last person's through being sick. Mama lights some awful smelling stuff in a tin plate; it foams over and a foul smelling yellowish smoke begins to curl upward. All the windows and doors to the room are shut tight. Stuffing is packed at the bottom of the door so the smoke won't get out. The bugs must really hate being in there, breathing that bad smell. But Mama says it also kills the sickness germs, which are so tiny we can't even see them.

I don't like thinking there are things crawling around inside me that I can't even see, and try to think it's not really true, that if we can't see something, it's only make-believe, like in fairy tales.

After all the stuff gets put back in, we have a nice clean room, which seems so much bigger. It's especially pleasant to slip under bedding that has hung outside, and lie on a mattress with the dirt pounded out of it.

Fresh air comes into the room now, too, as screens have replaced storm windows. Once more, we can open the windows and hear all the sounds from outside, like people talking as they walk by. I miss that during winter. Plus, it's nicer to sleep knowing the bugs have been chased away, even though we still say to each other before we close our eyes, "Don't let the bed bugs bite."

Spring house cleaning is a ritual for most in our town. On the way to and from school, I can see neighbors' yards filled with furniture. Some wash their lace curtains and lay them flat on big curtain stretchers, wooden frames which stretch the lace tight, the sun making wavy lacey shadows on the ground underneath.

Everything is getting a new beginning, all because it's spring. Winter colds have gone away. The bottle of homemade Pinex cough syrup no longer sits on the pantry shelf. The thick heavy blankets are stored in the big attic blanket box that always smells like mothballs.

The snow's gone—winter's gone. But there's still the ever-present thought—Christmas will never be gone. It has just been put away for a while, and even in spring, we await its return.

~ MEMORIAL DAY ~

Already, it's the end of May. This feeling inside, that something exciting is going to happen, gladdens each morning. Today, it's the parade. I can hardly wait.

"Can you see them yet?" I tug at the short sleeves of Buddy's torn shirt as he peers down the street. He's taller, and can see better. We've been waiting for what seems like hours, getting here early to get a good curb spot.

"Not yet," he says, shading his eyes against the morning sun. "Just stay sitting. I'll tell you when they're coming."

He walks away to talk with some of his friends who are goofing around on the grass. I'm not interested in joining them, not those guys.

It's a national holiday, so there's no school today. We're gathered at the curbs of Main Street, anticipation and excitement rippling up and down the people-lined blocks. Some men wear hats and suits, and women are in Sunday dresses. Kids are in play clothes, which are more comfortable for sitting on the curbs.

There's always lots of people lined up for any parade in our town, since there's not that much to do. Any time there's a free event, everybody comes. Kids and grown-ups all want to get out of their houses and be part of public goings on.

People have flags stuck in their grass or waving from their porches. Those living along the parade route bring out chairs, boxes, and blankets to sit on. Pitchers of lemonade are already on porch tables.

I hear drums thumping in the distance, upping our excitement. Soon, we see instruments glistening in the sunlight, and trombones begin blaring.

I get caught up in the whole rhythm of the annual Memorial Day Parade as it comes closer and closer, right down the center of Washington Street. The band players wear colorful uniforms and walk in perfect step, looking straight ahead. There's soldiers, too, marching stiff and precise in different kinds of army clothes. Some even carry guns. A few ride horses. There's empty spaces between each group, but we don't mind, cause each is worth waiting for.

There are no clowns today, because this isn't that kind of parade. We keep looking for more groups, but all too soon, there's the big American flag flapping and we know the end is near. Red, white and blue, the flag is waving in the breeze, the pole held in the leather belt of the flag carrier.

Respectfully, we follow the adults in saluting the flag as it passes by. Some put their hands over their hearts. Some bow their heads. Everyone is solemn, remembering the dead soldiers who fought for our country. This is live history, without any words, which is more impressive than reading about it.

The band marches into the distance. We can hardly see the fluttering flag anymore. The parade has ended, and the watchers start moving away.

For the past week, there've been men with soldier caps on street corners, selling small red paper poppies with little tags on them. American Legion, I think they're called. People buy the poppies and stick them onto their jackets, hats, or shirts.

When we ask, Mama tells us about Memorial Day and the poppies which are sold to honor the soldiers who died in the World War. There's a whole field of poppies planted in a cemetery in France that honors American soldiers who were killed there, called Flanders Field.

I don't know if I'd want to see a field of poppies planted on top of dead soldiers. It should be something more sad, not bright and dancing poppies. I remember when I was a poppy in that operetta, and died at the end of the first act. It was sad, but had nothing to do with soldiers dying, as it was mostly just wilting. No, I wouldn't want to wear one of those small poppies today, or ever. I like to remember only the happy poppies from that operetta.

In Grandma's living room, there's a big picture of a soldier in uniform in a gold oval frame. It's only the soldier's head and the top part of his uniform. He looks stiff and sad, and his eyes keep watching you.

"That's Uncle Nick," Mama says, "He got shot in France during the World War, and died over there."

Grandma had many children, some who died when they were very young. But Mama says having a child killed in a war makes Grandma the saddest, because she never saw him again after he was shot. He never gets any older than he is in that picture, so that must be how Grandma remembers him, before the bullet, not after. I only know him from the picture.

Mama and Daddy go to the cemetery on Memorial Day, which some people call Decoration Day, because they decorate the graves with flowers or flags. The day was first started to remember the soldiers who died in the Civil War, soldiers who fought each other in their very own country. We learned about that in history class.

We remember war on days like today. Reading about war is bad enough, or seeing it in the movie news. I would never want to be in one, ever. Most wars are far away, so I feel safe.

Mama says, "You kids don't have to go along to the cemetery. It's for remembering, and you don't have that much to remember. But someday you will."

I think I have lots to remember, but not very much about dead people. I only hear about them. I'm not old enough yet to go to funeral parlors, or even to a neighbor's house that has an open casket with the dead body displayed in it. I'm glad I can't go.

We never beg to go along to the cemetery either, because it doesn't sound like a place where we'd have much fun. When we walk past the cemetery, I always go extra fast, and try not to even look inside. Some of the bigger boys pick up sticks and run them along the black iron fence spokes, making all kinds of weird noises. Sometimes, they howl strange sounds, making the whole place scarier, even in the daytime.

No, I can wait a long, long time before I want to go visit the cemetery. I would rather spend the rest of the day going to the park, where we can ride on the merry-go rounds, slide down the slide and swing real high on the swings. And if we have any money, we go over to the root beer stand for a big glass of foaming root beer, two of us sharing one mug.

It's fun. But the morning sadness lingers. I don't try to push it away. Sometime it's nice to have two layers of feelings at the same time.

~ THE LAST DAY OF SCHOOL ~

I don't like endings—of anything. Stories. Movies. Radio programs. I don't even like the day to end, disappearing, dissolving into the dark. When I get into bed, I'm sad the day's over. No way to bring it back. That's why I'm heartsick now, because in a few days, school's going to end. Everyone else is happy about it, but not me.

They try to make the day before the last day a fun time. The nuns and some mothers prepare a nice picnic in the playground for the whole school. There's food and games. The best part is seeing the nuns run around in their long black robes, laughing and playing with us. I think this is the only time they get to do that. There's Kool Aid in a big pail and a giant steaming kettle with plenty of hot dogs. There's also candy, peanuts, and prizes. There's no schoolwork either, so it's a pretty good day. Still, I'm not happy about tomorrow.

The very last day of school, we bring bags or boxes from home and clean out our desks. I've taken most of my stuff out already. It's creepy empty.

"Make sure to go through the lost and found box, in case anything of yours is still in there. Last chance," Sister Regina calls out. "Otherwise, all of it goes to the poor children."

I go through the box and find ratty-looking mittens, dirty socks, broken hair barrettes, soiled hankies. Nothing of mine. Let the poor kids have the stuff. Even they wouldn't want any of it.

The walls look bare. All of our hand drawn pictures and stories have been taken down. Gone. Our names won't be left anywhere. Kids who tried writing their names or carving their initials on their desks got caught and had to work extra hard to make sure they removed every mark. Desks will be re-varnished during the summer, and floors newly waxed and polished. Not even our footprints will be left behind.

I want to stay in this room with Sister Regina. She's my favorite nun. She hardly ever hollers, and she reads aloud to us every Friday from fun books that don't have church stories. Sister Regina likes what I write, too, especially my made-up stories.

I'm going to miss her, but I dare not say that too loud around Geraldine. She's always complaining about Sister Regina. Geraldine never keeps quiet about much. But I still like to be with Geraldine. It's almost as if she's my other voice, saying things I would like to say, but never dare to.

Next fall, I'll have a new desk, new room, and new nun. I won't have my escape window to look out of when I want to think about far away things. I hear the desks will be bigger, and the work harder. If I flunked, I could stay here another year, but it wouldn't be the same.

"School's out—School's out—Teacher let the monkeys out!"

The chanting goes on throughout the day. I pretend I'm happy it's over and go along with everyone else singing the song. But I really like school, and look forward to going there each day. It's as if I have another family I'm joining in another place.

Our class goes to Mass in the nearby church every morning before school. I can also go over to the church at recess or lunch and pray for things I want. I think God hears me better from inside the church. It's where He mostly lives.

Geraldine is already planning things we can do this summer.

"I have so many things for us to do this summer, and will be so glad when school's finally out," she keeps saying. I can't keep up remembering all Geraldine tells me, because she talks pretty fast. I just keep saying "yes" and "okay."

"I'm going to the Brownie Girl Scout camp this summer. Why don't you go with me and we'll have such a good time together."

I had already asked Mama. "No, Brownie camp costs money that we don't have. And I'll need you to help take care of Sonny and Mitzy," is her quick answer. I'm not sure if I want to go to Brownie camp anyway. I'd have to sleep with girls I don't know, swim in a lake that has big fish in it, and live in a tent in the woods with wild animals around. Yet, there are new things that sound exciting when Geraldine recites them. Making leather purses, singing all kinds of songs together, eating around a campfire. So I'm kinda glad Mama made the decision for me. It makes it easier.

Geraldine is the only child in her family, and her father still has a job. But she doesn't think she's better than anyone else, and she does share things with me. Sometimes she's pretty bossy, so in a way I'm looking forward to some vacation time by myself while she's away at camp. She promises she'll write. But I don't want to hear about all the fun she's having, knowing I'll never get there. It's better not knowing.

I walk home slowly, dragging the paper bag along the sidewalk, tearing holes in the bottom. There's nothing in it I want to save anyway. All I wanted to save was every day spent in Sister Regina's room, but that's not possible.

~ SUMMER ~

"In the good old summer time...In the good old summer time..."

Mama's voice floats out over the warm breezes as she sings in the kitchen. All the doors are wide open and the windows raised, so even when I'm playing outside, I can hear what's going on inside, as if our yard was another part of the house. And when Mama's singing, I know she's happy, and that makes me happy too

Summer is a good season. I hope it goes on for a long, long time, because there's so many things I want to do.

First, get rid of extra clothes, especially leather tie shoes. Barefoot's best. Mama and Daddy think so, too, because then we don't wear out the only pair of shoes we each have, and by summer, they're getting smaller and the holes in the soles are getting bigger. Usually we have to wait till school starts before we get a new pair of shoes—if there's enough money. I don't worry about such things right now, since there are so many wonderful things to do in summer that don't cost money at all.

My favorite thing to do is going to the library, where everything's free. Even though school's out, I still love to read. Once a week, I walk over to the branch public library in this small red brick building and pick out new books, or maybe old ones. I carry my blue library card with my name printed on it in my green leatherette purse.

Sometimes I pick out books about Christmas, if I see one I haven't read. Just reading about Christmas spreads smiles inside me, no matter the season.

The lady at the checkout desk is always nice and talks to me just like I'm a grown up. "You must like to read," she says with a smile as she stamps the cards in the fronts of my books.

"Yes, I do," I say, then skip out of the library, hurrying home with my armload of treasures.

Mama says I can only take out four books at a time, because I shouldn't be spending all my hours just reading when it's so nice outside.

We have stacks of books at home, mostly ones Mama buys at rummage sales. But I've read them already, right when she brings them home. Some are too babyish. I read those aloud to my little brother. Sonny just loves the Uncle Wiggly books, and knows exactly which shelf they are on. He even knows if he's heard the story before. I don't always remember myself. But I like sitting on the sofa as he nestles close to me while I read. Little Mitzy gets up there too when she hears my Uncle Wiggly voices.

My own favorite rummage book is *Shaugn O'Day of Ireland*, about a little boy who has to dress like a girl so the fairies don't capture him. There's even photos of the boy and Ireland. I would surely like to go to Ireland someday—they believe in wee fairies and other magical things.

Way back, before she was an orphan, Mama's relatives came from Ireland. Mama collects different Irish things, and sings Irish songs.

"When Irish eyes are smiling. . . " brings smiles to all of our eyes when we sing it together, swaying our heads back and forth like silly dipsies. There's big green smiles too, when we eat our green mashed potatoes on St. Patrick's Day.

As soon as I get home with my library books, I find a spot in the shade and sit and read. The stories are sometimes so good I forget where I am. Right now, I'm reading *The Runaway Rocking Chair,* a book where pieces of furniture talk and have adventures, just like real people.

During the school year, I mostly play with my Catholic school friends at their houses after school. Evenings are spent with family. But in summer, I have friends that go to Lutheran school too. My best summer friend is Caroline, who lives right across the street.

Everybody from the whole neighborhood gets together during summer vacation, playing in each other's yards or houses. Boys have their clubs, the girls theirs. Well, it's not really a club, but we girls all have dolls that come in stand-up suitcases, with hangers for doll clothes inside.

We meet up at each other's houses, bringing along our suitcase dolls. It's much better than playing dolls by ourselves. We even sew clothes for them and trade doll stuff.

Nobody has a Shirley Temple doll, not yet, but next summer I'm sure I'll have one. If I don't—well, I might stop coming to the doll meetings. Each doll has her own name. Of course my new one will be named Shirley.

Every once in a while I still wonder about the Christmas Club Mama said she belongs to. I'll ask her again, nearer Christmas time—maybe she'll tell me more then.

Some days Caroline and I knock on the back door of the house on the corner and ask Mrs. Calloway if we can come in and play with Nancy, her new little baby.

"She's just up from her nap," Mrs. Calloway says, "and she's ready for company."

She holds the door wide open for us. Right away, we go to the sun porch where baby Nancy lies on her pink blanket. She's so cute. She laughs and coos as soon as she sees us. She's too little to move about yet, but her voice is big when she cries.

Mrs. Calloway likes having us there, because then she can get her housework done. Babies need lots of care. And the nuns always tell us we should go out of our way to help others, and this is what I'm doing. I'm not sure what the Lutheran teachers tell Caroline at her school, but I think she likes helping others too. We don't talk about religion much. I just know I'm not ever allowed to go to Caroline's church.

It's fun playing with Nancy's baby toys, plus we get graham crackers to eat, and sometimes a small glass of soda pop. We even feed Nancy her bottle of milk. It's easy being a mother. But one baby seems enough to take care of. Still, I would like lots of babies when I grow up. That's why I think this is good practice, taking care of babies in a different house. I get to see how other mothers do things. It's nicer than playing with dolls. But you have to be much more careful with babies than dolls, and make sure you never drop them.

Caroline and I get invited to summer tea parties too.

There's this older lady, Miss Birch, who lives in a smaller house on our block. Her grayish hair is pulled back into a tight bun. She wears funny high top black shoes and lives all alone. "The old maid" is what Mama calls her, because she's not married. We call her that too, but not when we're with her. It doesn't mean she's not nice, just not married.

Miss Birch has this screened-in front porch where she keeps a little table and small chairs. As we walk by, she sometimes calls out, "Would you girls like to stop in for a tea party today?"

We quickly say, "Yes!" and go right up the steps and into her porch. I've never seen the rest of her house. Sometimes I peek inside from the porch. The next room has a piano. The lid is closed, with open music sheets on top.

As soon as we come into the porch, Miss Birch puts an embroidered white cloth on the small table, sets out tiny glass dishes, then serves us sugar water and frosted animal crackers. Miss Birch joins us in our tea party, sitting in a bigger chair and munching on animal crackers too. Sometimes she tells us ahead of time to bring our dolls along, giving each a doll chair to sit on by the table.

Miss Birch has her own dolls that she keeps on shelves on her porch, and sometimes one of them joins our party, but never the same one. She has different sets of small dishes too, in flowered boxes on the shelves. We never know which ones she's going to set out. There's crystal clear green ones, and a shiny white set with painted flowers.

Sometimes, if it's someone's birthday, usually one of the dolls', she uses the good blue dishes with gold rims, adding tiny cupcakes with unlit candles. We all sing "Happy Birthday." But it's not like a real birthday party, just make-believe fun.

There are other fancy unused toys on her shelves too, but she never brings them down.

Miss Birch only invites us in summer, so we don't know what she does in winter. Some days her walk isn't even shoveled, and there are no footprints at all in her snow.

My favorite thing to do, as soon as the weather's warm, is go to the beach. We live only a few blocks from Lake Michigan, and Manitowoc has a nice public beach that's easy to walk to by ourselves. We speed through our chores, gather our bathing suits and towels, pick up some friends and walk the few blocks together, talking and laughing all the way. Sometimes the hot sidewalks makes us dance about in our bare feet, and warm tar on the street makes us hop and jump so we don't get sticky stuff on our foot bottoms.

There's an old gray wooden bathhouse at the top of the beach. You stand at the open window and someone behind gives you a big cardboard box with a number painted on it, then you get a small tag with the same number so you can pick up the box later. You have to make sure not to lose the tag, or you can't get your clothes back, which would cause big trouble at home.

Inside the bathhouse are separate little rooms where you change into your bathing suit. There's always this mucky smell, like dried fish and spoiled lake water, and even stinky bathroom smells. The damp wooden floor is covered in gritty sand. We each pick a separate cell to change in; all the while hearing squeals and yells from nearby stalls.

I always feel as if people can see me undressing—because there's lots of room under the short doors and big cracks in the walls dividing the cells. There's a bench attached to the wall in each stall. Sometimes kids jump up on the benches and peek over the tops. So I change real fast, anxious to get my bathing suit on, put my clothes in the numbered box, and get out of there and down to the sand and water.

We stake out our spot, usually the same place each time, and put our pails, towels, and any other stuff there. Then we run to the lake's edge to try out the water, jumping back and forth with each wave. Usually the water's pretty cold, at least till the end of summer. I splash around a bit at first. Brave ones go out deeper. I'm never that brave. It's enough to wade in up to my knees, always watching out for waves that might swoosh over me. Maybe next year I'll go deeper.

The best fun is digging in the sand till we hit water, then building our little cities and castles out of wet sand, or burying each other in it. There's always a search for pretty stones and treasures, in case someone lost money, or a watch. But others are looking too, so nobody finds much.

One time I did find a tiny gold ring. I never wear it, just keep it in my green purse, and always wonder who it belonged to. I'd give it back if I knew. Maybe it's a magic ring, one I can wish on. I wish on lots of things, but I'm saving this ring to wish for something special. Maybe nearer Christmas?

There's kids we get to know only from being at the beach with them. They live in other parts of town and have their own groups, so here's the only place we see them. We stay away from the bully groups, if we can. The lifeguard, high up on his stool, is always yelling at them through his big megaphone, "Stop what you're doing!" And they do, for a while. They're really bad, but seem to have more fun than anybody. They even play football in the sand, screaming and hollering, telling us to get out of their way or get knocked down.

After we get tired of playing on the beach, and maybe start feeling hungry, we turn in our number tag, get our box of clothes, change quickly, and start home, swinging our wet bathing suits round and round to get all the water out. Damp towels are hung over our shoulders as we happily zigzag home.

On the way, we have this game, picking out houses that we'd like to own and live in some day as we walk by. I always pick ones that look like those in fairy tale books. We make up stories about the houses and the people who live in them. Sometimes we just talk about what we'd like to be when we grow up. Of course, we all want to be rich and have big fancy houses and maybe servants, and food we can only dream about now. I want to have lots of children and wear pretty dresses like those I see in the movies and magazines.

My friend Caroline's mama looks like the ladies in the movies, and dresses like them too. Mama says she's another Jean Harlow, with her blond wavy hair and fancy clothes. She even drives a car. Mama doesn't know how to drive, and says she wouldn't even care to learn. Not too many ladies drive cars, or smoke, but Caroline's mama does.

Sometimes, Mrs. Simmons, Caroline's mama, will drive Caroline and me, my brother Buddy, and her brother Fred, to another beach, way on the other side of town. It's bigger, and has a better playground and a nicer beach. There are always more people there, too. Caroline's mama wears her colorful beach pajamas, a matching big floppy beach hat, and fancy sandal shoes, with her red painted toenails sticking out, looking like teensy cherry candies on each toe. Mrs. Simmons sits on her big flowered towel, far from the water, reading, looking just like a picture from a magazine ad.

Caroline's mama always brings along this decorated round tin box filled with all kinds of store-bought cookies and offers them to us every time she opens the lid, which I can hear from far away. I eat them slowly so they last longer, and it's not polite to take too many. Caroline says her mama doesn't have time to bake cookies. She's too busy doing other things.

"There she goes again, going to who knows where," Mama comments as she sees Mrs. Simmons drive away.

Caroline's home by herself lots. But that's okay; we don't need mothers around when we play.

Some days, we even stop for an ice cream cone after going to the better beach. We don't have to pay, because Caroline's daddy still has a job. "A good one," Mama says. I make sure I never get in fights with Caroline during the summer.

After a day filled with play, we settle down for a simple supper in our kitchen, not using the stove. We might have Kool Aid, lard and sugar sandwiches, lettuce and radishes from the garden, and peanut butter or oatmeal cookies. Anything cool tastes good.

We don't have an icebox, so when we hear the ice truck stopping on our block, we run out, begging for ice chips, as the busy iceman chips away at his big ice blocks. We stand nearby to feel the cold air from his truck blow over us, crunching our chips, watching him hoist the big ice blocks onto his shoulders with metal tongs. Then he goes into houses that have cards with numbers stuck in their windows, telling him how much ice they need.

After supper and dishes, we gather outside for group games like

Kick the Can, Red Rover, and Captain May I. We mostly play in the street, till our parents call us. We know that when the streetlights come on, it's time to quit our games.

"See you tomorrow," we call to each other, picking up our things and heading home.

Sometimes we spend warm evenings sitting on our front porch. If it's really hot, Daddy announces, "I think one of you can go to the ice cream stand tonight."

We've been waiting for him to say that. He reaches into his pants pocket and digs out some money. We go with Buddy, who always carries the money, to the small white wooden stand on the next block which sells ice cream, candy, popcorn, all kinds of good things. As we wait our turn, I sniff the delicious smells coming from the open window, while checking out everything on display on the inside shelves.

Once our ice cream's in the paper bag, we run home quick so it doesn't melt, anticipating the cool taste.

Daddy always says to get a pint of vanilla ice cream. Mama divides it into eight thin slices, with Daddy getting the biggest slice. We fight over who gets to lick the carton, which sometimes tastes better than the thin slice of ice cream we get on our saucer.

When we have money of our own, which isn't often, we go to the stand by ourselves and buy an ice cream cone, or Eskimo Pie. We save Eskimo Pie wrappers and send them in for prizes, always checking the curbs for old wrappers. My brother collects lead foil from cigarette packages and candy bars, molding the pieces onto his big ball of lead foil, which he sells for money. Mama collects string in a big ball, but she doesn't sell it, she uses it.

After ice cream, it's time for bed. First we wash our dirty feet in a pail of cold water, then get ready for bed. Only we're not quite ready to go to sleep just yet. We play games in bed, take turns rubbing each other's backs, and tell stories. The girls are in one bedroom, Catherine and me in a big bed, Betty Jane in her own, and Mitzy in her crib. Buddy and Sonny sleep in the same bed in a small room next to ours. We rap on the walls to each other, and visit back and forth, having to be real quiet and keep our giggles down so Mama and Daddy don't hear us.

Then it's off to dreamland, trying to remember our dreams so we can tell them to each other the next morning. My dreams usually slip away, and I never know where the dreams went, or how to recapture them.

I sometimes think about that. What happens to dreams and the times that went on before?

As I fall asleep, expecting the brand new next day brings up this nice feeling that something exciting is going to happen, and I'm always anxious to see if it does.

~ SUMMER STORMS ~

I wish summer would never end. Even if there's patches of clouds or cool weather, each day is most welcome. "Good morning, Mary Sunshine," we greet each other, and end up together with the finish. "You used to come at ten o'clock, and now you come at noon." But there are also days I dread, when there's storms, those dreaded thunderstorms that shake the whole house in the middle of the night.

Crackling bolts of lightning flash through our pulled-down window shades, lighting up the whole bedroom in flickering terror, followed by booming thunder crashes. Rain pounds heavily on the glass panes. Winds howl fiercely, rattling the windows, as if the storm is trying to get inside our house.

I lie wide awake in bed with the covers over my head. I know the rest of the house must be awake by now too, but no one says anything, not even Catherine, who's in bed next to me. Her breathing sounds different when she's awake.

Soon Mama begins her ritual walk through the house, checking doors, making sure windows are tightly closed. I take a quick peek as she tiptoes into our room, watching her shadow move about in the darkness. I want to call out, "I'm afraid." But I know her answer would only be, "There's nothing to be afraid of." And even though we don't talk, I feel a bit safer after she leaves.

I feel much more protected inside the house, under my covers. But that's when storm stories begin rattling around in my head. There's this one Catherine tells about the night she was sleeping in this old cast iron bed, her window open just a crack.

"A bolt of lightning streaks in, lights up the whole room. The bed sparks all over, then the bright spinning fireball streaks out the same way it came in, all in just a few seconds." Catherine claims she was stunned stiff and shudders each time she retells the story.

Mama tells her, "It was probably just part of a bad dream."

Catherine swears it really happened and she usually doesn't make up stories. Being the oldest, she's the most serious, the one we look up to.

We sleep in a wooden bed now. Even the cross above our bed is wooden. I'm not sure why we don't have the iron bed anymore, or whatever happened to it. Mama says it was just too old to keep.

Mama tells us stories too, about farms that were hit by lightning. All the buildings burned up, even the animals. She saw it happen once, from far away.

"No telephones, no fire engines, and no way to save those farms," she would always lament.

She says that's why barns and houses have lightning rods on their roofs to direct the lightning into the ground. I often wondered why those tall thin spires with round glassy balls were on top of farm buildings. Could people maybe wear lightning rods? Might that keep them safer?

Benjamin Franklin once got lightning to hit his kite and key, but he did that on purpose and lived to tell about it. There are people who don't live to tell about such things, according to Mama and her stories. There was even this man who had his hair turn white from lightning. Another had all his clothes burned off.

After Mama leaves, I close my eyes real tight and stay hiding under the covers.

But the thunder still rumbles, and I can see lightning flash right through my closed eyelids. I lie stiff, not moving; praying over and over, till it finally dies down. I'm still afraid to go to sleep, because sometimes storms come back. But after a long while, I do sleep. Waking up the next morning, it all seems like a bad dream.

But the big daytime storm I remember most was not a bad dream. It was real.

Every once in awhile, Mama goes to visit Auntie Stacia, who lives a few blocks away. Mama says she needs to get away from family sometimes. She usually takes Mitzy in the baby buggy, and one of us kids can go along, but only one. I always beg to be the one, because I like to go visiting. Even though I don't talk much, I still like to listen, and Mama and Auntie Stacia talk about things I never get to hear otherwise.

It's a warm breezy day. I have on my new red and white sun-suit with a matching hat Mama made for me. Mitzy is in her new pink jumper, and Mama has on her Sunday dress, summer hat, and nice shoes. Mama puts the sponge cake she just baked into her metal cake carrier, then puts it into the baby buggy. It's for Auntie Stacia's birthday, which is not today, but Mama says, "It'll keep."

Sometimes she lets me push the baby buggy alone. It's a gray wicker buggy with a fat round hood and nice blue lining. Mitzy likes to sit up and watch everything along the way. People stop and look at Mitzy.

"What a cute baby," they say. She's wearing her pink summer bonnet, and her cheeks are rosy. She shakes her rag doll all around. I think she's cute, too.

As we walk along, I'm so happy to make this trip I feel like skipping. Then, all of a sudden, I hear it—thunder! Mama quick looks up at the sky. I do too. There's big black clouds moving in fast and it's getting darker. Mama begins to walk faster and keeps looking at the sky. There's a big flash of lightning, followed by a loud crack of thunder. I've never been away from home in a storm before.

What are we going to do?

"Hurry," Mama says, "We only have three more blocks to go."

I try to keep up, helping to push the buggy, my feet stumbling. Then the rain starts, pouring down in thick, heavy drops. The sidewalks are soon sloshing with water.

Little rivers stream down the curbs, then bigger ones. Mitzy is under the buggy hood. I'm soaking wet. Mama takes off her hat and puts it in the buggy, over the sponge cake. Now the thunder's closer, louder.

I'm scared and want to cry, trying not to. I know we can't go home, and we can't get to Auntie Stacia's in time either. We're caught in the middle of the biggest storm ever and there's no way to get out of it.

Tree branches are bending. The wind whips all around us. Now big hailstones start falling, hitting the buggy hood in fat ice balls, beating all over me in shivering chunks.

What are we going to do? We can't even run, not with the buggy.

An empty garbage can rolls sideways past us. I scream as I jump out of its way, swerving the buggy. Everything's blowing all around us.

What if it's a tornado, like in *The Wizard of Oz*, and it blows us away—where would we end up?

"We have to stop," Mama says, water running down her face, and giant hail hitting her head.

How can we stop? Just stand there in the middle of this big storm? I look up at Mama for an answer—she always has them.

We're in front of a big house with a wide porch. Mama turns the buggy around toward the house and tries to get the buggy up the concrete steps, pulling it backwards up the wooden porch steps with great effort. Mitzy is screaming wildly. I'm shaking all over. I try to help, so afraid the buggy will come back down, tip over and Mitzy will fall out. Two more steps to go. Mama gives one more shove, I give an extra push, and we're on the porch, shaking off rainwater.

It's still hailing, white balls bouncing on the sidewalks, but we're safe on the porch where the hail can't get us, and there's no metal around to attract lightning, only white wicker chairs.

Mama checks inside the buggy and tries to quiet Mitzy. There's still thunder and lightning.

I'm cold, I'm wet, but at least I'm out of the rain. I feel like bursting out crying, biting my lips hard as I can.

The door of the house opens and I see a lady in an apron standing there. I'm thinking the lady might say we can't stay on her porch—

that we don't belong here. She doesn't know us, and might tell us to go home.

The lady steps out, holding the door wide open. "Would you like to come inside, at least till the storm's over?" She doesn't look mean at all.

"Thank you, but we'll be all right," Mama says. "We're dry here, and out of the storm. Thank you very much."

I would have liked to go inside, to get further away from the storm and see all that's in her house, but dare not say anything.

The lady goes back inside, then comes out again, this time with some big bath towels.

"Here, you can dry yourselves off," she says, handing Mama a big blue towel, and wrapping another smaller pink one around my shoulders. It feels so cozy and warm.

Then she puts her hand in her apron pocket and takes out a fat gingerbread cookie. "Here's something for you, little girl."

All of a sudden, the storm seems far away. That cookie is what's close right now. I manage a smile and say, "Thank you," quickly biting into the sweet cookie.

Mama's busy drying off Mitzy, the buggy, her hair, then my hair. The lady has gone back into the house, but the door to the inside is still open.

"You've been a brave girl, Lulu," Mama says. "That was a big storm we just came through. You helped lots. I couldn't have done it by myself."

Yes, I was brave, wasn't I, never letting on how scared I really was. Right now, the scaredness is down inside my stomach, mixing up with the cookie pieces.

The lady comes back out without her apron, and sits on a wicker porch chair next to Mama. I play with Mitzy, giving her a bite of my cookie. I don't even try to listen to Mama and the woman's conversation, because all they're talking about is the storm, and I don't want to hear anything more about any storm, thinking it might even bring it back if we talk about it.

"Well, I think we'll be on our way," Mama says after a few minutes. "Before another storm comes up." She gives the towels back to the lady.

"Your little girl can keep that towel", the lady says. "She'll be too cold without it." It's a nice warm towel, without any holes like ours have.

"Thank you, ma'am," I say, hugging the towel tighter. Two presents in one day from a very kind stranger.

The lady helps Mama get the buggy down the steps. Going downstairs is always easier than going up. The sidewalks are all wet, stacked with fallen leaves, and tree branches all over. It's hard pushing the buggy over them, so I run ahead, dragging things out of the way. When we get to the corner, there's deep water all across the street.

"Looks like everything's flooded," Mama says, and pushes the buggy right through the lakes. Our shoes are squishing with water. We continue going to Auntie Stacia's, but it's much slower than before. Nobody else is on the street.

Finally, I can see her yellow house. Yard ornaments are blown all over, and plants and bushes are bent way down. Her big birdhouse is on the ground, broken, and her birdbath is overflowing.

Auntie is sitting on the porch in her big green swing. Right away, she waves to us. "Thought the storm might have kept you away," she calls out. She's wearing the pretty blue dress she made out of silk from China.

"A little storm doesn't scare me," Mama says.

But I know Mama was scared, I could tell. Grown-ups never like to say when they're afraid; they have to be the brave ones, especially if there are children around.

Mama takes the cake tin from the buggy and sets it on the porch table. "I hope the rain didn't drip into your birthday cake," she says.

I'm wondering about that too, but Mama doesn't take off the tin cover. Next, she takes Mitzy out of the buggy and holds her real tight, kissing her all over.

I stand looking at the sky as the sun starts to break out from behind clouds. I'm hoping to see a rainbow, a sign from God that there won't be another big flood. But there is none. Maybe we just can't see the rainbow today from where we are. Like the sun and moon, we know they're up there, but they're not always visible to us, just at certain times. It must be the same with rainbows—we have to believe there's always one somewhere, even if we're not able to see it.

Religion makes you believe in lots of things you cannot see.

We all go inside, and right away Auntie shows Mama around—the rooms she's just painted over, using a sponge and two colors of paint, the new flowers she made from tin cans, and some large colorful ones from crepe paper, summer dresses she's sewn. She gives Mama some of her old dresses each time we visit.

"You can either wear them or make them over for the kids," Auntie Stacia always adds as she stuffs them into a bag.

One of my favorites, a made-over dress, used to be Auntie Stacia's satiny purple one. Silk feels so slippery soft when you wear it, and when I do, I always think of the teensy silkworms winding the threads around their cocoons, and the Chinese ladies unwinding the same threads—just to make this lovely material.

Auntie Stacia doesn't have any children. She did have a little boy many years ago, but he died from eating fish. His throat swelled all up and he couldn't breathe, but they didn't know it was because he was allergic to fish. Now we all know, and have to be careful about new children in our family, because they could have caught this fish allergy thing. Mama never lets little Sonny eat any fish, with strict orders, "Don't you ever give him any fish—ever! He could die like little Joey did."

Auntie has a big picture of little Joey on her sitting room table, but we never talk about him; yet it always seems like he's in the room, looking at us.

Auntie Stacia has this empty oatmeal box filled with wooden spools from her sewing which she always gives to visiting kids to play with. I don't want to pile up spools anymore, especially today. I always ask if I can look at her books. There's a whole bookcase of them. She lets me, even though she mentions, "Those aren't books for children. There aren't even any pictures in them." She shakes her head, as if wondering why I find books so fascinating.

Sometimes I sneak peeks at her romance and love magazines, when I'm sure Mama's in another room.

After touring the house, Mama and Auntie Stacia sit at the kitchen table having their regular tea and muffins. Auntie gives me a muffin with lots of strawberry jam on it on a little saucer, with a paper napkin, putting it on the floor where I'm playing with Mitzy. I feed muffin pieces to Mitzy, and she gets jam all over her face and keeps yelling for more. I think maybe Auntie will give me another one, but she doesn't. One is all I ever get.

Mama and Auntie Stacia talk about relatives, mostly ones who are sick or dying. I can't keep track of all their different names. And they talk about the bad conditions that are going on in our country, how poor so many people are. They don't mention the storm, as if that's already a closed chapter that doesn't have to be read again.

Pretty soon, Mama says, "I think we better be on our way. Enough visiting and storm-dodging for one day."

It's earlier than we usually leave, but Mama looks tired, and we won't be looking at Auntie's garden of flowers as we usually do, not today. I put the books and other things away, and help get Mitzy ready.

"You take care of yourself, Lulu," Auntie Stacia says, giving me a big hug, "We don't want anything happening to you." She says that every time we leave.

We walk fast on the way home, going the same way, but everything's different. There's evidence of the storm all around.

It's good to be back at our own house once more. If I'd been there during the storm, I'd have gone down into the basement, which I do sometimes, saying I'm looking for something, or making some project with Daddy's tools. It's much safer down there than upstairs—no windows and heavy block walls. But I'd never go up into our attic during a storm, that's for sure. It's scary enough up there, just any time.

I can't wait to tell everybody about all that happened.

I put on different clothes and rush outside to join the kids who are already out in bare feet, running up and down the curbs as streams of water rush down the gutters into over-flooded sewer hole grates at each street corner. While splashing about, we talk about the storm.

I make my adventure sound even worse than it was. Now I have a story I can repeat over and over about something unusual that happened to me. Grown-ups do that all the time.

A few days later, Mama says she's taking the newly washed pink towel back to the porch lady.

"She said I could keep it," I protest.

"It was just borrowed," Mama says, "just like we borrowed her porch for a bit."

The lady gave me the towel, she did not borrow it to me. But it would be hard explaining to Mama my difference between giving and borrowing.

I guess we don't have to keep things forever, only for the time we need them, then let them go.

~ FOURTH of JULY ~

JULY—It's there on the wall calendar. I never look forward to July, even if it's that much closer to Christmas.

Why? Because I dread the Fourth of July.

I never tell anyone about my fear of the Fourth, as most of my friends can hardly wait for the holiday. If I told them it's a day of terror for me, instead of a time to celebrate, they might even think I'm unpatriotic, which I'm not. I just would rather celebrate the birth of our country in a much quieter way.

A couple days before the Fourth, our backyard gets busy, with everyone gathering to decorate bikes, coaster wagons, even doll buggies. Kids plaster them with anything red, white, and blue. Some kids are making costumes to go with their decorated wheels.

Fred is turning his coaster into a covered wagon, wearing his cowboy suit. Sally, in a long blue silky nightgown, tries to become the Statue of Liberty, except her hat, with glittery pointy star ends, keeps falling off. Skippy's dressed like Uncle Sam, with a painted oatmeal box for his high top hat. Everyone has cloth flags on sticks which they place all over their bikes and wagons, careful not to let the flags touch the ground.

"Don't ever let your flag touch the ground," Buddy warns. "It's against the law. They tell us in Boy Scouts." Buddy becomes the backyard boss, because Catherine's busy sewing new summer clothes these days.

Even though it's fun helping, I don't really care to decorate my doll buggy, or dress up my dolls or myself. I don't want to be in the holiday parade. Mama doesn't tell me to either—she mostly lets us kids decide what we want to do.

Mama comes out during the decorating. "You kids will never win. Those judges have the winners, their favorites, all picked out ahead of time. You have to be rich to win, and we certainly aren't rich. We can't afford fancy decorations like they can. But you have fun anyway."

That's her speech before the Fourth, the same words every time. When Buddy was building his soapbox derby car, she gave almost the same speech.

"Those winners didn't build those derby cars by themselves, their fathers did most of the work, and they have the money to build an expensive winner. Poor kids never win anything."

Are we really the poor kids? Maybe she just wants to keep us from feeling bad if we don't win in these contests.

Buddy doesn't care if he wins or not, he just wants his bike looking spiffy, his wheels spinning in colors. If you do win, you get prizes and your name printed in the paper. Mama always reads the names out loud, muttering, "I see nobody from this part of town won. Same old thing. What makes poor kids keep entering?"

Then it's the Fourth. How do I know? The first thing I hear, even while I'm sleeping, are loud bangs. I just want to stay in bed all day, but know I can't do that, unless I'm sick.

Well, the explosions really do make me sick. My stomach churns and I feel like throwing up. I can't even eat breakfast. Nobody notices, because they're too busy getting ready. I'm silent amidst all the bustling. I have to get away from the smell of food. That's how I know I'm afraid. Even if I tell myself I'm not, my stomach tells me different.

I go out on the porch. Instead of birds singing, I hear blasts of firecrackers going off from every direction. Gangs of boys run up and down the block, putting big firecrackers inside empty tin cans and lighting the string. Bang! The can goes flying way high and no one knows where it'll land. I'm afraid to step off the porch, thinking I might get whacked by one of those flying cans, which could hit my eye, or cut my head. I make sure to cover my eyes each time I hear the sizzle before the bang.

There's giant firecrackers that shake the whole ground when they go off, sounding like thunder. Cherry bombs, the king of firecrackers, make the biggest noise. Tiny ladyfingers are bitsy ones all strung together. When they get lit and explode, they sound like machine guns going "rata-tat-tat." Like popcorn popping, only much louder.

The boys get excited about loud noises. They all have cap guns, and sometimes they take out the rolls of caps and pound them with a hammer on the sidewalk to make them explode, one right after another. They even sneak kitchen matches, break off the heads, then hammer bunches of them on concrete for giant bangs. It's not just a Fourth of July thing, either. That happens all year round.

Buddy and his friends always save up to buy fireworks at the corner stand, trying to see who can get the biggest and best. They never buy pretty sparklers, or colorful rockets, or roman candles, which I like to see at night, from far away, sitting on the porch. No, they like ear-splitting crackers, the badder the better.

Most are wrapped in decorated thin red paper. Sometimes I sneak peeks at the paper, before they're opened, because there are strange Chinese designs and weird Chinese writing on the colorful packages. To think—these firecrackers came all the way from China, without exploding. I'm very careful when looking at the packages, in case they might explode if I touch the packages wrong or drop them.

My brother laughs at me, saying, "They have to be lit before they can go off, Lulu, you goof."

But I don't always believe everything he says, and he sometimes says things just to get me scared.

When I hear those loud explosions, I feel the same way as when I hear the guns in movie newsreels about wars. I close my eyes and cover my ears.

I know I can't stay home all day by myself. Mama wouldn't let me. No one wants to wait for me to go to the parade with them. They're all anxious to get going and show off their decorated bikes. I'm left to walk to the parade by myself, which is better, since nobody will make fun of me if I jump when I hear exploding sounds.

I step off the porch, looking both ways like I do when I cross the street, then almost tiptoe along the sidewalk, afraid of stepping on a stray firecracker that could still be lit, praying along the way.

"Just let me get through this block safely, I'll give up candy for a week." The next block, I pray the same prayer. I hear lots of bangs, but none are that close. The prayers worked.

Finally, I'm on the parade street. Everybody's already there. I sit down on the curb, making sure I'm by lots of other people for protection. I can breathe easier now because no one's allowed to shoot firecrackers on the parade street. Policemen are all around.

"Keep the street clear. No loud noises!" The policemen go up and down repeating, "You will be arrested if you shoot off any firecrackers!" I sure hope so. They also say, "There's horses in this parade, and bangs scare them, make them run wild."

If big horses can get scared from firecrackers, then why can't I?

Pretty soon, I hear drums. The parade begins. I forget about being afraid and enjoy the bands, baton twirlers, horses, and clowns. Last comes the kids' parade, with decorated bikes, wagons, buggies, even toddling kiddies dressed up in costumes, looking so cute and pretty. Right now I kind of wish I was marching with them. I wave to friends in the parade, who seem to be having such a good time.

Being in the parade would be okay, but getting there's the problem. How do you run away from firecrackers if you're hanging onto your decorated doll buggy? It could tip, and your doll could break.

The flag goes by, and everyone salutes. The parade's over.

After, everybody goes over to Washington Park, where the judging is done. One section of the park gets filled with all the decorated entries. People are taking pictures.

Last week, the city gave out tickets to kids to get free ice cream and candy after the parade. My ticket's tied in my hanky, which is tied on my wrist. I didn't want to take my green purse today, in case I had to run. I didn't want to lose it.

I stand in line to get my ice cream cone and candy, and feel silly for being such a fraidy cat. Eating a delicious ice cream cone can scare away just about any bad feelings.

The band sets up in the bandstand and begins playing nice music. The firecracker sounds are far away now.

Why am I so afraid of them? Why do I keep thinking about kids who have their fingers, eyes, and legs blown off by fireworks?

Mama tells stories about these accidents every year. Other mothers repeat the same ones, and we kids do, too.

After eating all the free stuff, I find I have to go to the bathroom. I never use the park bathroom. Sometimes I've gone in with my sister, but it's not a very nice place. Smells bad, too.

Mama says I'm never to go in there alone, even if I have to pee in my pants. So I have to make the dreaded trip back home by myself, as no one else is ready to leave yet. In fact, most families stay at the park all day, bringing picnic lunches, playing games, and listening to the music.

I begin my walk home. As soon as I cross the street, the firecrackers get louder. Dogs decorated in crepe paper are running all around too, barking and jumping. There's something to be afraid of on both sides of the street. I go as fast as I can. It's hard running, trying to hold my legs together, jumping at every sound. There's not many people outside either, just their flags. Everybody's at the park.

Who could save me if something bad did happen?

I finally make it home. I run up the porch steps and rush to the bathroom.

I've made it through one more Fourth of July. Luckily, it'll be another year before I have to go through it again.

The next morning, there's burnt firecracker shreds everywhere. Leftover decorations, dented tin cans, and bits of red, white, and blue scattered all over the place.

It may have been a celebration for some, but I still think I'd much rather read about the birth of our country in a book.

~ PICNICS and FISHING ~

It's a jumping Sunday morning when Mama announces, "I think it's a good day for a picnic."

Before the words are out of her mouth, we're all yelling, "We want a picnic! We want a picnic!"

Daddy likes picnics too because he enjoys fishing. Right away, he's out in the garden digging for angleworms, putting the squirmy little brownish-red snakes into an old tin can, ground on top, but they keep wiggling underneath.

"Don't let me forget those worms," Daddy says to anyone listening.

Then he's gone with the car for a while, and comes back with a huge watermelon, a couple of lemons, and a candy bar. Mr. Goodbar's his favorite. Ours too, because it's marked into little squares that can be broken apart, one for each of us.

Mama gets busy making lemonade in the old giant dented thermos jug. We don't have an icebox, so there's no ice for the lemonade. That doesn't matter, lots of sugar's what matters.

Catherine starts making sandwiches, spreading sandwich spread, which comes in a large glass jar from the store, onto the piles of homemade bread slices she laid out. We never get to have this sandwich spread any other time. Everything's special about picnics.

We're all eager to help. Betty Jane carefully gathers the old towels we use for napkins. Buddy puts together old tin and glass plates and raggedy blankets, stacking everything into the picnic bushel basket he brings up from the basement. We put our own things into paper bags and wait at the door. Then the yelling starts.

"I get the window seat!"

"No, I do, you had it last time."

I don't care where I sit and don't like shouting, so I never win that game. Going on a picnic is winning enough.

After church and a quick breakfast, we change into play clothes, put everything into the car trunk, then wait alongside the driveway. Daddy putters a bit in the garage, lifts the hood of the car and tinkers with the motor, closes the hood with a bang, and gets into the car. He better not forget us. Soon he's backing the car out of the garage. He shuts the motor off and we all pile in. Doors slam shut. Daddy gets out, shuts the garage door, and then places long bamboo fishing poles across the outside car doors, tying them onto the door handles, and away we go, ready for a day of food, fun, and fishing.

Everybody's favorite place for a picnic is the Ten Cent Place. We don't even ask if that's where we're going, because we already know.

As we drive along country roads, everyone's talking, pointing to things in the fields and alongside the road. We check out license plates of the cars passing by to see if they're from another state. Once, there was a car all the way from Alaska. The big winner.

Then we see the wooden sign on the side of the road with large painted red letters: "TO ENTER—PAY **IO** CENTS."

The farmer's house is close by. Daddy honks the horn and the farmer comes out, walking real slow, his big collie dog jumping all around and barking.

Daddy pays him ten cents. Without saying anything, the farmer opens the wobbly wooden gate across his gravel road and waves us to go ahead.

We're in, which makes me happy, because one time the farmer wasn't home. He never came out after lots of honking and we had to turn around and go back home. I think someone—or one of his cows, had died, the farmer told Mama next time.

We drive down this winding road next to the river. Mama keeps telling Daddy, "Don't drive so close to the river bank! You're getting too near the edge!" Which rather scares us kids, too. We don't want our car to fall into the river with all of us in it, not before we have our picnic. I can't swim, either. My big brother can. I'm not sure if Mama or Daddy swims. I've never seen them in a bathing suit.

Finally, we arrive at our favorite spot and park under the beechnut tree. As soon as the motor's turned off, and Daddy's removed the fishing poles, we scramble out both doors, ready to find new adventures.

Mama stands by the car for a minute, breathing in deeply. "It's worth ten cents to be here. No crowds of people like those public parks. There's something different about the country. It's always so nice and quiet."

Daddy likes quiet too. He says the fish bite better. We kids make sure to play far away from him when he's fishing because we don't like to keep quiet, not at a picnic anyways.

First thing, we take off our shoes and go down by the water, where there's a big rock we climb and sit on.

"Don't you kids fall in that water," we hear Mama call out, which she says lots while we're here.

Right away, we begin looking for shiny clamshells sticking up in the sand at the river's edge. Sometimes we find unopened ones and search inside for pearls. There's minnows swimming around, polliwogs, and sometimes a big fish leaps up, making spreading circles in the water. We poke sticks in the water and shout to each other any time we find something interesting. Everyone comes running over.

Dragonflies and other bugs are jumping around on top of the water, and you can hear frogs croak, but we never see them. Butterflies flit about, stopping atop colorful wildflowers. Sometimes there's bees, but I never see any mosquitoes or flies. Mama says the frogs eat them, quick as they can.

It would be nice to bring some frogs home, cause we have lots of flies around our house. This long sticky curly flypaper thing hangs from the ceiling above our kitchen table to catch flies. Lots of dead flies get stuck to it. I don't like eating under dead flies. A frog would be nicer.

If we walk around in the mud or dig, I worry about quicksand, which can swallow up your whole body, so I usually stay on the grass part. But in the grass, I'm always on the lookout for snakes. My brother found a snake here one time and really scared me with it, but Mama made him let it go. I don't think she likes snakes either. Who does, except boys?

After, we do other things, like skipping stones in the water, running games, and maybe play cards for a while. Mostly I just sit in the grass and read my books, listening to the sounds of the river gurgling by, tree branches swishing in the wind, birds calling in different voices, and breathe in the scented fresh air that only blows here.

Across the river, there's cottages and piers with row boats. Pretty soon people come out of the cottages in bathing suits, and even though they're far away, I can hear them shouting and laughing from across the river. I watch their tiny figures as they swim or row their boats, and start to imagine lots of things about them.

Who are they? What do they really look like up close? Could any of them be my friend?

They must be really rich to have a cottage, and a boat too. Maybe that's why they're having so much fun. I always think it must be fun to be rich.

But Mama says, "We have our own kind of fun, and they have theirs. You don't want other people's troubles either. Rich or poor, we all have them."

Sometimes Mama brings her Kodak camera along and takes pictures. You have to be outside in the sun, so here's a good place to snap pictures. And we don't have to pose, like at home. Mama clicks surprise pictures here.

After a bit, Mama takes off her shoes and sits in her stocking feet on a blanket under the tree, wind blowing across her dress and hair. She's not doing anything, just looking into the distance, or up at the sky, as if nobody else is around. She looks so different here. We hardly ever see her just sitting still, doing nothing, at least not at home.

Daddy always brings along an extra fishing pole for Mama, but she scarcely uses it. Sometimes my big brother does, but he doesn't like sitting around waiting for fish to come, when he can be doing so many other things.

None of us like fishing, even though Daddy tried to teach each of us. I didn't like it all, putting on worms, taking off the fish, waiting for something that might never happen, then if it did, not truly wanting it to happen.

On the way in, we drove past cows. I see them now, coming closer to the fence by the river. I move away, afraid they might break through the rickety barbed wire. They look at me and moo real loud, as if I shouldn't be there. Now they're going down to the river to drink water.

"Daddy, that big cow, he's down in the water now, right next to that rusty broken fence," I yell out to him.

"Don't worry about any of those cows, long as there's no bull with them," he tells me.

But a bull could get mixed in without us knowing. So I get away from that part of the river and that group of bellowing cows.

Later, if Daddy thinks he's caught enough fish, he's happy. If he didn't, he says, "They just aren't biting today," and winds up the long fish line around his pole. He puts the fish he catches in a pail with water, after taking the sharp hooks from their mouths. It must really hurt. Fish always look like they're crying, but it's hard to tell when water's all over them. Daddy catches mostly bullheads with pointy whiskers, which I make sure not to touch.

We'll be having fried fish for supper tomorrow, and maybe the day after, too. I look forward to that, as fish tastes quite good after Mama dips the pieces in flour or corn meal and fries them till they're crunchy. Only you have to watch out for bones. I try to keep away from watching the degutting part before they're cooked. Best not to think of that when eating them, too.

If there's too many fish, Daddy gives some to our neighbors, the Yaegers, who have a grown-up daughter, Mabel, who isn't right in her head. They never get to go too many places because they always have to stay home to take care of her. They're nice people, and so is their daughter, though I never know what she's saying when she does her talking. Mama says that's because she's tongue-tied. Her legs wobble when she walks too, as they're kind of bent in parts.

I go over and visit the Yaegers by myself sometimes. There's always peppermint pillow candy in a sparkly pink glass candy jar with a cover on it on the parlor table by the window. It's always full, too. It wouldn't stay full at our house. I never see Mabel eat any candy. Maybe it's because her tongue is tied. I keep wanting to see her tongue, but know I shouldn't ask.

Mrs. Yaeger always gives me a piece of candy every time I come and visit with Mabel, which makes it worthwhile going over there. Mabel doesn't know how to play, but she's a good listener and laughs a lot, which doesn't need her tongue, I guess. Some of the kids in the neighborhood are afraid of her. I tell them not to be, and that they should visit her too, because she must get awfully lonesome, staying inside the house all the time, or in the yard by herself. Even telling them that they'll get candy if they visit doesn't change their minds.

"We don't want to catch what Mabel has," they say.

I don't either, but Mama says, "What Mabel has is not catching." And Mama should know, because she was studying to be a nurse before she met Daddy and got married.

When the sun starts moving downward, we help Mama take the

bushel basket of picnic stuff out of the car trunk. She spreads out an old blanket for our tablecloth and puts the food in the center of it. We can eat wherever we want, but everybody likes staying around the blanket eating and talking, sometimes even singing or telling stories.

Mama pours lemonade into aluminum measuring cups with handles. Daddy got lots of those cups when he worked at the aluminum factory. Rejects, he calls them. At home there's all kinds of aluminum rejects. Once they were all shiny, but they're getting dull now. Since the factory closed down, we don't get dented aluminum stuff anymore.

Daddy cuts the watermelon into big chunks with a sharp butcher knife, and hands them out. It's so delicious, biting into that first piece of watermelon, the sweet juices running down my mouth, sliding along my throat. It's the best part of summer.

We spit the seeds too, as far as we can, asking for another piece quick as we can, till it's all gone. But we never get a second piece unless the pink stuff's eaten right down to the rind. "Wasting food is a sin," we've been told by Mama, who adds, "Children in China would be glad to have that much food."

There's oatmeal cookies for dessert. Next we wait, without asking, for Daddy to bring out that Mr. Goodbar. He breaks off the small squares, putting them in our outreached hands. "Thank you, Daddy," we say and let the chocolate slowly melt in our mouths.

Then comes quiet time around the blanket as we watch the sun set. The nighttime birds start to fly about. "Look, there's fireflies, way off in the woods," Buddy points, and all heads turn that way.

I always keep a lookout for bats, not wanting any to get in my hair. I keep a towel handy at picnics for lots of things. Swatting bugs, wiping off mud, and in case I need something to put over my head real quick, if anything flies near my hair. Mostly, I just wrap treasures I find in it to take home—shells, flowers, and unusual pretty stones.

Daddy lies down for a while. We all whisper so we don't disturb him, but pretty soon he gets up, brushes off his pants, and says, "Time to be heading home."

The pail of fish and other things go into the car trunk, making the whole car smell like fish, but we don't care. Nothing can spoil our take-home joy.

Catherine points to the sky, "There's the first star." We all turn to see it blinking brightly in the darkening sky.

"It's wishing time," Mama says.

We all chant together, "Star light, star bright, the first star I see tonight, I wish I may, I wish I might—" then each make our own private wish. Mine is always the same—a Shirley Temple doll.

We snuggle together in the back car seat, glad it's still summer, glad we got away from home, glad we spent the day at the Ten Cent Place. And once we're home, we'll spend our time in bed rethinking the whole day, talking about it, and falling asleep happy.

~UNCLE STEVEN'S FARM~

Our family never takes vacations to far-away places, or even nearby ones.

But we do know people with cottages "up North" where they go in summer to fish or swim. It's hard to believe anybody can be that rich, to have more than one house, especially when some people have no homes at all.

Daddy frowns upon vacations of any kind. He believes a person should be working when awake, or at least doing something to keep busy. When he calls someone "lazy" it's a pretty bad name to call them. So I sometimes keep my hands busy while my head's wandering all over in daydreams and stories, so Daddy won't think I'm not doing anything.

Even now, when Daddy doesn't have a regular job, he never sits around, and he keeps reminding us we should always be doing something worthwhile, except when sleeping.

His father, my Grandpa, came over from Poland on a boat without any money, so their whole family, even little ones, had to work extra hard for everything they got. Keeping busy, working hard, they were told, was the only way to get ahead.

Relatives tell lots of stories about Grandpa, good and bad. Some are told in Polish, which I don't understand, but still like listening to. When Daddy's mad, he yells Polish words real loud. I think they're swear words.

So Daddy keeps himself busy every day of the week, except Sunday. That's a day of rest for all of us, well, except Mama, who still has to do cooking, making a big Sunday breakfast after church, and a hearty supper. We don't eat lunch on Sunday, so at least that gives her some time to rest.

After Sunday Mass and breakfast, the day is usually ours to do what we want. Sometimes, we visit Uncle Steven on his farm, my favorite place to go. For city kids, it's almost like traveling to a foreign country. There are acres to run around in, a river to fish in, and woods to explore. The farm has dogs, cats, horses, pigs, cows, and five country cousins, who dress different than we do, and talk kinda different too.

As soon as it's announced, "We're going to Uncle Steven's today," we all get ready quick as we can and pile into the old shined up Ford. Daddy says it's okay to polish the Ford on Sunday, because it's the only day he takes the car out of the garage, and we should look our best on the Lord's Day. Even a car.

Daddy makes sure the tires are pumped up, and the gas and oil are filled, then slowly backs out of the garage. With the motor still running, he calls through the open window, "Okay, kids, pile in."

And away we go, happily chugging out of the city. We sit glued to the windows, watching the countryside go by, the cars whizzing past, not talking much, mostly listening to Mama and Daddy.

"I wonder if Steve's fishing or farming today," Daddy says as we're nearing the last turnoff. I always marvel that Daddy knows how to get to such far-away places without getting lost. Bigger people must have bigger brains.

"Never saw anyone farm like Steve does," Mama says. "That oat field of his—full of mustard!" She makes it sound like mustard's something bad, but the field looks yellow and pretty to me.

The highway soon becomes gravel, and dust shoots out behind us. In the distance, we see Uncle Steven's log farmhouse and his old faded reddish barn. Daddy drives slowly down the narrow bumpy road to their large front yard, where the grass is never cut. Wildflowers, big bushes, trees, and all kinds of old farm machinery are scattered all over. We park in the deep grass.

Since we don't have a telephone and neither do they, they don't always know we're coming. Sometimes, on special occasions, Mama sends a postcard, writing real tiny, telling them all kinds of things and naming the Sunday we'll be visiting.

As soon as the car stops, dogs begin barking and the cousins run out to greet us. There are four girls and a small boy. They like having company as much as we do. When we get out of the car, there's lots of greetings and handshakes.

Cousin Delores, who's my age, runs up. "Hello, Lulu!" She grabs my hand. "We've got a whole day to play together." Off we go for a day of fun with our favorite cousins.

Adeline, who's a bit older, grabs my other hand, "Let's go ride on the swing first, so we can talk for a bit."

Behind their house is a creaky old wooden lawn swing, with bench seats on both sides. We sit there, working the swing back and forth with our feet and arms as we talk. Nearby is a tire on a rope, swinging from the twisted apple tree, for those who like wilder single rides.

Next, we go into the barn and play in the haymow for a while. The high soft piles of hay are perfect for somersaults or fearless jumps. Shafts of dusty sunlight reflect vertical spotlights on all of us. I prefer to watch rather than doing any jumping. Still, it's fun being in that big barn with high ceilings, old wagons, and strange noises. There's even birds flying around in there. If they were bats, I sure wouldn't stay.

When we're tired of the barn, we run over to the empty granary, which is a cool place to be on a hot afternoon. Before harvest time, when the grain gets piled up in there, it's empty and turns into a big summer playhouse. There's always this peculiar smell, like dried chicken feed, moldy leaves, and leftover grain. Some grains still hide in cracks and corners.

There's rickety furniture, big and little toys, some of them rusting. Piles of books and games are everywhere. They come from their Uncle George, who isn't married, and buys each kid a present every birthday.

There's dolls too, but no Shirley Temple doll. I don't think they even know who she is, because they've never seen a movie. We skate across the skiddy grain-polished floors, or have wagon races in there. I've never seen playrooms as big as this, or so many toys, with new ones added each visit. Lucky cousins.

Behind the log house is the second best play place. Junked stuff is kept out here—an old kerosene stove, with the knobs and doors still working, trashed pots and pans, a few wobbly chairs.

Here, among the hollyhocks and tall weeds, we make our summer play kitchen come to life, putting together mock meals, using green apples, mud, and stones, decorating the dishes with wildflowers, sticks, and berries.

Some things are different on the farm than at our house. There's no faucets for water. You have to pump water from the iron pump outside. Inside, you get it from a pail with a dipper. But the water's cool and tasty, no matter where it comes from.

Their bathroom's outside too, in a small wooden building. The seats are above round holes that go way down deep into the ground. It's dark, buggy, and smelly in there, and I wait as long as I can to use the place, having someone stand guard outside the door, always hoping I won't fall in. There's no toilet paper, just a Sears catalog. I have to use the pages to wipe myself, which I didn't know at first, thinking it was for something to look at while in there, till my older sister explained it all.

The time goes fast. Soon Uncle Steven's calling, "Children—time to go get the cows!" We pick up nearby sticks and start walking to the far pasture, a parade of kids hop-scotching across the giant rocks sticking up in the fields. We play games as we go along, sometimes singing crazy songs.

"Come boss! Come boss!" we call across the fields, as we get closer to the cows, who begin mooing back and start coming together. Each cow has a special name, which our cousins know, but I just call them "bossy."

We trudge back slower, the herd moving ahead of us. I feel so important that we, with our big sticks and loud shouts, are controlling this group of huge fearsome animals.

Milking time's next. Cows march into their own stanchion stall, without anyone telling them which one is theirs. They just know. They eat some hay and wait for milking. I watch, fascinated, as white streams squirt into metal pails with a rhythmic "swish, swish" as adults sit on stools, milking them. Meowing cats soon emerge from cobwebbed corners of the whitewashed interior. Sometimes they get fresh milk squirted right into their open mouths. I make sure to keep my mouth closed tight when I'm watching.

After the chores are done and the animals bedded down, everyone migrates to the farmhouse kitchen.

"A few eats before you go," Auntie Ellen coaxes.

We all sit around the long plank table, kids on a wooden bench on one side, adults on the other. A flickering kerosene lamp is already lit. It's pretty in here by lamplight. The patterns on the cracked oilcloth are worn away, and the dishes don't match, but for me it's always a looked forward to time, gathering at this table with all these happy people. It's as if we have found a perfect way to keep the day from leaving, even though the sun is nearly down. A cool breeze comes in through the screen door, crickets are already chirping, and there's much talk and laughter. It all sounds different inside these thick log walls.

There's strong coffee for the adults and colored sugar water in old jelly glasses for the kids. The table's covered in plates of homemade bread, a soup dish heaped with pale butter, and a mixing bowl with thick oily peanut butter that Uncle Steven buys in five-gallon pails from the country store. Ours comes in smaller stingy jars, and we're careful how much we spread on our bread at home, knowing Daddy's watching and will say, "Don't put so much on." But here we pile it on.

145

If it's someone's birthday, there's a crumbly lopsided chocolate layer cake with drippy frosting. Auntie Ellen isn't a very good cook, Mama always says later, but whatever Auntie Ellen puts on the table tastes good to me. I never care how it was made.

Sometimes the grown-ups play Sheepshead after dinner on the cleared away table, banging the cards down hard with their fists, shouting "Schneider!" or "Game!" when they win. We kids play cards or other games on the floor near the lamplight, or just sit and tell stories. Sometimes we go out on the porch steps to get away from their noise.

One time, our whole family stayed overnight at Uncle Steven's. It was threshing time. Daddy was needed to help out the next day, and Mama needed to help with the cooking, as there's always lots of hungry men on threshing day.

Mama and Daddy slept in the kids' downstairs bedroom. So we kids slept on the floor in the attic, getting up there by a ladder that went through the ceiling. We lay on quilts that were spread over straw, and had so much fun we hardly slept. I could see the moon shining through the tiny window at the far end, and felt much closer to it, because I'd never slept that high up before.

However, we're not sleeping over tonight, even though we kids beg to stay longer. "Time to start getting on home," Daddy's saying. We finish our game, maybe having to stop right in the middle.

After drawn out goodbyes and last minute chats through open car windows, the motor starts up. The car lights turn on, shining up the whole yard. There are no other lights around, except the stars in the pitch-black sky, glowing like distant sparklers. Even night time is different in the country.

We wave and wave till we can't see them anymore, then settle our tired bodies into the crowded back seat, as the car lulls us with its rocking motions.

The road ahead is pitch dark, but the bright headlights open big patches of light as we motor along, and soon our tired eyes begin to close. The voices of Mama and Daddy break through our drowsiness, taking away the pleasantness of the day when they mention how days on the farm are not always happy days.

"He's never going to get his hay in." Mama uses her scolding voice.

"Not him," Daddy agrees. "When the sun shines, it's a better day to go fishing than cut the hay." I've heard this conversation before and can almost predict what the next words will be.

"He's going to lose that farm," Mama says every ride back. "That field of cucumbers; he's let it all go to weeds already."

"He could make those kids work harder, too." Daddy feels they play too much.

"You can't run a farm the way he does!" Mama says. Even in the dark, I can see her head shake in disapproval.

However, I like the way Uncle Steven runs his farm, and every summer I count the calendar days until I can spend my one-week vacation there.

Adeline and Delores spend a week at our house, too. Though it's hard to believe, they like the city better than the country. It's fun showing them city things when they stay with us—the big downtown stores, parks and playgrounds, and of course the ice cream stands.

The week before my trip, I spend lots of time getting things together, packing it all in a big cardboard box. My best clothes, clean and folded, a nightgown without holes, my favorite bath towel, toothbrush, candy treats I've been saving up, pencils and writing paper.

I don't take books, because I'd rather read the ones they have, and their pile of old magazines. They have stacks of big-little books, too, which read fast. It's almost like going to a different library, except you can't take their books home. My cousins say I can, but Mama says I can't. She makes the rules, even when I'm at a different house.

The trip begins like our regular Sunday visits, only at the end, I don't go back with my family. I stand outside the car while Mama, Daddy, and the rest hug me and say goodbye.

I want to go with them, yet I don't. I get anxious for them to leave so my week can begin. My lips begin to quiver as I watch their car drive away. I turn around quickly and go off with my cousins, all of us running toward the house—my new home for one whole week.

My things are already in the cousins' bedroom, and I pass out treats Mama sent for each of them.

Days on the farm are fun, right from early morning, when roosters crow us awake, the birds calling in cheery song, till late night storytelling in the wooden beds, accompanied by cheeping crickets, hooting owls, and the beagle dog, Tuffy, snoring loudly on the rag rug by the side of our bed. Tonight I sleep with Adeline, Delores, and little Stevie in their big bed, on a straw mattress that prickles lots. But by the end of this first day, I'm so tired I could sleep on rocks.

Still, the noises in the country are different than those I hear at home. When I wake up during the night, hearing strange sounds, it takes a minute to remember where I am. But I still don't know what most noises are and I'm too sleepy to check them out—or too afraid. The best thing about being here in the night is knowing I'm not alone, snuggled with all the cousins. Being alone in the dark is the worst feeling.

Each day, there's something different to do, like opening a surprise package every morning. There's work, too. Everybody works, even if you're on vacation. We have daily chores in the house, barn, and fields. But when you do chores with others, it never seems like that much work. Feeding the chickens and pigs, cleaning the cow barn, doing the dishes in cold water, pumping water for the animals and the house, hanging clothes on the wash line—we do it all together.

Daddy was wrong. Uncle Steven works hard. I know, because I see him do it, every day.

Today we're going out in the fields to bring in the dried hay. I pick out a straw hat from the big box. We climb onto the empty wooden farm wagon. Uncle Steven sits up front, driving the two large horses. Ahead is the field with long rows of hay drying in the morning sun.

Uncle Steven stops the wagon, helps us out, and gives us pitchforks. He grabs his own pitchfork and begins tossing large forks of hay onto the wagon. Sweat trickles down from under his torn straw hat. He wipes his face and neck lots with his big red bandanna that he keeps tied around his neck, then gets back on the wagon and moves it ahead to the next batch of hay, the load getting higher and higher.

I'm not too good at using the pitchfork, even if it's a smaller one. Sometimes I do get some hay onto the wagon, or Uncle Steven asks me to scrape the loose hay into bigger piles on the ground instead. The cousins are more practiced at all of this.

Luckily, work stops for lunch at noon, when the sun beats down hottest. We all go back to the shady house for a quick lunch of cold meat, bread, and milk, which is kept cool in a large stone crock jar in the basement, which has big rock walls and is reached by an outside cellar door. Nobody stays down there very long. At least, I don't.

There's little talking at lunch.

After, everyone sprawls out in the patch of unmowed grass in front of the house, under the shade of the large chestnut tree. Uncle Steven flips his straw hat over his face to keep the flies away while he's resting. I do the same thing. We all rest. An unheard of idea at our house, where lying down is never done in the daytime, unless you're sick.

Even while working in the fields, there are pauses for rest. We can stop when we wish, take drinks of cool spring water from the battered turtle-green thermos jug, using the dented cover for a cup. Sometimes Uncle Steven stops and lights up his brown-stained corncob pipe and just sits under a tree in the field, doing nothing, eyes squinting from the sun, a smile on his face.

"Gives the horses a chance to rest too," he says.

Uncle Steven laughs a lot. With his kids. With the animals. He's always making little jokes about almost anything. He never gets mad, not like Daddy does sometimes. It's hard to think of them as being brothers. Maybe living on a farm makes the difference, because Uncle Steven doesn't have to worry about getting a job—the farm's his job.

Maybe Daddy should move to a farm?

One time, we find a nest of baby snakes when we turned over a shock of hay. My immediate fright is eased by Uncle Steven's mirthful laughter, as he gently pushes the snakes out of the way with his pitchfork.

"They won't hurt you," he chuckles, "They're good for the grain. They eat the mice."

Daddy would have scolded me, "Don't be such a fraidy cat. You're bigger than they are."

Being bigger than a snake doesn't make me feel any less afraid.

After supper, once the dishes are done, we kids play games around the kitchen table, or read old magazines by the kerosene lamp. It's a winding down time, punctuated by the ticking of the kitchen clock on the wall shelf, and the constant squeak of the rocking chair as Uncle Steven rocks and smokes his pipe, eventually dozing off, his face still smiling.

One by one, everyone leaves to go to bed; first to the outhouse, then washing up in the tin wash pan, and off into the bedroom. We giggle and talk in the dark till we fall asleep.

Every morning, after the cows are milked, Uncle Steven has to put the big cans of milk in the back of his pickup truck and take them to the creamery. I always ask to ride along. The others have ridden in that truck so many times it's not that special for them anymore. But it's special for me to spend time alone with Uncle Steven and pretend he's my dad. But it's only pretend.

We drive on winding roads to the creamery and cheese factory and have to wait in line to drop off milk cans. Uncle Steven waves and talks to the other men waiting in their trucks. Lots of them chew tobacco, and spit out their windows. I try not to look when they do. Mama calls it a "filthy dirty habit" whenever she sees anyone spitting.

One time, I asked Uncle Steven if I could go inside the cheese factory with him, instead of waiting in the truck.

"Sure," he says, "but you be careful you don't fall into one of those big cheese vats. We'd never find you."

The minute I step inside, the terrible bad smell overpowers me in this hot room. It doesn't smell at all like cheese, more like stale stinky sour milk. Gaggy stuff. And the thick soupy gunk in the big shiny kettles doesn't look like cheese either. Men in white aprons and round white caps have big wooden paddles, stirring the goop around. I make sure I don't get too close, and don't stay in there too long.

We always get cheese samples when Uncle Steven goes to the high counter to sign slips of paper for his milk. They give me a big piece of fresh white cheese, which I munch on after, while sitting high up in the front seat of the truck. It tastes much better than it smelled.

Sometimes, before going back to the farm, we stop at the country store, a place that has all kinds of different things, from corn shellers to needles and thread, not like our small corner grocery store, which Mama calls "Hinky Dink" because they have so few things in their dinky place.

There's always lots of people at this country store, chatting noisily with one another. Everybody seems to know everyone else too, but they don't know me.

"Whose little girl is this?" someone asks. "She ain't one of yours, is she, Steve? One you've been hiding?"

"Nope, this is Felix's girl," Uncle Steven says, patting my head, "My brother's. She's staying by our place, for vacation."

"Vacation? Farms ain't no place for a vacation." They laugh. "Farmers, heck, they never get no vacation, any time."

"Looks just like Felix, don't she." A tall skinny man bends his head down, looking right into my face. I can see he's missing lots of teeth. "Can you smile for us, girlie?"

I try to hide from the glare of his attention, but there's no place to go, except maybe behind the big cracker barrel in the corner. I'm all right with Uncle Steven, but don't like being among strangers, and usually don't say anything, keeping my head down.

The toothless man asks, "Cat got your tongue?"

I don't answer that either, even though I feel like sticking my tongue out at him, to show that I do have a tongue.

Sometimes I walk around the store, looking at different things by myself, mostly on the bottom shelves. I don't have any money, so I'm not even tempted to think about what I might like to buy.

No Shirley Temple dolls here. Not too many toys at all, mostly farm stuff. Hanging across one wall are wide rolls of pretty dress material. Some day I'd like to have a dress made from such silky material, and pick out whatever design and color I wanted.

Who buys such fancy dress cloth in a farm store? There's hardly ever any women here. Probably busy doing work at home.

Uncle Steven buys a few things, but he doesn't have much money either. Still, a trip to this store can be interesting whether you buy anything or not.

There's special days at the farm too—when Auntie Ellen announces, "I think we can all go cherry picking tomorrow." The cousins get all excited. This will be my first time. They tell me all about it, and I get excited too.

Everyone gets up early and does their chores real quick. Auntie Ellen packs peanut butter sandwiches, ripe tomatoes, and fills the thermos with colored water. We all squeeze into their rusting and rattling regular green car and drive up into the Sturgeon Bay area to pick the reddest, sweetest cherries I've ever tasted. We stop along the roadside before we get there for a sit-in-the-grass picnic. If we have to go to the bathroom, we go in the deep grass. "We've a long way to go yet," Auntie Ellen warns.

Big signs soon appear along the highway—"PICK YOUR CHERRIES HERE."

When we get to their regular cherry place, we all cheer.

The owner gives us each a tin pail. You have to pay for each pail you fill. He also tells us not to eat the cherries when picking them, because that's like stealing. There's a big sign saying that too.

You have to go up on a ladder and pick cherries from small trees till you get your little tin pail filled. It's hard not to eat a cherry every once in a while, because they taste so good right from the tree. But because you have to spit out the stones, it's not easy doing it without anyone seeing you. I keep the stones in my mouth as long as I can, trying not to choke on them. Mostly we just eat the cherries that have fallen on the ground, which I don't think is stealing. We have to watch out for wasps though, which look for cherries on the ground too.

There's other families picking cherries, yelling, calling to each other. I guess it's cheaper to pick cherries than buying them in the store. More fun, too. There'll be lots of cherry pies, cherry jam and other good things made for the winter ahead, but nothing tastes as good as right from the tree in summer.

"Can she bake a cherry pie, Billy Boy, Billy Boy, Can she bake a cherry pie..." we sing loudly in the car riding back, packed between peanut butter pails brimming with cherries and red-stained children with bittersweet feelings in their stomachs.

Uncle Steven's old log house has never been painted. Their furniture's not half as nice as ours. The sitting room has a sofa, but that room's hardly ever used in summer. In the corner there's an old pump organ from their Uncle George. Sometimes, on rainy days, Gladys, the oldest cousin, brings out the songbooks. She plays the organ, and we all sing around it. Their beagle dog howls along with us. We forget all about the rain.

But even during rain, we have to go bring in the cows, and go outside to the outhouse. There's a white enamel pail with a cover kept under the bed that we can use at night. But I haven't used it, afraid I might tip it over in the dark. But just knowing it's there helps.

I wouldn't mind living here at all, I keep thinking. But then I also think I would miss Mama, and just maybe, my brothers and sisters. A one-week vacation is probably best. Like reading a book, you can step into another world for a little while, but then you go back to your own.

Bad things happen on the farm, too. One afternoon, Uncle Steven doesn't eat lunch with us because he is still in the fields trying to finish his work before the rains. Farmers always worry about rain. Sometimes they need it, sometimes they don't want it. Today, even though Uncle Steven doesn't want it, it is going to happen anyway.

We can see through the kitchen windows that the sky's turning coal black. Thunder begins rumbling and lightning streaks across the suddenly swaying tree tops. One by one, we go outside to watch, not saying much. I'm not sure what's going to happen next, or what I should do when it does.

The wind howls fiercely, and the windmill spins wildly. We stand on this small rickety porch, rain drenching us.

"He's coming," someone shouts.

We see Uncle Steven running from the barn. Pelting rain plasters his striped overalls to his skin. His straw hat's gone. His dripping hair's spread every which way.

He huffs and puffs as he joins us on the porch, leans against the post, and covers his face with his hands. Nobody says anything.

My heart beats fast inside. I want to go into the house, but instead just move closer to the door. I'm not sure what you're supposed to do on a farm during a storm, this is my first one. I forgot to even look to see if there was a lightning rod on the house.

"I got the horses in the barn—" Uncle Steven says, then stands and watches the storm with a grim face.

All of a sudden, hail begins to beat down angrily. Big white hail stones bounce across the grass. Thundering bullets of hail hammer on their tin roof.

"Oh, dear Lord, that's the biggest hail I've ever seen!" Gladys sounds frightened and backs closer to the house. The others do too.

Uncle Steven looks out. There's no smile on his face as he watches the continuous hail. Finally, he breaks the silence.

"The hail—Ellen, I only got half the grain cut—" His voice is trembly, sad. He stands there, holding Auntie Ellen's hand tightly.

"That hail—it's flattening every piece of grain. Pounding it to hell. It'll never come back." He shakes his head slowly. "It's lost, Ellen. All that work—gone, just like that."

"We'll make it through," Auntie Ellen says in her quiet voice. "Somehow."

The raindrops rolling down Uncle Steven's creased face make him look like he's crying. But grown-ups don't cry.

Uncle Steven doesn't make any jokes the rest of the day, just sits in his rocker, staring ahead. The rest of us are quiet too, as if the storm was still around, hovering, shrouding the whole house in a new kind of gloom.

That was one of the saddest days of all of my summer vacations.

~ "THE WORST VACATION" ~

There is one summer vacation I don't even like remembering.

Mama still visits the people who adopted her. If anyone asks her why, she answers, "You can't hold grudges all your life. You learn to forgive, even if you don't forget."

The old couple still lived on the same farm, near Cooperstown, where lots of Irish people settled. I never like going there, remembering Mama's stories about living in that dreadful house.

Her stepfather had died, but the stepmother—the "old lady" (that's what Mama calls her) is still there. She's all wrinkled up, and never smiles.

Her nephew lives with her now. Mama calls him Big John. He's a State Senator and he's gone away to Madison most of the time, so we hardly ever see him when we visit.

Big John never smiles either. But there's a huge grinning photo of him on the front room wall.

"His fake election pose," Mama comments, wrinkling her nose.

Anyway, in spring, Big John writes Mama that the old lady is going to need help in summer, because of some injury, and would Catherine be able to come and work there as a hired girl?

Mama doesn't like the idea of Catherine hiring out, but I hear her tell Daddy, "Well, the old lady really needs help, and we sure can use some extra money."

Catherine's all excited about going, and I help her pack the family suitcase. She hugs me so hard before getting into the car, then drives off with Mama and Daddy. I just keep waving and crying.

Mama gets a letter from Catherine the very first week, saying she's homesick and doesn't like being there alone. That's the only part Mama reads to me before saying, "I think you should go to the farm and stay with Catherine. It'll be a nice vacation for you too."

I really miss my sister. Surely we can have all kinds of new adventures together in this different place.

So I pack my few things in a cardboard box and drive off with Mama and Daddy to the old lady's farm. It isn't the same happy feeling I have when I'm going to Uncle Steven's, and once the place comes into view, scary feelings begin to jump around in my stomach.

The house looks like it's falling apart. Mama's stories are extra loud in my head today. And now I'm going to have to live in the very same place she did.

How will I be able to get through the coming days—especially without Mama?

Catherine's so glad to see me. Her big hug quiets my worries. Catherine will be my Mama while I live here, making everything better.

The old lady sits in her rocker, talking only to Mama. Daddy's anxious to go fishing, so Mama repeats instructions to me, kisses me goodbye, and she's out the door.

What if they never come back to get us?

Soon as the car's gone, Catherine takes me upstairs to the attic room. It's an empty space with a rusty iron bed and raggedy quilts. The ceiling is made of rough wood rafters with big nails showing through. There's a small grimy window. Right away I know I don't want to sleep in that bed, but there's nothing I can do about it anymore.

I cry myself to sleep that night, thinking so many disturbing thoughts. Am I in the same bed Mama slept in when she was a little girl? Did her Christmas morning story take place in this room? Everything keeps repeating in my head, making me cry more.

Thus begins my worst summer vacation.

So many things are dreadful. Especially the food. There is no ice box, so we have to go down into the dark musty basement where the awful edibles, with strange tangled names, are stored.

Breakfast is mush, which Catherine cooks in a big iron pot. After breakfast, what's left hardens in the pot. Catherine cuts it into thick slices and fries it in bacon fat for supper. She cuts pieces of moldy bacon from an old bacon slab hanging in the stinky smokehouse that has lots of bugs crawling in it. I think there are rats, too.

I eat very little. But Mama left me some bags of special candies, which I've hidden under my pillow. At night I suck on them before saying prayers. Both help.

Some farmer brings over milk, butter, and eggs. Sometimes Catherine makes pancakes, muffins, or bread, which I look forward to, especially when I sniff the savory aromas circulating amidst the ever-present foul ones. In the pantry is a tin pail with thick gooey syrup we use on the pancakes. It tastes funny, but still has a sweet taste.

Catherine has to feed the old lady each meal, which I don't like watching, so I keep my eyes focused on the holes and cracks in the old wooden floor, thinking up stories, trying not to listen to the slobbering sounds the old lady makes as she slurps food into her mouth. Catherine's jobs are to make the meals, clean, wash the clothes, and get the old lady ready for bed, which she tries to do as early as possible. She also has to take care of the chickens and weed the scrappy garden. I help when I can, sweeping the kitchen's rickety floor, washing dishes in cold water from the outside pump, using a bar of hard gray soap.

I follow Catherine around so I can help her and to never be too far away from her.

"It's break time," Catherine announces after lunch and supper each day. And we get away from the house quick as we can. Mostly we go down to the pond and sit on torn blankets and talk, or watch the ducks paddling around. I take my pencil and tablet along and write stories. That way I can escape into my imaginary self, and forget all the troubling things at the house above. But if the big bell clangs, Catherine has to go quick and see what the old lady wants.

There's this large bull running around loose in the unfenced yard, bellowing and snorting. He has a large ring in his nose and a clunky chain dragging from it. He's really scary. When he comes close to the house, I can hear his chain rattling as he paws the ground. I'm always afraid to go outside if he's near, but I have to when I need to use the outhouse.

I hate being inside that little place. It's smelly and hot. Flies and bees buzz around. But if I hear that bull, I stay inside, peeking out to make sure he's gone, then quick dash for the house.

Mama never did tell me how long I'd have to stay. Catherine doesn't know either. "Don't worry, you'll get back home in time to go to school."

School and home—they seem to be in another country now, with no way to get there.

When the moon and stars begin shining, and the crickets start chirping, we take the kerosene lamp and go up the creaking stairs into the dark attic. I'm mostly glad when night comes, because then I can cross off another day. I try to get to sleep quick as I can, and try not to remember the bad dreams.

Catherine says there's mice in the attic, so she sets traps. Every once in awhile during the night, we hear the trap snap and a big squeak. I can't move after that, waiting for daylight to see what's in the trap. But Catherine's already removed whatever it was.

"Nothing to be afraid of," is all she'll say. But I'm sure it was a big rat, and pull the covers over my head nightly.

There are two bachelor brothers who live down the road in an old gray farmhouse that has all the paint worn off, and a long front porch with rickety stuff piled around on it. Catherine and I walk down there to visit them one day. Mama said we should.

"They're kind men, and were good to me when I was little."

They're very glad to see us, and tell us lots of stories about Mama as we sit on the porch.

"She was such a nice little girl," Patrick comments with a smile.

"Yes, she was," Mike adds, spitting tobacco juice off the porch.

"But those two what took her in—well, they weren't nice at all."

They give us some funny tasting cookies, also fresh corn from their garden to take back, and find me an old broken doll from inside a big hinged wooden box.

Patrick takes Catherine aside, but I can still hear, cause his voice is pretty loud. "You make sure you lock that door to the attic when you sleep at night. The girl they had last summer, well, Big John—he got her in trouble." There's silence for a bit. "That's all I'm saying. Don't want to get you too scared. Just be careful of him."

What kind of trouble did Big John get a girl into?

"If you two ever need any help up there, you be sure to come down by us," Mike says as we leave. "Day or night, you come down here."

How would we find our way down there in the dark? What if they were sleeping? When I ask what Patrick said to her, Catherine dismisses his words as "just old man talk."

But she double locks the attic door each night after that.

I want to go back to see the bachelors again, but Catherine says, "The old lady was really mad when she heard we went there, yelling at me, 'Your job is to work here and listen for my bell, not go visiting others.'"

I try not to complain too much, keeping most hurts inside so Catherine won't be sadder. Even when my stomach feels sick, I don't tell her. Or when the bee stings me. Or the strange dog chases me. Or the night I hear wolves howling right outside the window.

There's always something unexpected happening, and none of it is good.

One night we hear this loud hollering coming from inside the big barn, as if someone's yelling for help.

Catherine quick sits up in bed. "You stay here. I'm going to see what's going on out there."

I know the bull's sleeping, so I put on my shoes real fast and follow her in the dark, not wanting to stay alone.

The shouting's even louder now. Slowly Catherine squeaks open the big barn door. All of a sudden a thundering voice screams at us. "What are you two doing out here at this time of night!" A dark figure that had been moving back and forth comes nearer.

"You have no business being in this barn! I'm practicing my speeches for the Senate and do not want to be disturbed! Get out! Now!"

He says other things too—big swear words. We both run back to the house fast as we can.

"I didn't even know he came home." Catherine's out of breath. "And I never heard him practicing his speeches in the barn before, just in the house."

Once upstairs, she holds my shaking body, trying to comfort me.

"He's just a mean man, so stay out of his way. He thinks because he's a State Senator he's so important, and everyone has to bow down to him. Well, Mama and I know things about him other people don't."

Now I have new fears about staying here. They just keep adding up and up. Big John hollers at me for lots of things after that. But he doesn't yell at Catherine too much.

"That's because he's afraid of Mama," Catherine tells me. "She knows stuff he's done that wouldn't be good for his elections."

Mama has so many secrets and I know she won't tell me this one either. I don't even try to think what it might be. I don't understand elections, nor do I understand Big John.

Sometimes I sit on the rock outside the house, under the kitchen window, watching the sun go down, waiting for fireflies, always wishing I were home. But I don't want to leave Catherine here alone. She needs me. Mama said so.

This one night, I hear the old lady and the Senator talking by the open kitchen window. I can't hear it all, but catch some.

"I don't know why Lizzie sent two girls here. We only asked for one. Expecting us to feed them, and pay them besides." Big John is talking.

The old lady mutters, "I think it's because Lizzie's family has no money. Felix isn't working, you know. So, they thought they could get free room and board here for the summer for those two lazy girls."

"Well, I don't like leaving you here alone when I have to be gone away on business."

"I'm better off alone than having to watch those two. See that they don't steal our food, or go into your office and snoop through your important files."

"She went through my files!"

"Yes, Catherine did. I caught her snooping in there one day." I can't hear the rest, hard as I try.

That night in bed, I tell Catherine all I heard.

"Snooping! All I was doing was cleaning up his filthy place." She's really mad and even forgets to set the mouse trap, and I hear mice scampering all night. I even hear someone rattling on the attic door knob.

Could Big John break through the door lock?

I sleep very little that night, and my dreams are worse than ever.

When Mama and Daddy come two days later, on Sunday, to check up on how we're doing and see if we need anything, I begin crying and tell Mama what I heard by the window. How Big John screamed at us in the barn. About the big bull. The terrible food. I'm crying too hard to continue.

Mama questions Catherine in the next room afterwards. I listen around the corner. "What Lulu says is true, Mama. Only, she didn't tell you what Patrick told me—about the girl that worked here last summer. . ." Catherine whispers the rest.

A few minutes later, Mama announces, "You two pack your clothes, you're both going back with us. Today!"

Then she talks with the old lady. I don't listen, because I'm already scrambling up the attic stairs, quickly throwing my things into my cardboard box.

Catherine's soon up there too. I can't tell if she's happy or mad. She doesn't say anything, just throws her things into her suitcase. She doesn't even make the bed.

We rush down the stairs with all our belongings.

"Don't worry about your pay," Mama tells Catherine, "I'll make sure you get it." In next to no time, I'm in the car with Mama and Daddy, driving away from that terrible place. Finally, I'm going home. The bad story has reached "The End," and I don't ever want to read it again.

~ BEAN PICKING ~

Bean picking time is one event that announces summer's almost over. I always look forward to working in the bean fields. It means I'll be earning money to spend at the county fair, and for Christmas presents, since Christmas is coming pretty close too.

Farmers grow acres of beans in the big fields surrounding our town and need lots of help picking the new beans that grow on the plants daily. Kids are best for picking beans, because they're shorter and will do it for less money than grown-ups.

I'm anxious to begin the picking, even if it means working all day in the hot sun. I get my stuff ready the night before. The next morning, I jump out of bed real early and scramble for breakfast. Pretty soon, Mama's at the door, calling loudly, "Time to go. We can't miss that truck. Farmer Kowalski doesn't wait for anybody!" Mama goes with us, for the extra money, she says.

I pick up my tin scrub pail, grab my lunch bag, straw hat, and a sweater in case it gets cold, and follow Mama out the door and down the block to wait at the corner for the old pick-up truck to come by. There's Mama, Catherine, Buddy, and me from our family. Betty Jane stays home to watch Mitzy and Sonny. She's not that good a bean picker anyway, and would rather stay home.

While we wait, other pickers gather. The rumble of the truck perks our ears, and it soon chugs to a stop. We climb into the back, picking our spots, sitting on our turned over pails, cause it's going to get even more crowded as we go along, picking up others on the way.

There's lots of chatter as we ride in the morning air, as if we're going to a party. People on the sidewalks turn and look at us. We wave to them. We don't care who sees us, because we're one big group, on our way to earn money, which is a good thing these days. Better than just standing on the curb, watching workers go by.

"They don't need to look their noses up at us," Mama says as we pass, "Working never killed anyone."

We stop at the edge of the farmer's field and can see the long, long rows—straight lines of thick green bean bushes. The sun's just coming up, and the air seems fresher, with dew still on the grasses. There's always more birds out here, and more bugs too.

We line up, ready to get going. The farmer gives us each a big dirty heavy gray cotton bag. We write our names in pencil on a tag that's clipped to the bag. I put my bag at the end of a row, making it "my row," choosing one next to kids my age, and far away from Mama, because she's always saying, "Pick faster, don't talk so much." Talking's the best part.

I get down on my knees and start picking the beans, finding big clumps of them under the thick leaves, grabbing a bunch at a time, dropping them into my pail. Mama and the farmer always warn us to "pick the beans clean," and make sure there's no ripe beans left on the bush.

As soon as we can, we begin telling stories, sharing jokes, and singing songs as we move along the rows on our knees, shoving the pails ahead of us.

When my pail's full, I carry it to my empty bag, dump it all inside, and go back to where I left off. We try to beat each other with the number of pails we fill. I also have to keep up with my new friends, so they don't get too far ahead of me in their rows.

Sometimes we help each other so we can stay close by, or just sit and rest till the others catch up. There's fast people who pick two rows at a time, but one's hard enough for me.

By noontime, it's really hot and I'm glad when the farmer blows his whistle, calling out, "Lunch time!" No matter where we are, when we hear that whistle we stop picking and go over to the grassy area under the old crab apple tree. There's a big jug of water we can pour drinks from, and a pail of water to wash our hands in.

We sit under the tree, eating our lunches, sharing some, and resting a bit, but the time goes pretty fast. All too soon we hear the whistle and see the farmer walking over. "Lunch is over—back to work."

Some people go to the bathroom in the deep grass, but I try not to, unless I know I can't wait, then we take turns guarding each other. I always worry about snakes, so I do it quickly. Bees and wasps are around too, adding more problems.

The afternoon sun really beats down now. My bare arms begin to burn and I try to keep them under the bushes as much as possible. Some women wear old cotton stockings on their arms to block out the sun. I put my straw hat on, which helps, but afternoons aren't as much fun as mornings. There's not as much laughing and talking, and we're already looking forward to quitting time. My bag's still not full. Others have filled two or three bags. But I just keep picking, because there's nothing else you can do once you're out in this field but pick the beans.

Finally, the farmer calls, "Quitting time."

Everyone dumps their pails into their bag, ties them up, then line up by the big scale the farmer set up. He and his helper weigh our bags and mark the pounds in a book next to our name.

"You picked 97 pounds today," Farmer Kowalski says, spitting out the tobacco he's always chewing. "That's one dollar and ninety four cents." That's a lot of money for me.

We get two cents for each pound. But we don't get the money right away, only once a week. So we make sure to be back on Friday, which is payday. We have to give half of our earnings to Mama, because Daddy's not working. I don't mind. It's a good feeling being a wage earner, being able to help out the family.

We're tired, sunburned and dirty, and the ride home in the truck is quieter than it was in the morning. We say "bye" to everyone as they're dropped off, knowing we'll see them again the next morning, and each day for the next two weeks, or long as the bean-picking season lasts.

Betty Jane has supper ready, but we tell her right away, as soon as we walk in the door, "We don't want any beans for supper tonight!"

I've had enough of beans and don't want to see, smell, or have any inside of me. I mark down the amount of money I've earned in my little notebook, plus how much I'll get to keep. Already, I'm planning how much I can spend on presents for Christmas, which keeps getting closer and closer.

Working outdoors brings on a whole new kind of tired. My body sinks gratefully into the comforting arms of the bed. There's hardly time to say all my prayers before I'm sound asleep.

~ THE CHILDREN *of* SIN ~

The County Fair is the biggest event of the summer. Everyone, young and old, looks forward to this week-long celebration that brings in people and animals from all over the state, plus carnival workers from all over the world.

When we were little, Mama and Daddy would take us, giving each of us a certain amount of money to spend to go on a ride, buy cotton candy, or maybe splurge on a crushed ice cone. Daddy still had a job then. The money went fast, but afterwards, we'd make sure to enjoy everything free at the fair, never wanting to go home, eager to come back another day.

Night time was a whole different experience there. Colored lights flashed and spun everywhere. The overhead sky was illuminated with circling lights from the Ferris wheel and sparkling patterns from other high rides. There was twinkling magic wherever I looked.

When Mama and Daddy stopped taking us, we had to go with

the bigger kids, who'd drag us all over to see stuff we didn't want to see, and do things we didn't want to do.

They were always giggling with their friends, dawdling in places we were anxious to get away from. They had to bring us home before dark, too, so I didn't even get to stay and see the dancing lights of night time.

The County Fair Grounds is on the other side of town. There's a big chain fence surrounding lots of barns, buildings, and a big grandstand. The day the Fair opens, you can hear the music and noise from most any part of town, and even see its glowing lights coloring the night sky. You just want to be there as soon as you can. Waiting seems to take forever, with an almost Christmasy feeling throbbing inside you the days before.

I decide I will beg Mama once more to let me go alone to the County Fair, without my older sisters.

"I know the way. I have my bean-picking money saved up, and—"

"You're too young to go there by yourself," Mama says, while I'm thinking of all the reasons why she should let me go.

"Geraldine's ma lets her go by herself. And Betty Jane and Catherine always walk ahead with their friends. They don't want me tagging along."

"Well—" I wait anxiously for the next words, which come after a long pause, "I don't know if you're big enough yet."

"I'm big enough," I say, trying to stretch up as tall as I can. "I go to the library by myself—to school, to church, way to the other side of town to visit cousins Vivian and Veronica—"

She stops me before I give my whole "I'm old enough" litany.

"Well—well, you can go there with Catherine and Betty Jane

tomorrow, then—" another pause, "then you can go off by yourself. But you make sure to check in with them, and tell them when you leave. And I want you home before dark, do you understand?"

"Yes, I understand," I answer, head bobbing up and down in happy agreement.

"But, you'll have to take Sonny with you, because the girls don't want to look after him all day, and I'll be busy canning peaches and don't want him underfoot."

"I can take Sonny," I say. "I'll take good care of him." I never mind watching Sonny, because he likes to see new things as much as I do. Besides, he's my favorite brother.

The next day, I get up extra early. I quickly eat breakfast, dress in my flower print dress and make sure Sonny has nice clothes on too. My saved-up money is tied in my hanky, already in my green leatherette purse.

Mama tells Catherine she can stay after dark this year, "But you make sure Sonny and Lulu leave before the streetlights come on."

"Take a sweater along," Mama tells me. But the sun is shining, so I don't think I need a sweater, something extra to carry around, and kind of forget it. Mama tells Sonny, "You be sure to mind your sister, and if you get lost, you go straight to a policeman." She's already starting with the peaches as we leave.

We walk on the sidewalk behind the older girls, who seem to be going awfully slow, giggling lots. Once I hear the music and all the other sounds in the distance, excitement mounts, and my steps get quicker. Pretty soon we're there, standing right outside that silvery fence, a day of adventure awaiting us.

We get our hands stamped with purple ink at the gate, but because we're younger, we don't have to pay like my sisters do, which they complain about. Sometimes being younger isn't so bad.

"Make sure you tell us when you leave," Catherine warns as she walks away, looking for her other friends.

I grab Sonny's hand and start taking giant steps in the opposite direction, feeling so very important and suddenly grown up.

I decide we'll look at the animals in the barns first. That doesn't cost money and Sonny likes animals. The smells in there are pretty bad, so I try to go through the barns quick as I can. The big bulls with chains in their noses bring up bad memories. I almost run past them. They bellow, following me with mean eyes. I stay away from the giant horses too. They're always stomping their big hooves, shaking their heads, and snorting loudly from their noses. The pigs smell the worst, grunting while they slurp and slobber their food. The nicest are the soft lambs. I stop to pet them.

Rabbits, chickens, and all kinds of colorful birds are moving around in their cages, filling the barn with a mix of strange sounds.

Sonny wants to stay and look at them more, but I tell him, "Maybe later," which is what Mama says a lot when we ask her questions, and we know "maybe later" means "mostly never." But it's already getting hot outside, making the barns even hotter.

Next, we walk through the outside game areas where there's lots of loud music. Men with mustaches and half aprons try to get us to play their pitching games.

"Come on, little girlie. You can win some nice prizes today. Your little brother would like one of those stuffed animals, wouldn't he?"

I try not to even look at them. Mama says the people who run carnival games are crooked and don't want you to win, so I'm not even going waste my good money trying. I look at people carrying their prizes, large stuffed animals, statues of sailor girls, wondering how many nickels they had to spend to win them. I like the big fat nickels the best, and hate spending any of them.

Pennies are easier to spend, and one of my favorite places is Penny Land, where you can play all kinds of games for just pennies. There's flashing lights and tinkling sounds coming from that big tent. Inside a tall glass box, there's a metal digger, which you can use to snatch trinkets and prizes in the digger's claws, which isn't too easy. Sonny, who takes lots of time, wins almost every turn. So I give him pennies to play while I look around at other things. There's fortune telling machines, and peep shows, which are too high and cost more, but big people are always looking in them. Penny Land is a fun place to be, but it's away from other things, so pretty soon I'm ready to go back on the midway.

We stand and watch the people screaming and hollering on the rides, some from way up high. It sounds like they're having fun, but I don't want to spend ten cents on something that's over so quick.

I let Sonny ride in one of the small airplanes hanging on chains that goes around and around in a circle. I stand by and watch, like all the mothers do. He waves to me and I wave back, then help him out after. He looks a bit dizzy, but he's still grinning.

"I was really flying that airplane, really—up soo high," he says, and twirls around with his arms flapping up and down. He's always been fascinated by airplanes. When he hears one up in the sky, he runs outside, pointing and shouting, "Airplane! Airplane!"

I decide we need some lunch and buy two grilled cheese sandwiches, one for each of us. This is my most longed for treat. I've never tasted anything so delicious anywhere else, and you can't make them at home because you need a special machine and store bought bread. The warm gooey cheese melts in my mouth in slow delicious bites. Sonny doesn't want to finish his, so I gladly do it for him. I buy him a five-cent bag of popcorn to eat as we go walking around the carnival.

I'm getting more anxious, because this year I promised myself that I would go to any sideshow I wanted to see. My sisters never wanted to pay money to see sideshows, claiming they're all fake, so we'd have to stand outside the tents and listen to the man tell about the wonders that were behind the big flaps. Sometimes the carnival people would come out front, dance, eat fire, and do all kinds of strange acts on this little stage, while the man talked about them in a big loud voice.

I always wanted to go inside and see more. These were people I couldn't meet anywhere else. They called such people "freaks," and though it isn't a bad word, it's something you really don't want to be, because if you're born a freak, your parents would sell you to the circus to make money.

How could parents do that—sell their own children? What if I had been born different?

Sonny is tiring out, so I let him sit on the grass while I stand in front of the sideshows, watching the fire-eaters, sword swallowers, and all the other strange performers in their different costumes. This is nothing like the circuses we put on in our backyards during the summer. Not at all. These people are real, not pretenders like we tried to be.

As they perform outside, you can see the huge painted pictures on canvas flaps behind them, advertising what's inside. The pictures are unusual, colorful, and wildly strange. Some are even scary.

One says "Siamese Twins," and the barker tells the crowd about twins who were joined at the middle when they were born. A thousand questions race through my mind.

How could two people ever live like that?

There's also a three-headed calf advertised. But when people come out, some are complaining that it was only heads of calves, pickled in a huge glass jar. "Rip-off," I hear many times from people leaving the tents. It makes me hold back. Even after listening to the man shouting all about what you could see inside, if you only bought a ticket. There's nothing I'm too excited to see—big snakes, little midgets, monkeys riding bikes—nope, not today. There has to be something more out of the ordinary that would be worth spending my money on, making my first time alone at the Fair something worth remembering.

We're almost at the end of sideshow row when I see it—the big flap that says "CHILDREN OF SIN" in huge red letters on swaying worn canvas picturing two gnome-like children standing in a primitive jungle setting.

"Come in! Come in! See the Children of Sin!" the barker is shouting.

Thoughts begin flashing through my mind. Would this be something like the penny arcade movies? Lots of them had "sin" in their titles. Or would they just be mummified bodies, like some of the other advertised attractions that weren't what they said they'd be.

Everything about the show intrigues me, but I still can't decide. Well, Sonny would enjoy it if they were children. He's been jiggling around so at the other places, laughing only at the free trained animal acts.

Trying to look as important as I can, I walk up to the lipsticked ticket lady, plunk down my two dimes, and say "Two please." (They don't have children's prices at this show.)

"Here you are, sweetie," she says. "You can go right on in. Show's about to begin."

Tightly fisting the red tickets and hanging onto Sonny, we follow the mostly adult crowd into the mysterious depths of the shadowy tent.

Wow! There, sitting on high chairs on a wooden platform, are two strange live creatures, only about three feet tall. I go closer to see better. One is wearing a little girl's dress, her hair drawn up tightly into a peaked topknot, making her head look like it comes to a point. The boy, in soiled grown men's clothes, is almost bald. Both have yellowish skin, crinkled like crepe paper.

So these are the Children of Sin! How awful! I move further away, yet stand gaping with the others. Sunday sermons about sin and punishment flicker through my mind. I look again, and notice that there are padded leather dog collars around their necks, with long chains attached.

A fat scruffy man, wearing baggy pants, wide suspenders over his dirty undershirt, and shoes with no socks, walks slowly onto the platform and gazes over all of us. He looks straight at Sonny and me. I'm afraid he might make us leave, so I try to get close to grown-ups so we look like we belong to them.

He coughs gruffly, then begins telling the story, really fast—something about a brother and sister marrying, living in sin. "And this is the result!" He points a finger at the downcast children. Adults around me whisper to one another.

"They're both forty-three years old," the man continues, "But they still only have the mentality of six year olds. . . And so they have to be treated like children." He laughs as he playfully tugs on their chains. They slap back at him.

"That's why we have to keep them chained up—for their own protection. Because, like children, they like to run away." He laughs again, tickling at them. They jump around like monkeys at the ends of their chains.

People are laughing too. Only, it doesn't seem very funny to me. Kids don't like being tied up, stared at, or made to do tricks on such a hot day. I sure wouldn't.

"Their mother abandoned them," he continues, "and if it weren't for the carnival, they would have been left to die."

I didn't want to hear any more such stuff, especially about being left without parents, so I edge away from the front with Sonny and sneak over to the side, where the little girl is sitting now, perched on her high chair, looking out over the crowd.

Something inside me responds, connecting me to this strange tiny person, and I wave to her. Her eyes catch mine. A childlike smile spreads across her scrunched face.

All of a sudden I'm caught up in these children's peculiar world, so different from mine, wanting to know more about them. But how? Certainly not from that burly man.

In the corner, behind a short canvas fence, I can see a child's table and chairs, messy dishes, half-eaten food with flies buzzing around. Nearby, on the ground, is a boxlike bed with two dirty blankets. This must be where they live.

Where did they play? Where are their toys?

"That's all folks," the man calls out. "Stay as long as you wish. But don't ever forget these Children of Sin! Remember what happens when man goes against God's laws."

The crowd begins slowly filing out, pausing to look at the display of pictures on the tent wall, reading the write-ups about the two. It's all too high for me to read, but I catch some of their words.

"Lucky the carnival keeps them—nobody else would."

"They don't even look human."

The man leads the children to the small table and chairs in back, and clamps their chains to an iron bar. I watch from a distance.

"Be good," he warns with a playful slap, then disappears behind a tent flap.

The wizened little man climbs onto his chair and buries his head in his hands. He looks like he's crying.

The girl notices me and comes over to the low canvas fence that separates us. Pangs of sympathy rustle through me. How lonely they must be. No other children to play with. Chained up all day. I decide to be nice to her, talk with her. I walk closer. I have to say something so she knows I'm friendly and doesn't go away.

"Do you like being with the carnival?" I ask. Traveling with a carnival had always seemed the most exciting thing in the world to me, even if I'd never do it.

She doesn't answer, just looks at me. Maybe she can't talk. Up close, her skin is dry and crackly. But her eyes, they look so human. I'm thinking—maybe I could have a new friend from the carnival, and write to her. How exciting to share her letters at school.

Then, all of a sudden, she reaches out a claw-like hand over the low fence and grabs my hand so tightly. I'm a little frightened as her claws dig in deeper. Unexpectedly, she speaks in a squeaky raspy voice.

"Help me," she gasps. "Help me get away from here!" She sounds really serious, her hands gripping tighter.

What the man said, about them always trying to run away—was that really why they were chained up? Or were they just being kept as captives? Quickly, I try to stop my scrambling imagination, thinking about what I should do, pulling my hand away.

"Tell somebody to get us out of here," she pleads, trying to lean over the canvas, straining at her chain.

"Who should I tell?" I hadn't expected this kind of talk. All I wanted was to make a new friend.

"Help me get away," she pleads, reaching out her hand again. "They beat us every day. Help us get away!" Her tiny eyes are watering. I'm sad all through; my soft heart truly believes her.

"Open my chains!" She shakes at them feebly, making rattling sounds. Her neck is red and raw where the leather collar is attached to the chains.

So, it is true! That evil man is keeping them chained up against their will and it's up to me to help free them. She probably never told anyone else this, but she trusts me, I can tell. What to do? First, I'll unfasten the chain.

Bravely, I begin to climb over the low canvas fence. Suddenly, their keeper appears from behind the tent flap.

"Hey, you kids!" he shouts fiercely. "Get away from there. Stop bothering them!" Like lightning, the little girl runs to her chair, jumps up and sits quietly, eyes downcast, never looking at me again.

Quickly, I grab Sonny. "We better go now," I say, rushing out of there before that man catches us and chains us up too. My heart is thumping wildly. I'm afraid to even look back.

My eyes can hardly see when we get back to the sunny midway, after being in that shadowy place so long. My stomach is queasy—was it that grilled cheese sandwich?

Carnival music is playing, but all I can hear is her crying voice saying "Help me!" It follows me.

Should I go back? What can I do? Somehow, I have to help her.

"Where are we going now?" Sonny tugs at my sleeve. "More shows?"

"No more shows," I say, walking rapidly. All of a sudden, I'm the heroine in an adventure story, entrusted to deliver a secret message, and it must be delivered to the right people, quickly.

Dragging Sonny behind me, I begin searching for a policeman. Already I can see the headlines—"Young Girl Saves Two Held Captive by Carnival."

I can't find a policeman. And I can't tell the Fair people. They're probably in on this too. They'd never let those children go.

I'll go home, tell Mama. She always knows what to do. She can call the police from the phone next door. I quickly find my sisters and tell them I'm leaving.

"Are you feeling all right?" Catherine asks. "You don't look so well."

"I'm okay, I just want to leave now," is all I say, not wanting to tell them about what happened, and start walking to the gate, wanting to get home quick as I can. There's an urgency within that I've never felt before. I rehearse my speech to Mama in my head as my feet fly along the sidewalks.

As soon as I get home, I tell Sonny to go play outside, then tell Mama about the chained up children, rushing my words out. She's busy canning peaches, pulling steaming jars out of boiling water with metal tongs.

She drops the hot jar back into the kettle. "What do you mean; you went to see the Children of Sin?" She's yelling, her face is red and steamy. "Taking your little brother in there with you too!"

"But, this bad man, he had them in chains," I try explaining with even greater urgency.

"I knew I shouldn't have let you go alone." She wipes her forehead with her peach-stained apron, saying all kinds of sharp things to me before going back to her work.

It wouldn't do any good telling her the rest. If she didn't believe me, that means the police wouldn't either. I'm probably the only person this chained girl has ever told her story to, because she liked me. I could tell. And now I can't help her.

Mama makes me stay in the house the rest of the day, with strict orders not to step out that door at all. The bad feeling stays with me. I keep hearing the words "Help me" repeating over and over.

I hardly sleep that night. The carnival overflows my dreams. The little girl is trying to claw at me. Their keeper is running to catch me. . . .

Early the next morning, before anyone else is awake, I get up and dress quickly.

I need to go to the fairgrounds. Maybe I can sneak in and still try to free my little friend. I have to at least try.

I run as fast as I can. Only, when I get there, everything's gone. The carnival is all taken down. Paper's blowing about. Empty popcorn boxes and broken prizes are scattered across the flattened grass.

Huge red trucks are rumbling out the double gates. Some trucks have open slats, like they hold animals. Others have windows and doors, as if people lived in them.

And in one of those trucks are the Children of Sin. Still chained up, because I failed them in their only chance for freedom.

What more could I have done?

I sit down in the tall grass outside the chain link fence and begin to cry. Somewhere in my head I hear that pitiful voice calling out "Help me!" I see that gnarled face with those pleading watery eyes. There's new pain in my heart as I watch the trucks roll down the road, going further and further away.

I'll never see them again. And I'll never know the ending of their sad story.

~ NINE O'CLOCK MAMIE ~

All too soon, it's back-to-school. I'm in grade three now. New shoes, new classroom, and a new nun—Sister Felicity. It's almost like starting a game over with the same players, but a different leader.

Autumn smells saturate the air. The furnace in the basement at our house is fired up, using coal from the coal bin and wood from Daddy's stacked up piles. Heat and the odor of fire burning filter up through the metal floor registers. Winter clothes, taken from attic storage, reek of moth balls. We sneak vanilla to sprinkle over the smell, till Mama says, "Who's wearing my vanilla?" Back to moth ball odors.

It's getting closer to Halloween, which has good and bad parts.

Dark October nights, with dead leaves falling and cold winds chilling, are the perfect setting for spooky and scary stories. We tell them at school and retell them at home. I search for hair-raising tales at the library, looking forward to being frightened, but only in the safety of our house, with lights turned on and family nearby.

The best and scariest stories are the ones Mama tells. She's such a good storyteller. Of course, she only shares those that really happened, making them all the more frightening. Any time you add the words "it really happened," shivers become realer too.

There's one story Mama tells us about Molly and Eileen, two Irish sisters she knew, who lived alone in this old farmhouse and took in washing to earn a living.

One night, they heard a strange knocking on their kitchen walls. They searched everywhere but couldn't find what might be causing the knocking. Night after night, the wall rapping continued, getting louder and stronger. They were truly frightened, not knowing how it started or when it would end.

The knocking kept them awake at night. They were afraid to be in the kitchen during the day, where they had to do the washing. People commented on how pale they were becoming, how jumpy.

Finally, someone recommended bringing in the parish priest to see if he might find out where the sounds were coming from. If demons were possessing their house, he could command them to leave.

They summoned Father O'Brien. He came to their house one evening with his candles, holy water, and prayer books. He prayed. They all prayed for a very long time. Then Father asked, in a loud and thunderous voice. "Who is it that is doing all this knocking on these walls? Are you the evil one?"

Silence.

Then a faint voice gave out a pitiful cry—"Pray for me." The voice continued repeating the request over and over. Finally, the sisters recognized the voice. "Tis the voice of our dear departed mother. Glory be! Dead already for so many years."

"Your mother is asking for your prayers," the priest tells them. "She says she won't be at rest till she receives them. You've forgotten to pray for her these past years."

Molly and Eileen had thought their mother was already in heaven, and didn't need prayers anymore. So after the priest relayed her request, Molly and Eileen prayed for their mother morning and night, every prayer they ever knew. The knocking stopped.

I always think of that story whenever I hear noises in our walls, making sure to pray for anyone I know who's dead, even if Mama tells us that the dead can't return in person, or with knocks.

"Once they're dead, they're always dead," she says. But I'm not so sure anymore. She also claims that these two sisters weren't always right in their heads anyway.

Still, I believe the story, and think Mama does too. It proves to me that there are spirits that we can't see all around. Also that prayers can solve many things.

I never believe in witches though, mostly because they're usually in fairy tales, which are make-believe stories. But there is this one person in our town the kids claim is a witch. I'm not sure what her real name is. Everyone just calls her "Nine O'clock Mamie."

The place where she lives is the perfect setting for a witch: a blackened-gray clapboard house on the corner, surrounded by jungles of gnarled trees and overgrown bushes. Poison ivy twists along the black iron fence surrounding her yard. The place looks like a picture in a scary storybook.

There are no curtains on her windows, just yellowed newspapers stuck over them.

"Watch out, she runs after kids with a butcher knife," one boy tells another. "Henry said he was so close he could see the shiny part of her knife."

"She kidnaps kids."

"I heard she boils cats and dogs, snakes and frogs."

The stories get wilder and wilder. I'm not sure whether to believe them or not, but I still listen when the older kids talk about her at recess.

It becomes a game for some, to stand in front of her house at night, taunting, "Old lady witch, fell in the ditch, picked up a rotten apple, and thought she was rich." Then they run like crazy before she comes out.

Halloween night, they get even braver, pounding on her door, rapping on her windows, hoping, yet not hoping, that she'll open the door so they can see what a real witch looks like on Halloween night. Only, she never comes out.

I have to go past her house on my way to the grocery store. Cautiously, I walk on the other side of the street, eyes warily watching her door, legs ready to start running. One day, I'm completely startled to see this strange figure walking toward me on my side of the street. It has to be Nine O'clock Mamie. No one else in our town dresses so strangely. She's wearing a long gray dress and a heavy fringed shawl, with tangled gray hair that seems to sprout wildly from her head.

She's coming closer. I don't know what to do. If I run, she'll run after me, catch me. I stand statue still. Now she's passing. I can hear soft whistling, or is that just the odd way she breathes? Curiosity to see what a real witch looks like overrides my fear.

I glance up quickly, without lifting my head, only my eyes. The short peek tells me she doesn't look like a witch at all. No evil looking face or long hooked nose, not even witch's warts. She has a sad face, resembling a faded rag doll. Her grayish eyes stare straight into the distance. She shuffles right past, not even noticing me.

I don't tell the others that I saw Nine O'clock Mamie up close, or how I thought she looked. They wouldn't believe me, because it doesn't fit their witch description at all. But after that brief encounter, I don't think it's very nice of them to repeat those sassy things in front of her house. Mama doesn't think so either and warns us not to make fun of her, or be with any of the gangs that do.

"Nine O'clock Mamie, sitting on a fence, trying to squeeze a dollar out of ninety-eight cents!"

That's another rhyme they chant. Some say she buys only two or three cents worth of sausage at a time at the Clover Farm Store, counting out her pennies carefully.

I always wondered about her name. How did she ever get it?

One summer evening, I'm sitting on our porch steps when the neighbors gather, which is even better than reading. Daddy's telling stories to the new renter from next door. The name "Nine O'clock Mamie" comes up. I listen more closely.

"The reason they called her Nine O'clock Mamie," Daddy says, "was because a fortune teller told her she'd meet her lover on the bridge, at nine o'clock."

Mama joins the conversation. "So, every day, at nine o'clock, there Mamie would be. Standing and waiting, all dressed up, on the Eighth Street bridge."

"Well, she did meet a young gaffer," Daddy continues. "Fancy clothes, dark mustache. They went out for a while. Got engaged. Then her folks died, leaving her the house, plenty of money, and one of the few cars of that time." Daddy pauses for what seems like forever. "Then the guy took off, just like that, taking all her money and the car with him. No one ever saw hide nor hair of him again."

"But Mamie still waited for him to come back. Waited every day on that bridge," Mama adds. "Eventually, she couldn't take the townspeople looking at her, pointing, whispering. So she stopped coming to the bridge. Began staying at home, hardly stepping out of her house at all. She has seldom been seen since then, except for getting food..."

Mama pauses, then adds, "She always was kind of shy."

That was all they said that night. But things shifted in my mind about her. I even think of visiting Mamie, discovering all the secrets that are locked up in that strange house. I could be like the heroines in these books about girl detectives. Nancy Drew checked out everything.

Only, I never went to her house. I was no Nancy Drew. I was a reader, not a doer.

Then it was too late. Mamie died that fall. Once the news is on the radio, word spreads through town speedily. The next day, Mama reads aloud the small death notice in the newspaper. I guess they use her real name in death, even if nobody did while she was alive.

"Nine O'clock Mamie's dead!" everyone tells everyone else. Once more, her strange life becomes the prime topic of grown-up conversations. I can't go knock on her door now, and regret never being brave enough to do it before.

Luckily, the day the trucks come to clear out her house is a Holy Day—All Saints Day, the day after Halloween, and there's no school. As soon as I hear, "They're cleaning out Nine O'clock Mamie's house today," I hurry over and become part of the crowds of onlookers gathered in front of her house one week after her death.

"The city has ordered her house cleaned out. For health reasons," one lady says. People are pushing for frontline space, and being small, I can squeeze ahead of most. It's been whispered that jewels and money are in that house. There are so many rumors about so many things, I can't keep track, just trying to listen, peering to watch.

It's mostly grown-ups that are crowded about. It seems kids still stay away from her place, which is okay with me. I don't even want Geraldine with me today. I want to be part of this event without talking to anyone, and absorb it through all my senses.

Every minute is fascinating, as they haul all the trash out from her first floor, moving huge mounds of strange looking stuff right through the front door with big shovels. There's a horrendous accumulation of dirt. Baskets of ashes, tree stumps, tree branches, rotten food, rusted cans. Piles and piles of newspapers. Stacks of magazines. Bundles of letters.

The men all wear gas masks.

"Lived right next door to her," an aproned lady is saying, "yet never saw the inside of her house. Ever. Mail began piling up. So, I got curious. Finally called the city. The police came. Had to break in. They found her on the floor, dying. All alone."

"Why didn't the health department do something about her?"

"She never let anyone inside. Not even to check her gas and electric meters."

"Don't think she used her gas or electricity, I suppose."

"Probably starved to death," another comments. "Pete, who runs the Clover Farm store, said she didn't buy enough to keep a bird alive."

"Well, what did she have to live for anyway," another shrugs.

The next day, I'm there again, even earlier. They're cleaning out the second story today. I see a completely different assortment of things. It seems she lived alone in all that downstairs mess the last part of her life. The first half, before the boyfriend ran away, was carefully preserved upstairs, almost like she never went up there again.

I think about a whole lot of things while I'm watching.

Love doesn't always have a happy ending, does it, no matter how long you wait for it.

The gas masks are off today. Men stand at the top of the narrow stairway, which I can see through the open front door. They shovel down endless trains of cardboard boxes, trunks, more bundled newspapers, letters, pushing the stuff past the gauntlets of curious onlookers, who are supposed to stay behind the ropes.

Necks crane as the workmen quickly search through each box for possible valuables before tossing everything up onto the garbage truck to be taken away to the town dump.

"Everything has to be burned. Health Department rules!" the men sternly warn as people reach past the ropes, trying to pick through some of the items.

The workers open up an old trunk on the sidewalk. The lid is lined with stained flowered wallpaper. Inside are layers of dresses—pale colored chiffon, white lace gowns.

Was one of them supposed to be for her wedding?

Also in the trunk are elaborate hats and yellowed corsets, which the men hold up and shake about, pretending they're wearing them. People laugh at their antics. I don't.

An older man nearby comments, to no one in particular, "She was rather a pretty thing, when she was young."

Another trunk contains men's clothing—dated, but fancy.

"Musta been her lover's clothes." The workmen are laughing boisterously now.

"Well, least he left those behind for her."

It seems so sad, all her years of accumulations, things she had cherished, kept hidden from prying eyes—in one day, everyone saw it all. And now it will be burned at the dump.

That's what they did to witches, didn't they? Burned them. Maybe they did it to their possessions too.

A pink embroidered hanky falls from one of the boxes onto the grass. I quickly pick it up and put it in my pocket. I'll keep it in my treasure box. Something pretty of hers has to be saved.

I stay till there's nothing more to be taken out and the last truck has pulled away. Scraps of paper and other bits are blowing about. People seem reluctant to leave, still muttering to one another. But I don't want to hear any more talk. The end has been reached. Her book's closed up.

I wonder many times after if she ever knocked on the walls of her house after she died, asking someone to pray for her.

Who could she ask?

I make sure to put her in my prayers sometimes, or whenever I walk past her empty house.

I still have questions.

Did she ever meet her lover after she died?

And could she possibly have died at nine o'clock?

Every time I walk across the Eighth Street bridge after that, I'm sure I see the faint shadow of a woman, leaning against the bridge rails.

~ POEMS and POOR HOUSES ~

Thanksgiving's getting closer, which means Christmas is closer, too. Yippee!

Shirley Temple's picture in the wish book is smudged with fingerprints and kiss marks. I can't wait till the new catalog arrives with a brand new picture. Toy departments will be opening soon, and then I can see my dearest doll in person.

"Make the days go faster," I silently add to my prayers each morning.

At school, we're drawing big fat turkeys and learning about pilgrims. We're also studying poems, memorizing them too. "Evangeline" by Henry Wadsworth Longfellow, and "Barefoot Boy" by John Greenleaf Whittier.

Most of these famous poems are quite long and mostly serious. Then the teacher makes us write our own poem for class. I decide my new poem will be about Thanksgiving, and I'll make it funny.

"Thanksgiving with Uncle Henry" is the name I give my poem,

and it turns out it's even fun to write. It's about an imaginary goofy uncle who comes to our house for Thanksgiving dinner with his ten bad kids. They have strange names, are sloppy, unruly, always fighting—not a family you'd want around your holiday table. Uncle Henry thinks they're "vonderful shildrens."

When Uncle Henry talks, I have him speak in German-sounding words. I don't know why, but in this rummage sale book of poems and recitations, the funniest poems are always written with German accents. "Ach" and "vonderful" are used a lot.

We also have an old German neighbor, so when I'm writing, I think in my head about how he talks, using his German speech sounds for my poem.

My poem ends with Uncle Henry asking each one around the table, "And vot iss you tankful for?"

Looking at the awful kids he's brought with him, how badly they've behaved, I have the child in the poem answer, "Uncle Henry—I'm thankful, I isn't you!"

Of course, we don't really have an Uncle Henry like that, but what's so great about writing is you can make up just about anything. Silly things that happen in your writing don't have to be real. Sometimes writing is even better than reading, because you're in charge of what takes place and how it turns out.

We hand in our poems.

Sister Felicity likes mine so much that the next day, she asks me to get up and read it in front of the whole class. It's an honor to be chosen, but I'm still not happy about doing it. Kids might think I'm goofy after they hear it.

I begin. "It done happened in the morning, pon Thanksgiving

day..." I read the German words in a man's voice, making them sound like my German neighbor. The kids start laughing, continuing their giggles till the end.

"That is a wonderful poem, Lulu," Sister Felicity says, "and you read it so well. I think the lower grades would enjoy hearing it too. So, tomorrow morning, I'll take you into their room and you can read your nice Thanksgiving poem to them."

I don't want to read to other grades. I know the students in my class, so it's okay to recite in front of them, but it's not okay to read to kids I don't know, especially such a silly poem. Younger ones might not understand the words, or the German accent.

The next morning, I take my lined paper with the poem I've written in pencil and walk with Sister to the room next door. She tells the puzzled group that I'm going to read them a poem about Thanksgiving, one I've written by myself, and when they're bigger, they can write poems too.

But this one isn't like real poems in books, I want to tell them, but don't. I keep my head close to the paper and begin. The words fall out of my mouth, sounding just like Uncle Henry. I forget where I am, as if I crawled right into the poem.

The kids begin laughing and I get louder and sillier. When it's over, they even clap, which keeps me smiling. Still, I'm glad to get back to my own classroom, hoping I never have to read that poem out loud again. I hide it quick when I get home. I like to keep my writings secret.

During play time, we kids always make up silly poems—the dipsier the better. I'm good at that. They just stay in my head, and don't have to even get written down. We singsong them to each other at recess, when the nuns aren't listening, and howl with laughter.

We make up different words and goofy rhymes for regular poems and songs too. So poems don't always have to be highfalutin—just when you're studying them in school.

Our principal, Sister Adeline, is in charge of our stage programs, which are put on a couple times a year. Just about everybody in all the classes gets a chance to be on the stage, mostly in a group song, with everyone strung out in rows on wooden risers across the small stage, wearing costumes to fit the song, with different actions to do while singing.

Sometimes, we do drills onstage, using flags or flowered hoops, or other colorful things that can be moved and waved about in rhythm, which looks colorful and pretty from the audience. But onstage, not everybody remembers all the actions, and you can get hit by the flag of the person next to you. So I don't like being in drills. Still, we enjoy practicing. It gets us away from studying. Sometimes we even come in to rehearse on Saturdays, which is kinda fun. We don't have to wear school clothes, or follow school rules about talking and sitting up straight.

Sister Adeline has a small organ in a black box, which opens up like a suitcase. It has a handle on top, so she can carry it around. As we practice on the stage, she pumps away on the organ down below, while shouting directions and motioning wildly with one hand. It gets kind of crazy on that stage sometimes. But by show time, it's all pretty good.

Parishioners buy tickets to these programs and the money goes to buy stuff for the school. The priest, Father Levitz, even comes to see these shows.

The fall program is being planned.

One day, Sister Adeline hands me some pages and says, "Lulu, I want you to do this poem for our next program. You can begin memorizing now, so you'll be ready when we start our rehearsals."

I look at the pages of the poem. It's called "Over The Hill To The Poor House." Why would Sister think I would be good at saying a poem like this onstage? I've never done any part in the program by myself before and I'm not anxious to start.

I count the verses—it's twenty-one verses long! I'm a good memorizer, but this is an awful lot to say in front of big people, without forgetting words.

I take it home and read all the verses. It's a sad poem about a poor old lady who is on her way to the poor house, because her children don't want to take care of her. It's not something I would've picked to read for myself, and certainly not in front of others.

Sister Adeline tells me that when I say the poem I have to sound like this little old lady, wear a costume, and act "old" on the stage. That might work better, because then I don't have to be me.

I need to tell someone about the poem, but not my friends, because I don't want them telling me why I shouldn't do it, so I tell Mama. She says I should be proud to be chosen and do the best I can, reminding me, "You've already had stage experience in the poppy play. That's probably why you were chosen."

She finds me an old granny dress from one of the neighbors, a raggedy knit shawl, an old lady's black straw bonnet that ties under the chin, plus a cane, and an old reed basket to carry.

I begin practicing by myself at home, then at school with Sister Adeline. She tells me I should sound older. I'm not sure how to do that. Then I think of the grannies I've seen in movies, and try to imitate them, making my voice sound old and quivery, adding a bit of an Irish accent, because most of the movie grannies I've seen sound Irish.

I practice walking around stooped over, with imaginary aches and pains all through my old body. After walking around like that, I feel real aches and pains, without pretending.

Sometimes I put on the costume for practice. The long dress and old shoes make a difference, especially in the walking.

The more I pretend to be this old lady, the more I start thinking it's not fun getting old, not fun at all, having all this stuff happening to your body. I would rather stay young for a long, long time. Jump all the rope I can, run around fast, hop and skip, before I get too old and rickety and can't do such things anymore.

The day of the program is here. The Friday afternoon show's for the schoolchildren, Friday and Saturday nights for the grown-ups.

I don't eat much lunch. The poem paper is all wrinkled up because I keep looking at it all the time, making sure I got the words right. Some older girls come in and put makeup on my face. To give me wrinkles, they draw lines on my skin with black and gray pencils. I really don't like having these wrinkles on my skin and try not to look in the mirror after the first time. They put talcum powder in my hair so it looks gray.

I just hope I can wash all this stuff away. Old people can't do that, but luckily I can.

Once I put on the stage clothes and pick up my cane and basket, I really do feel old, and even before saying the words, I'm already sad.

I wait behind the stage.

It's time. The pilgrim playlet has just finished and the kids in pilgrim costumes rush off the stage and go sit in the audience to watch the rest of the show.

I bend over, hunch my shoulders, squint, and try to look old and poor. I shuffle onto the stage with my cane and basket. I'm not supposed to say anything till I get to the bench. Sister told me to take my time getting there. "Let the audience wonder what this poor old lady is doing out there. Who is she?"

I'm not me anymore, I am now two people, the real me and this old lady who has lost everything, with nobody to care about her anymore.

I'm at the bench. I don't look at the audience, just keep looking down. I begin, the words quivering out...

> *"Over the hill to the poor house, I'm trudgin' my weary way,*
> *I, a woman of seventy, and only a trifle gray;*
> *I, who am smart an' chipper, for all the years I've told,*
> *As many another woman that's only half as old."*

No one makes a sound. No one knows who I am, either. Some must even think I'm an old woman who lost her way and somehow got onto this stage. I keep going, not missing a word. I'm already on verse four.

> *"I'm willin' and anxious an' ready any day*
> *To work for a decent livin', an pay my honest way:*
> *For I can earn my victuals, an' more too, I'll be bound,*
> *If anybody only is willin' to have me round."*

I sit on the bench, pause a bit. I remember I have to make this next verse sound different, because I'm looking back into my memories. I'm even supposed to look a little bit happy, but not too much.

> "Once I was young an' han'some—I was, upon my soul—
> Once my cheeks was roses, my eyes as black as coal.
> An I can't remember, in them days, of hearin' people say,
> For any kind of reason, that I was in their way."

I walk around while I'm saying all the other verses, about my children, and how they didn't want me. By the time I get to the last verse, I'm feeling very sad.

I stop, look out into the distance, trying not to cry, but tears fall anyway as I say these words.

> "Over the hill to the poor-house—my chil'n dear, good-by!
> Many a night I've watched you when only God was nigh;
> And God'll judge between us; but I will al'ays pray
> That you shall never suffer the half I do today."

I turn and walk off slowly. I hardly hear the clapping because I still feel I'm this old lady going off to the poor house.

It's a strange feeling, realizing you can turn into someone else, just like that. And I have to do it two more times.

What if I get older and older each time I do it?

Friday night, my family attends. After the whole program is through and I'm in the classroom changing back into my regular clothes, Mama comes in by herself. I'm so happy to see her. I know

I'm not really old, because I still have a young mama, and things are regular again. I've been through something new, and I came out okay.

"You were so good, Lulu. People can't believe such a young girl could play the part of an old lady, make her look and sound so real. You had lots of them crying." She hugs me hard. "Some of them want to come again and see it twice, it's so good."

It makes me happy that I could do something to make Mama proud of me, especially after failing at those guitar lessons. All those sad old lady feelings are now joyful ones.

The Saturday show is even better, and Sister Adeline says they're going to have a special matinee on Sunday afternoon, because so many more wanted to come, and there weren't enough seats.

After the Sunday show, I'm glad it's over, and never want to do it again. I say goodbye to the poor lady as if she were a real person, pack up her clothes, and fold up the poem, putting it away in my special box to save.

I'm glad to be a child again. If the poem was true, and you had to worry about going to the poor house, well, no wonder so many old people look sad. What if Mama and Daddy had to go to the poor house, because they were poor? They are poor, but I'm not sure how poor you have to be to be put in the poor house.

Later, I hear Mama telling Mrs. Kolancheck, "So many in that audience were really crying, because so many of them are on the verge of going to the poor house themselves. And like that little old lady Lulu was playing, they have nowhere else to turn."

"Yes, there was lots of sniffling going on, and such sad people leaving. Going to the poor house is not something to look forward to," Mrs. Kolancheck adds.

I wonder myself why something so make believe can make people so sad that they really cry. We really need a happier time in our country, and I'm sure Christmas will bring it to all.

~ THANKSGIVING AT GRANDMA'S ~

"*O*ver the river and through the woods—To Grandmother's house we go—"

We're learning this song in school. Only Grandma doesn't live over the river, she lives just a few blocks away, and we can easily walk there.

So when Sonny and I don't have much to do, I say, "Let's go visit Grandma." He's not too anxious to go, because during the school year he and Mitzy have to stay at Grandma's on Fridays while Mama works. There's never any toys there, just old catalogs and wooden sewing spools.

I always tell him, "We'll stay for just a little bit," adding, "Old people get lonely, so we have to go cheer them up." We're told at school that visiting the sick, the poor, and the lonely gains us extra grace, and I'm always looking for more.

We knock on Grandma's back door, and hear her shuffling inside. Grandma opens the door, holds her black rimmed glasses up close to her eyes. Soon, she's smiling.

206

"You children come to visit me?" she asks.

"Just for a little while," I say, walking into her clean kitchen. Strange smelling things are always cooking on her stove.

Grandma talks mostly in Polish, so it's hard to understand everything she says. She mixes her words up, too. Grandpa speaks pretty good English, only he's not always there. Sometimes, he's out in his backyard garden and doesn't even come in while we're visiting.

Daddy told us Grandpa came to America from Poland on a big boat when he was little. I'm afraid to ask Grandpa about those days, because he always sounds grumpy and doesn't talk much with kids. I'm still curious about that boat ride, though.

Grandma wears long dresses with large aprons over them. Her white hair is pulled back tight, piled on top of her head. Her teeth are missing, she has lots of wrinkles, and fat around her middle. But she's always nice to us. She seems mostly glad to see Sonny and me, but never hugs or kisses us. Mama says, "That family never was brought up to hug or kiss—I had to train your Dad different."

Right away, I sit in the rocking chair with arms, if Grandpa's not there, because that's his chair. Sonny sits on the small wooden stool. Grandma sits hunched over at the kitchen table.

Grandma asks about each in our family. "How's Mama doing? What's Papa doing? How's school? You both are getting so big already."

I do most of the talking, which isn't much. But it's just nice to sit there, listen to the squeak of the rocker, the loud tick of the old wooden clock on the kitchen shelf. It's quieter here than other houses. A nice place to visit.

I try to say things Mama talks about with her company. About the weather, what we'll be doing tomorrow, what we did before we came there, and how we're feeling.

There's long pauses. But that's okay; we're still visiting, even if we don't talk. The signal that the visit is over is when Grandma gets up. "Wait, I get you something."

She shuffles off to her back pantry, coming back with two big round sugar cookies. They're thick, hard, and not too sweet. But the sugar sprinkles taste good. We always lick them off first.

"Thank you, Grandma," we say as we take our cookies and go to the door. "Come back and visit me again, yah?" she says as she closes the door.

While walking home, I remember things Mama has said about Grandma and Grandpa and their house.

"Even though it's a city house, they still live like they're on the farm. They never turn the lights on, and sit in the dark at their table till it's time to go to bed. They make sure they read the paper while it's daylight—because they don't want to spend any money on electricity," Mama says after every visit there.

"So afraid they'll end up in the poor house. I should be as poor as they are."

Grandma's bathtub is filled with big plants in orange clay pots. She claims it's easier to water them there. Some of the vines crawl right out of the bathtub. I guess they must not use the tub for taking baths.

"Never took baths when they were on the farm either," Mama answers when I ask about it.

Sometimes, while Sonny and I are visiting, Grandma sits in her chair at the table, praying on her black rosary beads, mumbling words over and over real soft in Polish; fingers clicking along. She and Grandpa go to the Polish church, the one with a long Polish saint's name, which is up on the Polish Hills, where the Polish people in Manitowoc live.

One time, Daddy took me there with him. Inside, it looked different from our church. People dressed different too. The priest spoke his prayers and sermon in Polish. Everybody sang hymns in Polish, loud and good, even Daddy. I just watched and listened, feeling a little bit like I was in Poland, especially when I shut my eyes.

Mama won't go there, because she likes to hear her sermons in English, even if the rest of the Mass is in Latin. "When they're preaching, I like to know what I'm hearing."

This year, the relatives decide that instead of each family having Thanksgiving by themselves, they'll all gather at Grandma Rosik's. The aunties have many talks. Who should bring what food. How many dishes they'll need. How many they can fit at the tables.

We never have turkey on Thanksgiving. "Too expensive," Mama says. She always bakes two chickens for that day, and makes her famous fruit salad. It has bananas, oranges, whipped cream, nuts and other tasty ingredients. It's a secret recipe Mama won't give out, not even to us. I find that strange, keeping recipes secret, like it was some great invention, or a bad thing. But when Mama has a secret, she never gives it away.

That fruit salad is so delicious I yearn for it all year. I don't want to miss out on getting some for Thanksgiving, just because we're going to Grandma's. Then I find out that's the dish Mama's going to bring, making me thankful ahead of time. Yay!

The day before, we help cut up things for the fruit salad. It has to be three times as big this year. When I ask about the money for the ingredients, Mama says, "Well, I can spend a bit more, because I don't have to make all that other food. And Grandma's supplying the two turkeys!"

Two! I hope they're big enough, so we all get a piece. I've never tasted turkey before.

The two big bowls of fruit salad are set in the back hall in a large box to keep cool till the next day. Mama warns us, "Don't any of you touch that fruit salad, or even smell it." We've been busy licking our fingers while helping, and the temptation is hard to keep down.

Thanksgiving morning, there's snow all over. I'm thinking maybe we won't be able to get to Grandma's, and all we'll have to eat for Thanksgiving will be fruit salad, which is okay with me. Then I think further—fruit salad wouldn't be too good without chicken, or mashed potatoes and gravy, and hot buttered biscuits to go with it all.

Usually, Mama invites the renters upstairs to eat with us on Thanksgiving, because they don't have any relatives nearby. I wonder who they'll eat with today? With all the snow, they'll probably eat upstairs alone.

"No, they can't go to Grandma's with us, because they're not relatives. Besides, Grandma's house will be full enough," are Mama's final words.

After a hearty breakfast, so we don't "eat like hungry hogs" at the next meal, we get ready. Somehow, it doesn't seem like Thanksgiving. No smells of anything cooking. No tablecloth on the table.

Because of the snow, Mama decides we'll take the kids' sled. I'm the one picked to sit on it and hold the big box with the fruit salad.

"And you make sure it doesn't fall off. Hang onto it real tight."

I sit on the sled, hugging the box tightly. Catherine pulls the sled, Buddy pushes. Mama and Daddy walk ahead, carrying bags of stuff—I don't know what. Betty Jane, Sonny, and Mitzy walk behind, scarves over their faces, holding each other's mittened hands.

I'm concentrating on hanging onto that fruit salad and get mighty scared when we go over bumps. There's a slippery spot under the snow—Catherine falls, but Buddy quick holds onto the sled.

"Don't you drop that fruit salad—it's my favorite," he warns. That'll keep him from trying any funny stuff on the way, like he usually does.

Pretty soon, we're at Grandma's house. Cars are already parked outside.

"I see Steve and Ellen made it from the farm. Thought the snow might have kept them home," Mama comments as we gather on the sidewalk, stamping our feet.

I was hoping maybe they might come by their horse and sleigh. I was looking forward to it, till I noticed their rusting green car the same time Mama did.

Daddy takes the box of fruit salad, walking carefully with it. Mama tells him to put it on the outside back porch to keep cool. "Make sure that box cover's on tight."

We go right in without knocking. All kinds of people are already there.

"Got here early, cause we'll have to go back early," Uncle Steven greets us as we enter. He's smoking his corncob pipe. Curls of smoke mix with the streaming sunshine coming in the kitchen window. It seems even brighter today because of the sparkling snow.

"We brought along a big smoked ham too, in case there's not enough turkey," Auntie Ellen adds.

I don't like smoked ham, and certainly not on Thanksgiving.

Everybody seems to be talking at once. There's so many people I can't count them all, and more keep coming. We pile our coats on top of the bed in Grandma's bedroom. The pile keeps getting higher and higher.

The turkeys are already in the oven. They smell delicious. On the pantry shelves, there's pumpkin pie, mincemeat pie, frosted cakes, poppy seed kolaches, and different colors of Jell-O.

We're given strict orders, "Keep out of that pantry!" But I have to look, just once, before it's all eaten up. I've never seen so much good food gathered in one place.

"Okay, you kids and you men, get out of the kitchen, so we can get the food cooking," one woman calls out loudly, others echoing the same words.

I know Uncle Steven's kids are somewhere and go track them down. Men go outside and shovel snow. Others bring in more wood for the stove. Auntie Rose and Uncle Herby, with their two girls, Vivian and Veronica, dressed up real fancy and alike, just stand around as they usually do. Uncle Herby has a beard, and a motorcycle, but he didn't use it today, because of the snow.

I hear Mama talking to someone. "I see Rose brought her usual bowl of Jell-O, with lots of Relief oranges in it."

"Never takes much work to make Jell-O, does it?" the other answers.

"And that Herby, he made sure his case of beer got here—even if it had to come by sled," Mama continued. "Wonder how he gets that beer? Far as I know, the Relief Department doesn't hand it out."

The men shake off the snow, then go into the spare room to play Sheepshead around the wobbly card table, banging the table hard and yelling out every once in a while, but all in a fun way. Uncle Herby gives each one a bottle of beer. But if they want more, he tells them "You have to pay for it."

Auntie Stacia is sitting down, already knitting. She and Uncle Willard don't have any children, only Joey, who died. But there's lots more of her new tin flowers all over. The dining table is covered with a pretty tablecloth she embroidered, and a wobbly turkey she made out of crepe paper.

Uncle Pete and Auntie Leatrice are here too. I was hoping they might not come. I never liked Uncle Pete—he always seems mean. Mama once said that he does bad things to his children, but will never tell me exactly what. I don't like it when he looks at me with his beady eyes, and pinches his bluish lips. He always has stubbles of whiskers and shaggy hair. His voice is growly, no matter what he says. He's just not a very friendly uncle to anyone.

Mavis, their daughter, came with them today, wearing kinda dirty clothes and torn shoes. She's about my age, but never talks much, just hangs close to Auntie Leatrice, who's big and fat, and doesn't see too well, but can't afford glasses. They said their son Paul didn't come today because he had to stay home and take care of the animals.

I remember cousin Paul telling us about the time his father made him sleep outside in the pig's pen overnight for something bad he did.

How bad a thing could someone ever do, to get such a punishment?

When Mavis had her First Communion, relatives were invited to Uncle Pete's farmhouse. It didn't seem like much of a celebration, even if they were more dressed up. Everyone ate flat cake and drank warm Kool Aid. We didn't stay long. The house was dirty and shabby, with flies all around. They had a slop pail right in the kitchen.

Mama never likes going there, even if Uncle Pete is Daddy's brother. "That doesn't mean I have to like him, or like to visit there."

Daddy sometimes goes hunting with Uncle Pete and his wild hound dogs. Daddy uses Uncle Pete's shotguns, because Mama doesn't want such things around our house.

One time, I saw them come back with dead squirrels and other bleeding animals hanging on a big stick. The dogs were yelping and barking, covered in blood.

"No Daddy, I don't want any squirrel tails," I start yelling, "Keep them away from me."

"You city kids—always such fraidy cats," Uncle Pete says in his snarly voice, putting chains on his dogs, while I cling to Daddy, pleading, "Don't let those big dogs get at me!" Even when they're on chains, they still bark and leap, frightening me terribly.

Daddy says he goes hunting so we have some meat on the table. But if I know where it came from, I never eat it. Sometimes Mama doesn't let us know, just mixes it in with other things. Sometimes, it's best not to know.

I walk through the house looking for my cousins and find them on the sun porch, which has windows all around, but no heat. So we keep our warm clothes on and begin playing games and telling stories. I never get to see them in winter, so this is special.

Uncle Herby sits in a big stuffed chair, drinking one of his beers, reading a detective magazine. I hear him burp every once in awhile, with no "excuse me" at all.

The ladies are busy setting the table. Big people will be eating at the pulled-out dining table; kids will eat at a smaller table.

"We can't sit everyone down at once, so we'll have two shifts," Mama declares. "Those who live on the farms will eat first, because they have to leave early, then the second shift can sit down."

What if there's no food left by second shift? I don't ask, but I'm already worried. When we get too cold on the sun porch, we move into the living room. Uncle Frank is in there now. He lives upstairs at Grandpa and Grandma's. "And doesn't pay a cent of rent!" Mama complains.

"Well, he helps them out," Daddy says.

"Helps them out? Sure, helps them out of food and money," Mama retorts. Uncle Frank used to be married, but his wife died having a baby that died too. "That's when he started his drinking—after Sally died," Mama says, as if drinking is a bad thing to do.

"He only goes to the church where the prayer books have handles," Daddy always says with a laugh.

Uncle Frank owns a garbage truck, with the name "Rosik Garbage" painted in big letters on the doors. Catherine hates that, having her last name on a truck that goes all over town picking up garbage. Her friends tease her about it too, which makes her even madder.

Uncle Frank is nice looking, with a brown mustache. He brings out the photo books and shows pictures to us as we sit beside him on the davenport. He points out snapshots of all the relatives when they were younger and looked much different. There are lots of wedding pictures in there, baby pictures too. Then he shows us the book of postcards from all over. Shiny and pretty pictures on the fronts. Each one is worth looking at. Some messages are in Polish with foreign stamps.

In between, Uncle Frank tickles us, which I don't like, and punches at the boys. He's not like a regular dad. He makes lots of jokes and is always telling me, "I want to marry you when you get bigger," and puts his arms around me. I never tell Mama about this, but I don't think I'd want to marry him.

Mama says we should never be alone with Uncle Frank, but won't tell us why. Another one of her secrets?

We have to wait in Grandma's bedroom to go to the bathroom, which is next door. There are lots of pictures in big frames on all the walls. One of Jesus' head bleeding, with a crown of thorns. Another of the Blessed Virgin, just her head, with sun rays coming out, looking real holy. The dead soldier, Uncle Nick, is on the wall too, an even bigger head picture than the one in the living room. There's a fancy marriage certificate, written in Polish, on the wall above the bed. There are also crucifixes and holy water fonts in a couple of places.

The shades are drawn so the sunlight doesn't fade things, making the room dim and dark. I don't like staying in that bedroom too long, with all those sad pictures looking at me. I wouldn't want to sleep in there either.

My turn in the bathroom. The potted plants aren't in the bathtub today. Mama said she made Grandma put them in the basement when she went over the other day to help get things ready. She brought over extra dishes and our knives and forks too.

"Just hope we get them all back, and someone doesn't take our stuff because it's nicer than theirs."

Finally, I hear "It's ready! Time to come sit down and eat."

Everyone crowds around and we're told who can sit where and who has to wait.

Two big steaming turkeys occupy the center of the big table. I don't know if I can stand waiting to taste a piece. It looks just like a picture, and smells delicious.

Then we all hear a big scream. It's Mama, yelling outside the back door. "Some damn animal got into the fruit salad! Ate the whole top off!" she tells everybody as she comes in with the torn box.

"Well, just scrape that part off, " Auntie Rose says. "It'll still be okay."

"For you maybe, but not for me! I'm not serving my special fruit salad to anyone after some animal got into it! So everyone will just have to get smaller portions from the second bowl."

What about those eating second shift? Another new worry.

I'm back on the sun porch now, waiting my turn to eat, hearing the clink of dishes, talk and laughter, smelling the food. Finally, after what seems forever, they start getting up from their places. That means it's almost time for the second shift!

"You don't get to sit down to eat till they're gone," Auntie Rose tells me. "So stop asking." Farm relatives hold everything up, getting into their clothes, taking a long time to say their goodbyes. I don't even want to talk to the cousins, and hear how good all the food was, so I stay on the sun porch, pretending I'm reading.

"Okay, the second shift of kids can come in!" Auntie Stacia calls.

I rush in, then stand and look at the turkey platters—two cages of empty bones. Unless—maybe there's some meat saved somewhere else, on a different plate for the small table? I feel like crying, but bite my lips, lips which have just been drooling for turkey.

I sit down on a wobbly stool at the kids' table. Vivian and Veronica are already seated there, prim and proper.

Auntie Rose is dishing up our plates. None of them match.

"Here, Lulu, you can have what's left on this nice turkey leg. Mavis didn't eat it all."

She sets down the plate holding a half-gnawed turkey leg, cold mashed potatoes, gooey gravy, chunky stuffing, and watery red cranberry sauce.

Mama quick grabs the plate away. "Just one minute there, Rose! Lulu is not going to eat anyone's leftover food! If she can't have fresh things, don't you give her anything at all. Our family does not eat food other people began eating on!"

"Well, then they've never been hungry, have they?" Auntie Rose says as she slams down the plate. The food slides all around, cranberry sauce sloshing over everything.

"We've been hungry, but never hungry enough to take food out of the mouths of others. Like those who are too lazy to work for their food, and would rather go on Relief!" Mama is really angry now. Her voice sounds different.

She and Auntie Rose go into the bedroom, slamming the door, but you can still hear them yelling back and forth.

Auntie Stacia gives me a new plate of food. "Sorry, Lulu, the turkey's all gone, but here's some nice smoked ham for you."

I look at my plate—cold stuffing, runny gravy, grayish smoked ham, and soggy vegetables. I'm not hungry anymore. I even feel kind of sick. But then I think—I could still eat some fruit salad.

"Can I have my dish of fruit salad instead, Auntie Stacia? I helped make it."

"Sorry honey," she answers, "I think that bowl got emptied first thing. But there's lots of Jell-O, pie, cake—"

I shake my head "no," begin to cry, and can't stop, quickly holding my napkin over my face so no one sees.

When someone comes to our table to lead a Thanksgiving prayer, I just bite my lips harder, because there's nothing now that I'm thankful for. I feel even worse than the family around the table in my funny poem about Uncle Henry. Only here, there's nothing to laugh about, and nothing to eat.

I decide I don't ever want to spend another Thanksgiving at Grandma's. From what I hear Mama say later, I don't think she does either.

Even after we get home, Mama still rants about the fruit salad, and what Auntie Rose said to her.

I try to break in. "I didn't even get a tiny taste of that fruit salad, Mama," new tears forming.

Forgetting about Auntie Rose for a minute, Mama comes over and pats my head, "Nothing to cry about, Lulu. Tell you what—I'm going to make fruit salad for Christmas this year. And I'll make enough for everybody. But not one smidgen for any thieving animals!"

That brings out the smiles and "Yippees" all around.

So Thanksgiving's over, and hopefully it will be the first and last one held at Grandma's or anywhere else away from home. Home's always the best place, for just about anything.

Now all we have to do is wait for Christmas.

Who cares that I didn't get any turkey or fruit salad for Thanksgiving. I'm going to get fruit salad and a Shirley Temple doll for Christmas!

~ WINTER ~

It's here! December! The most awaited month of the year.

Everything's shifting. The sun's moved further away, and the world is darker when we get up. The house takes on a permanent chill. But even in these dimming days, sparkles begin to blink in the distance. Christmas lights come closer and brighter, as they dance about in our heads, crowding almost everything else out.

One of Daddy's favorite sayings when we're pokey is: "What are you waiting for—Christmas?" That's exactly what I am waiting for, and have been all year. Anticipation tingles in my bones, jingles all through me. Only this year, the joyous expectations are marred by all that's happening around me, and doubts push in to dim some of the dancing lights.

To save heat, our sitting room and bedrooms are closed off, their heat registers shut. The kitchen, with the coal and wood burning cook stove, becomes the family gathering place, from the time we get up in the morning till we warm our pajamas on the open oven door at night.

We kids all sleep in the spare room, also our play room, off the kitchen now. The daybed's opened up, and four of us sleep in it sideways. Buddy sleeps on the floor alone, under the thick goose down blanket. Mitzy's also in there, in her crib.

We go to bed earlier, anxious to snuggle under those fat layers of covers—giggling, telling stories, rubbing each other's backs. Only a curtain separates this room from the kitchen, so heat and light seep through.

Mama stays up late, working in the kitchen. I hear her moving back and forth. I like having her that close at night. It sometimes warms me even more than the covers.

No one talks about it, but so many things tell me we're poorer than ever. Daddy doesn't work with the junk man anymore.

"Nobody has money to even buy junk these days," he mentions to Mama.

He keeps telling us, more than before, "Don't keep those lights on so long...Close the doors tight, so heat doesn't get out...Shut that water off, we have to pay for that water, you know..."

We share bath water, adding more hot water from the reservoir in the kitchen stove till the last Saturday bath is taken. Mama even makes her own soap from ashes, lard, and lye.

The daily paper's stopped coming. Our neighbor, Mrs. Yaeger, brings her paper over when she's done with it. She lets us use her telephone, too, if we need to. But we don't know anybody who has a telephone, so there's nobody to call, unless we need to reach the police or fire department.

The burlap bags of leaves we gathered from the parks in the fall are piled around the basement windows and the chicken coop to keep the house warmer and the chickens from freezing.

"We really need these eggs this winter," Mama says, carefully counting those I bring in, my chilled fingers lingering on the warm shells. "And no Sunday chicken dinners for a while—at least not till next spring."

Meals are stingier too. Breakfast is still a pot of cooked oatmeal. Mama buys cans of condensed milk by the case. She punches a hole in the can top, pours the contents into an aluminum pitcher, then fills it with water, making a big pitcher of pale milk, which seems more watery than usual these days.

We hardly go for secondhand bakery anymore, or even to the grocery store. Most of our food comes from what's stored in our basement: bins of potatoes, carrots, apples, and Mama's jars of canned food, colorfully lined up on wobbly wooden shelves.

"I just hope that basement stockpile lasts through the winter," Mama keeps saying.

There's a big stone crock of sauerkraut in the pantry, topped with a plate and a big rock. It smells pretty stinky, but we don't complain. It wouldn't do any good. Besides, it tastes much better than it smells, especially with spare ribs—when we have them, chewing into the insides of the soft bones.

We all come home from school for lunch at noon. Usually it's a big kettle of homemade noodles Mama just made from flour and eggs, adding tasty red sauce from her jars of canned tomatoes. Sometimes, there's cottage cheese mixed in, my favorite, well, after macaroni and cheese with a crunchy top. There's even freshly baked bread most days. Mmmm. Tastes specially good spread with melting lard, then dipped into the spaghetti sauce.

Supper is mostly potato soup these days. We sop it up with dried bread. Sometimes, if there's lots of eggs, Mama makes Yayetska—beaten eggs, onions, and bits of bacon, all put into the big iron skillet. It swells up and gets crispy, then she cuts into pieces like a pie. We all like it. It's Daddy's favorite too.

"A good Polish dish," he says, wiping up the last yellow bits with his crusty bread. Sometimes Mama cooks Daddy a ring of Polish sausage. It smells good, but we don't get any.

"Daddy's the one who needs meat the most," Mama says, "because he works the hardest." Mama works hard too, but she never gets any either.

Sometimes at night, we kids make fudge or taffy, dipping cups of sugar from the big 100-pound bag sitting on the pantry floor. Taffy's such fun to make. We pull it into long, stretched-out shiny twists. But it's getting near the sugar bottom, and Mama says to wait each time we ask if we can make candy.

There's still popcorn left on the cobs we grew. We shell off enough each time to make big kettles of popcorn on the kitchen stove. The popping sound brings everyone in, and warm popped corn fills us up pretty good. We can't put butter on it, like that good stuff we smell at the movie theater, because "We can't afford butter, that's why."

I like to imagine there's butter on my home popped corn, even licking it off my fingers. You can imagine a lot of things about food, making up what it might taste like, holding those thoughts in your mouth, till you can almost smell and taste them on your tongue.

We also make root beer at home, using a bottle of Hires Root Beer Mix and yeast, keeping the mixture in a big crock in the basement till it's ripe. Then it's put in saved root beer bottles, capped with the bottle capper, and stored in the basement—waiting for Christmas, when we each get a bottle of our own. Sometimes, the bottles pop ahead of time, sounding like an explosion in the basement. I don't even like thinking of all that good root beer going to waste. If possible, I'd try to scrape it up from the basement floor and put it all back in the empty bottles.

Washed clothes hang on ropes strung across the kitchen, because Mama can't hang them outside now—the clothes would freeze stiff.

We bundle up before leaving for school, huge scarves wound around our necks and over our faces till we can hardly see. Whatever galoshes fit our feet become ours to trudge through the snow that is already piling up on both sides of our sidewalks.

We hardly play outside when it's so cold. We'd much rather huddle around the kitchen stove. In the evening, we shell dried beans, or crack hickory and beechnuts that we gathered in the woods in fall, for holiday cookies and fruitcakes.

I even help with darning socks, because Mama can't keep up with all the holes. Catherine might read aloud to us, part of a book each night, as we do our busy work. We do homework or play games around the kitchen table on the worn, cracked oilcloth. So far, we can still listen to the radio, even if we sometimes have to listen in the dark to save electricity.

We're busy making Christmas presents for each other, trying to keep them secret and hidden. Buddy's down in the basement, sawing and hammering. Catherine's busy at the sewing machine, the treadle going up and down. Last year, she made me the prettiest dress with pink bows. I hear Mama sewing late at night now too.

I take out books from the library showing how to make different things into gifts, from milk bottle caps to safety pins and old pieces of cloth. For Daddy, I'm cutting up an old bed sheet and hand-sewing squares into big handkerchiefs. For Mitzy, I'm making monkey dolls from Daddy's old work socks. There's a recipe for flour and water that you can form into figures and then paint them. I'm trying to make Buddy some toy soldiers without him finding out, using the molds he uses to make lead soldiers.

Mama's gift always has to be something store bought. I made sure I saved ten cents from my bean picking money so I can buy her an extra nice gift this year.

On Saturdays, Sonny and I sometimes go downtown and walk through the stores to see what they have. I mostly look at things in the Kresge Dime Store. The store lady behind the counter asks if she can help me, but I say, "No thank you, I'm just looking," which is what Mama usually says.

Then one day I see it, at the dish counter, on a higher shelf—a beautiful ruby red wine glass, sparkling like diamonds. The sign says "Ten Cents."

"Look, Sonny," I point, "Isn't that beautiful? Mama could put it on the kitchen window sill, and when the sun shines, it'll sparkle, just like the stained glass window at the doctor's house." My mind's made up—no more searching. "That's the present I'm going to buy for Mama, but not today."

I just hope nobody else buys it before I do. I enjoy anticipating and thinking about something before I get it, so I don't mind waiting.

We go downtown again the next Saturday. This time I ask if I can look at the wine glass, saying "please." The store lady takes it down for me. I hold it, oh so carefully, turn it around, marvel at its beauty, then hand it back. Mama doesn't have anything as pretty. Our sugar bowl, goldish Carnival glass, is the nicest dish she has, but it's old, the sparkle's dull, and the cover's gone too.

There's Christmas music playing in the stores now—"Santa Claus is Coming to Town" over and over. They're beginning to put up decorations inside and outside the stores. Huge green arches hang across the downtown streets, with shimmering lights and dangling tinsel. You can look down the street; the same decorations are repeated far as you can see, as if it were endless mirror reflections.

A really big manger is put up on the Court House corner, with a large sign in front that says "PEACE ON EARTH." Nearer to Christmas, different groups sing Christmas carols in front of the manger. I like to go and listen, to hear real people caroling, instead of the radio or record singing. Baby Jesus isn't in the manger till Christmas Eve.

Toy departments open in the big stores. Mama's not too happy about this. "Can't get their stuff out early enough to sell, can they? Pretty soon, they'll be decorating way before Thanksgiving!"

I don't tell Mama, but Sonny and I go to the toy departments any time we can. It's like stepping right into Storybook Land. There are so many big, beautiful, brand new toys. It's even better than looking in the Sears catalog. Here, we can view them close up, touch them. We watch the small trains go round and round and the windup toys jiggle about. But my favorite thing to do is stand and look at the Shirley Temple doll, smiling at me from her cellophane box on the top shelf. I can't wait to hold her.

She just has to be mine for Christmas.

This one night, I can't get to sleep. I hear Mama and Daddy talking around the kitchen table. I sit up and try to listen harder, catching only some of the words.

"It's not right, to lose the house now, after all these years paying on it. It's just not right," Mama keeps saying.

"I know," Daddy's talking now. "Lots of families are losing their houses these days."

I don't understand—how can someone lose a house? They're just too big to lose.

"Where would we go, with six children?" Mama sounds worried.

"I don't know—I just don't know." Daddy's quiet for a bit, then says, "If we didn't have the house, we'd be able to get Relief."

"Go on Relief! Oh no! That's not for us! We need this house for the kids more than we need Relief."

"At least we're not starving. And we still get the rent money."

"Ida's not sure how long her job's going to last—people aren't buying as much tinsel this year."

"This month's mortgage payment is all we need to get past right now."

"And the one after that, and the one after that. Every month, the same old bills. Then comes year-end taxes—"

"Maybe I can chop more wood this week. Sell some of the extra."

"You're not going out chopping wood, not in this freezing weather. You just got over the influenza. I don't want you coming down with pneumonia! That's all we need—pneumonia for Christmas."

Daddy was real sick for a while with flu, and we had to stay away from him so we wouldn't catch it. I don't know why Mama didn't catch it, since she's always so close to him.

"But my influenza's better."

"Only because Dr. Mack took such good care of you—even if we can't pay him." Mama then adds, "I don't know what we'd do without his help, with the kids getting sick all the time."

I didn't know you had to pay doctors, just that Dr. Mack comes to our house when we are sick. I thought it was because he liked us. He's big and tall, and carries a black bag filled with all kinds of doctor things. He stands over our beds, pounds our chests, looks down our throats, then talks to Mama.

That's what doctors do, don't they—take care of sick people? Why would you have to pay them?

"The wood's going down pretty fast," Daddy continues. "We'll need more wood soon."

"Can't shut off any more rooms."

"You'll want to heat the sitting room for Christmas."

"Yes. That's one day that room has to be warm."

"I can try checking for loose coal at the coal yard again."

"There has to be some place we can borrow money from."

"I tried. Banks need collateral. Our only collateral—six children." I don't know what the word "collateral" means. Why would banks need children? I never understand much when they talk about banks and mortgages.

"How can they foreclose, when there's no work anywhere!" Mama sounds mad at somebody.

I don't know what happens when they foreclose. Does it mean they close up the house? Why would they do that?

It's quiet for a while, then Daddy says, "Lizzie, what about the Christmas Club?" I listen more intently.

"The Christmas Club?" Mama lowers her voice, "Oh no, that money is never to be spent for anything else."

"I just thought—"

"That Christmas Club money stays right where it is. I work hard for those dollars. Set them aside each week, so the kids can at least have one happy day a year. Every penny is pinched and squeezed till there's no more squeal left in them."

I know about pinching pennies, but it's the words "Christmas Club" that stay in my head. I remember the time Mama mentioned it at the doctor's house. I can't hear the rest as they talk more quietly.

I need to know more now. It's important. I poke Catherine in her back. She stirs in her sleep.

"Catherine, I need to know. Tell me, what is the Christmas Club? Why does Mama need money for the Christmas Club?"

"I don't know," she answers sleepily.

"Is that when they have their friends over at Christmas time and play cards?"

"I don't know, I guess so." She goes back to sleep.

I can't stop thinking about it. Why would Mama need to spend money on friends and think that would make us kids happy? Why would she work so hard to save money for the Christmas Club? Their friends coming over—that doesn't make it a happy day for us children. Maybe Mama thinks we're more happy because we get the leftover food and drinks? Must be some reason.

I want to ask Mama about it, but then she'd know I was listening to things I shouldn't be listening to. And these weeks before Christmas, I have to be on my best behavior, because just maybe, there might still be a chance of getting my Shirley Temple doll.

I try to get back to sleep, so all this new talk circling in my head will be gone by morning.

~ SANTA ~

"Jolly old Saint Nicholas, lend your ear this way..."

That song prances through my head every day now, especially on December 5th, the eve of St. Nicholas, when we hang our long stockings over kitchen chairs, since we don't have a fireplace. The next morning, they're filled with candy, popcorn balls, and sometimes, if you weren't good, the dreaded coal and wood, which Buddy got one year. Still, it's a fun time, but nowhere near the big day coming up.

In school, we're told about St. Nicholas—how he took gifts to the poor, how he got to be called Santa Claus, and how he still really is St. Nicholas.

I don't care who he is, he's my favorite person, especially this time of year. The poem I read over and over is "A Visit from Saint Nicholas." It starts with, "T'was the night before Christmas, when all through the house—" Later, it describes Santa.

SANTA

*He had a broad face and a little round belly
That shook when he laughed like a bowl full of jelly!
He was chubby and plump, right jolly old elf...*

It describes him exactly. Just seeing his picture makes me feel jolly, as if gladness pours out all around him.

Santa's picture is everywhere now, waving from signs, pasted on our school windows. His helpers stand on street corners downtown, ringing bells, wanting people to put money for the poor into the big black kettle. Because Santa's so busy this time of year, his helpers dress up like him to do these Christmasy things—at least, that's what Catherine tells me when I ask.

Santa's in stores now, too. He wears a red suit and strokes his silvery beard, sitting on his big fancy throne in the toy department, ho-ho-ho-ing loudly.

You can sit on his lap and tell him what you want for Christmas, but only if your parents are with you, so Sonny and I just stand and watch. I'd feel kind of funny sitting on Santa's lap anyway. Besides, we each write letters to him, telling what we want. That's better than telling Santa, because he'd probably forget what we asked for after listening to so many kids.

Geraldine and I talk about Christmas lots when we get together at each other's houses. Today we're playing jacks, bouncing the small ball as we try to pick up as many jacks as we can.

"I'm getting a Shirley Temple doll for Christmas," I tell Geraldine. Before, I always said I was "hoping" for one. But now I'm so sure, I decide to say it out loud, to make it even surer.

"Who says?" Geraldine stops picking up jacks.

"I do. Because I'm asking for one, in my letter to Santa."

"Well, Shirley Temple dolls are expensive, more expensive than most any other doll."

"Doesn't matter, not if it comes from Santa."

Then Geraldine says something which really puts a stop to all my expectations. "I don't believe anymore."

"What don't you believe?" I think I know, yet don't want to hear.

"In Santa. I don't believe in Santa anymore."

"How can you say that? Everyone knows he's real. You can't just make up someone like him—not for so many years." I start singing, "He sees you when you're sleeping, he knows when you're awake—"

I keep singing, not wanting to hear any more, because sometimes I wonder too, but try not to think about it, especially this year.

"Well, I heard my cousin—" Geraldine stops quickly. "Maybe I shouldn't tell you. You're younger than me."

"Tell me." I hate being younger than her all the time.

"Well, my cousin says—" she pauses for a moment, "She says there ain't no Santa Claus."

"No Santa?" Nobody's ever really said that out loud to me before. I want to throw each word right back into Geraldine's mouth, but have to ask, "Well, then who brings all those presents?"

Geraldine looks around, then whispers in my ear, "Your parents." I don't believe her and tell her so.

"Our parents could never afford all those toys. They don't have any money. Especially this year."

"Well, they must have money from somewhere. Secretly, they must have money."

"They don't! I know that for sure. I would know such stuff better than you."

"Then how come your family always gets more and better toys than anybody else on the whole block?" Geraldine's voice becomes louder.

"I don't know." I really don't, but never worried too much about it.

"Every Christmas, everyone in your family gets something really terrific. Something brand new!"

"Maybe it's because we've been so good."

"That's not true, and you know it."

"It is so. Because, the Martins next door, those kids fight all the time, and they hardly get anything for Christmas." I get up, ready to leave.

"Well, you kids fight too."

"But never near Christmas time." I start putting on my coat.

Geraldine continues her questions, hardly listening to my answers. "How come poor families gets used toys, and you never do?"

"Maybe Santa's elves fix ours over better."

"My cousin said the firemen fix up old toys for poor kids," Geraldine sounds like she's telling a big secret. "That's where most toys come from—the fire department, not Santa!"

I'm really disturbed about the whole conversation. I don't like having my dreams spoiled. "Well, we're just as poor as anybody. You tell me then why we get so many new toys?"

"I don't know, Lulu. I don't know why your Christmases are always so grand. Better than mine, even." Geraldine opens the door for me and I rush out into the cold air, not wanting to hear any more.

After that, I don't go to Geraldine's house that much. I don't want to hear her repeat what she's just said, not so close to Christmas anyway.

Our Christmases are fabulous, but only because of Santa, not our parents. Mama does do lots of extra baking and cleaning. But it's Santa and his helpers, not Mama, who carved and glued the tiny furniture for my big wooden dollhouse last Christmas, made the lace curtains, and crocheted teensy rugs.

If it was true—that Santa didn't bring the toys, that our mother and father did, then any hopes of getting Shirley Temple this year—

It would be useless to even think about it anymore.

The glowing lights in my head begin to dim. There has to be some way to keep my hopes alive. I still believe in miracles, and Christmas Eve is the time for miracles, so maybe...

I keep remembering Mama's Christmas story about Santa not coming to her house because she was an orphan. But I'm not an orphan. Santa always came to our house before.

For just one more year, this year especially, he has to be real.

~ THE WEEK BEFORE ~

The calendar reads "Wednesday, December 18, 1935." One more week, then it's Christmas!

I'm jingling all over. Everything's jingling—inside stores, outside stores. Women wear tiny bells on their coats. Kids put tinkling bells on their caps. Jingle bell music plays on the radio. We bring out the old Christmas records, playing them over and over on the windup talking machine. The needles are getting worn, and we can't afford new ones, but the songs still sound good, even if they're a bit scratchy.

In school, we're practicing for the Christmas program. I'm going to be an angel at Bethlehem, which is better than being a shepherd. But right now, appearing in a school play is not top on my list, because there's so many other things to think about.

The Christmas program will be Friday afternoon, with the gift exchange after. I'm worried about that, because Mama says there's no money for school gifts this year. We've used up all the Big Chief tablets we usually give as birthday gifts, which I'm glad of, because I don't think tablets or pencils are very good gifts to give or receive.

Sister Felicity tells us to bring only small gifts, write on the package if it's for a girl or boy, put it on the pile, and take a number. Only those who bring a gift get to take one home.

So what if I don't get a gift from the pile? Some of them aren't that good anyway. I'm planning to get Mama's wine glass this Saturday. Last Saturday, I went downtown with Sonny, making sure it was still there. It was, even prettier than I remembered.

On the way home, we stopped outside the movie theater to look at pictures under glass windows. There's a big poster announcing a new Shirley Temple movie coming for the holidays. Only I won't be seeing it. I have no money left, only the dime saved for Mama's gift.

I stand and look at Shirley's picture for a long time till Sonny complains. "You've looked at Shirley long enough. I'm getting cold."

It doesn't matter if I don't get to see this movie, because pretty soon Shirley Temple will be right in my house. She'll be with me all the time.

~ THURSDAY ~

Thursday is a busy day at school. We're doing final show preparations. I'm still worried about not bringing a gift. Geraldine's already told me how her package will be wrapped.

"Make sure to pick mine, it'll be something you'd really like."

I'll just tell her, "I forgot to bring my gift," or lost it—or something.

When I get home, Mama says she has a surprise for me. Surprise? Whatever could it be? And why for me?

She brings out an old shoe box. "Open it."

Slowly, I take off the cover. Inside is just a bunch of brown fur. Some surprise.

"I made you something, for the school gift exchange."

I don't want to give someone a piece of old fur, even if they don't know who it came from. I take the thing out of the box, trying not to look too disappointed. Suddenly, it turns into a soft kitten. Mama made a precious little kitten out of pieces of fur from an old coat she cut apart. There's glass buttons for eyes, a long furry tail, and yarn whiskers. Around its neck is a collar of tinsel with little bells. It's so cute, I want to keep it for myself.

"Do I have to give it away?" I ask, hugging it tight.

"Yes, you do," Mama says. "I made it for some child in your school, not for you."

"I just hope whoever gets it likes it much as I do." I keep petting the soft fur.

"Just remember, there's more joy in giving away something that you yourself want."

I hope that's true, because I'd rather give away things I don't want.

~ FRIDAY ~

On Friday morning, it's still dark outside when I wake up. The radio's playing, and even though I'm still half asleep, I pick up some of the words.

"Big blizzard out there today, folks…All city schools are closed… Most roads are blocked…Snow expected to continue all day…"

I sneak out of bed and peek out the window. All I can see are big chunks of white, blowing every which way.

Usually I'm happy when they close school, because then we get to do all kinds of fun stuff at home. Only today, the fun stuff was going to be at school. It was our last day there before Christmas.

What about our Christmas program? The gift exchange?

I hear Mama talking to Daddy. "They're closing everything. I don't know how I'm going to get to Dr. Mack's house to clean."

"There's no way you can go out in this weather," Daddy tells her.

"I've been out in worse storms. It'll just take me longer to get there." Mama's always brave about everything.

"This is a really bad one," Daddy says as he shakes the grates in the kitchen stove. "I was planning to cut wood today, too. Even if it stops, the snow will be too deep to get at the wood now. I'll just have to wait—maybe till spring."

It's quiet for a bit, then Daddy says, "Take that coat off, Lizzie, you're not going out in this storm."

"We need the money. We need it this week more than ever."

"Just wait till tomorrow. Maybe you can get through then."

"I can't wait till tomorrow. They want the house cleaned today, because their holiday party is tomorrow afternoon, and I always bring my fruit cake for that party, too. Monday they're off to Florida."

Who goes to Florida for Christmas?

Probably only rich people who don't have children. Kids want to stay and wait for Santa where they normally live.

I peek through the door curtain into the kitchen. Mama already has on her coat with the fox fur collar, galoshes, a big scarf wound around her neck, and a wooly cap over her ears. Her mittened hands hold her shopping bag with cleaning stuff and the fruit cake.

"You're never going to make it," Daddy says.

I hear the kitchen door slam. When Mama makes up her mind, there's no stopping her. I feel terrible that Mama has to go out in this storm. It's not right. She could fall down, get buried in the snow and nobody would ever find her. It's a long walk to the doctor's house. Somebody has to help her.

We need Mama. We need her here for Christmas.

I decide to get my clothes on and go out and see if I can catch up to her, help her in some way. It's up to me, because the other kids are still sleeping, and Buddy has a bad cold. He was coughing all night.

I dress quickly and go into the kitchen to get my jacket from the coat hooks by the door.

"Where do you think you're going?" Daddy comes out of his bedroom with his overcoat on, surprising me. "Don't you know there's a big blizzard out there? There's no school today. So take those clothes right back off."

"I'm not going to school," I say. "I'm going out to find Mama—she might get lost in the snow if she can't see her way."

"Well, you won't be able to see your way either. So just stay put. I'm the one who's going to go out and look for her."

Daddy gets his flashlight, tests that it works, then puts on his cap with ear flaps and his heavy black gloves. Before he can get his gloves all the way on, the kitchen door blows open. There stands Mama, covered in snow.

"I couldn't make it. Not even to the corner," she says, huffing, sinking into a chair with snow falling all around her.

"I was just getting ready to go after you," Daddy says. "Lulu wanted to look for you, too."

"I didn't want you to get lost, or buried in the snow," I say. Yet, I'm kind of glad I didn't have to go out there, and happy she's back.

"I tried. No way I could get any farther. No way I can clean their house today. No fruit cake for them, either."

Mama shakes snow from her head. Trickles run down her face. I can't tell if it's melting snow or tears.

"So, there won't be any money at all this week. I was counting on it to buy makings for the fruit salad for Christmas. One more thing we'll just have to do without."

I wish I hadn't heard that. I wish this day was over already. I won't get to be an angel. Some girl won't get that nice furry kitten. But worst of all, there's not going to be any fruit salad for Christmas. All I've been praying for is the Shirley Temple doll. I didn't even think of praying for anything else, and now it's too late.

Mama gets everyone else up. During our oatmeal breakfast, she announces, "Since you're all home today, it will be a good day to bake Christmas cookies, and the oven will keep the house nice and warm too."

Before, when we'd stay home from school, we'd get to listen to radio serials like "Ma Perkins," "Guiding Light," and other good ones.

"No radio today," Mama says. "The storm makes too much static." But we know the real reason—electricity costs too much money.

It's best listening to the radio in the evening anyway, cause you never get to know the endings of the daytime serials. Luckily, Daddy still lets us turn on "Billy the Brownie" each night. I wouldn't want to miss that.

Mitzy's in her high chair, eating and playing. Daddy's down in the basement, pounding away and sawing. He's lit the little oil stove down there. I can smell it upstairs; maybe I'll go down and stand near it later. Buddy's down there helping cause he doesn't like doing baking, or any kitchen work. "Women's work," he calls it.

We girls get our aprons on and begin helping Mama.

First, we have to get down the battered box of aluminum cookie cutters. There are Christmas trees, gingerbread men, stars, and other holiday shapes.

"It'll be gingerbread and sugar cookies today," Mama says. "Till we run out of time, or sugar."

The frozen cookies were baked last week, and they're already stored in big tins. To make them, you pack dough with nuts real tight into long wax-paper rolls, freeze them outside, then slice the frozen dough real thin and bake it. The cookies come out crispy and delicious. I always sneak a few before they're locked away.

The fruit cakes are already done too, wrapped in cloths dampened with Daddy's whiskey. Maybe that's why I don't like fruit cake, that strong whiskey taste. Mama always serves it to her company during Christmas time. Of course, didn't she say she saves money for her "Christmas Club," making sure they have something special? It's not fair, spending money for company fruit cake, with no money left over for our fruit salad.

The whole house begins to smell cookie good. We hardly notice that the snow's still pounding outside. We sprinkle colored sugar on top of the sugar cookies before they get baked. This afternoon, we'll frost gingerbread men and other shapes. Christmas trees get decorated real fancy, any way we want. I save pieces of candy cane from my St. Nicholas stocking, smash them up and put tiny bits on the trees to look like ornaments.

We get to eat broken cookies, but Mama hollers if she thinks we broke them on purpose.

It turns out to be not such a bad day. Mama seems happier—she always is when she bakes.

"Sounds like Ida didn't go to work today either," Mama mentions when we hear steps from upstairs. Mama worries that if Ida didn't work today, maybe she might not be able to pay the rent, which is due on the first of each month. "And this is one month I could use that money before the first." Mama pounds the rolling pin extra hard on the baking board.

Around noon, Ida comes down. "I couldn't get to work today, Liz," she tells Mama, "and as long as my lunch is packed already, I thought I'd have lunch with you, if that's okay?"

"Glad for the company," Mama says. "I couldn't get to work either. The snow's kept everybody home." Mama pulls out a chair at the kitchen table. "Sit down, Ida. Have some tea and fresh baked cookies with your lunch."

The table is filled with racks of drying cookies. Mama clears off one end so she and Ida have a place to eat, and gets down the nice tea set, the one with painted Japanese scenes. Pretty soon she's pouring hot tea into fancy cups.

Ida opens her lunch box and takes out liver sausage sandwiches wrapped in newspaper. Then she screws open a big thermos bottle and pours out soup that's still steaming, into the metal top, offering Mama some.

"I'm sorry there's not enough to share with you children," Ida says, as we stand close by, watching and sniffing. "It's only ham and bean soup. We've been eating it all week, using up that skinny old ham bone."

"You children go, eat your own lunch now." Mama pours some soup into a cracked soup bowl. It smells better than our daily potato soup.

Catherine fixes us leftover bread pudding with brown sugar on top, and hot Postum to drink. We have to eat on the floor in the spare room, making a table by putting a big game board on top of a low stool. It turns out to be fun, like a picnic. We each get one chipped gingerbread man. I eat mine slowly, thinking of the gingerbread man story with each bite, hanging onto the spicy gingery aftertaste.

We can hear Mama and Ida talking in between our eating and giggling.

"I don't know what I'm going to do," Ida says, "I was going to go shopping after work today to buy a present for Ginny, Dorothy's little girl. You know she's been sick with the scarlet fever, real bad, and Dorothy was going to stop by here tomorrow. There's not gonna be much Christmas at their house this year, the way things are going. Charlie's been out of work for so long. And now, little Jenny won't even be getting a gift from me, cause I can't get out to buy one."

"I think I have something nice you can give little Ginny," Mama says. "Lulu was going to exchange gifts at school today, but since she can't get there, that gift can go to cheer someone else up."

"Oh, I don't think I could take it. Lulu might want the gift for herself."

"Well, I didn't make it for her."

Mama calls out, "Lulu, get the box with the fur kitty."

I bring the shoe box, open it, and hand Ida the kitty, still wanting to keep it for myself. Ida strokes the soft fur.

"Why, it's beautiful. Perfect! Ginny will just love it. She's always wanted a pet, but pets cost money. Where did you buy it? I can pay you—if it's not too much."

"It's not bought," I interrupt, saying proudly, "Mama made it. She makes all kinds of nice things out of old stuff."

"You don't pay me anything, Ida. This is our gift to Ginny. Later, we'll send up some frosted cookies for her too." Mama gives Ida the box. "Something led me to make that kitten yesterday. Now I know why."

I feel okay about the kitten going to a sick little girl, even happy about it. Sometimes things turn out better than you think they will.

~ SATURDAY ~

On Saturday morning, the snow has stopped, and the sun's out, making everything bright and glisteny. I can hear snow shovels scraping, stampings of feet, neighbors calling to one another. One day can make such a difference.

"Okay, let's get those shovels moving," Daddy yells. He has a hard time getting the front door open, so much snow is piled up against it.

Pretty soon, Daddy, Buddy, and Catherine are shoveling snow, piling it into high hills on both sides of the sidewalks. Luckily, we only have three shovels, so the rest of us just run around in the snow, getting yelled at if we make chunks fall back on the sidewalk.

Even Frank from upstairs is helping. He's big and strong, but doesn't shovel too fast, stopping every few minutes.

"I don't think he's ever had a real job in his life," Mama always says. "He's just not the working kind. Lucky, Ida is."

Daddy calls him "a lazy lunk," but not in front of him.

Things are better all around. But I can tell Mama's still feeling bad about not working yesterday. I feel bad too when she tells me I can't go downtown today.

"No, there's still too much snow. You just wait till Monday." I can't tell her I have to go to get her present. "Today, after paths are cleared, you can deliver Christmas cookies."

Every year, Mama wraps up packages of cookies in soft brown paper Daddy used to get from the aluminum company. They used it for wrapping tea kettles, but they let him take home piles that got wet or dirty. We still have stacks we use to draw on and for other things. The packages are tied with tinsel ribbon from Ida, then put in an open cardboard box.

I volunteer to deliver because I like going to other people's houses and they're always glad to get our cookies, sometimes even inviting me in.

Around noon, there's a path on the sidewalk and the plow has opened a single row on the street.

"Okay, you can deliver cookies now. But be careful. Don't drop them in the snow! You won't get to eat those broken ones." Mama hands me the box. "And make sure you wish them a Merry Christmas. If they ask you to come in, make sure you wipe the snow off your feet. People want to keep their houses clean for Christmas."

My first stop is the Yaegers' house next door. I have to bang hard on their storm door. They don't have a doorbell because it scares Mabel. Pretty soon, Mrs. Yaeger opens the door. "Why, hello, Lulu. Did you bring us some cookies? Come right on in."

I stamp snow off my feet, walk in, and set the box of cookies down carefully, picking out Mabel's package. Mabel, still in her night gown, peeks into the room. She sees the cookies and starts jumping up and down, then runs in saying something that sounds like "coookieesss."

She grabs the package and rips it open. Cookies fall all over their clean carpet. But Mrs. Yaeger doesn't yell at Mabel, just helps pick them up. Mabel right away starts eating the gingerbread man, making all kinds of slurping sounds as she does.

Mrs. Yaeger brings the pink candy bowl over to me. "Would you like some candy, Lulu?"

Mmmm. Today it's filled with all kinds of Christmas candy. Striped ribbon candies, round hard candy with tiny colored pictures in the middle, cream-filled mint straws, filled raspberries—kinds we never get at home. Which one to pick?

"Take a whole handful," Mrs. Yaeger urges, then gets a little sack and fills it up with candies. "You can share these with your sisters and brothers. Would you like to stay a bit and play with Mabel? She hasn't seen you for quite a while."

I like playing with Mabel, but I'm getting pretty hot in my thick jacket and snow pants. "I'd like to, but I still have more cookies to deliver."

"You go right ahead then. And thank your mother for us. I hope Santa brings you some nice gifts."

"Oh, he will," I say, almost dancing out of there, then turn back, remembering to call out, "Merry Christmas!" I think Mabel yells it back to me. At least, it sounds like it. She must know about Christmas, because every year I get a Christmas postcard from her—the only mail I've ever received. "MABEL" is printed in scribbly letters.

Next stop is Caroline's house across the street. While writing out cards for the cookie packages, Mama comments, "Caroline's mother doesn't seem to have time to bake cookies, and that family needs some 'real' cookies at Christmas."

Since Caroline is Lutheran, she goes to a different school, and I mostly see her only in summer. I'm not sure how Lutherans celebrate Christmas, but just about everybody does, no matter what church they go to—even those who don't go to church.

Their porch isn't shoveled off yet, and you sure couldn't get a car out through that mountain of snow in front of their garage door.

Mrs. Simmons answers the door. She looks half-asleep. Her face doesn't have makeup on, so she isn't pretty as usual. She's wearing a crumpled silky kimono with lots of big flowers on it.

"Why hello, Lulu. What brings you out in this snowy weather?"

"I brought some Christmas cookies for Caroline and Freddy. You too, if you like them."

"Well, isn't that sweet of you. And you know, I haven't even been able to get the car out to go buy some cookies. Caroline's still in bed with a bad cold. But I'll tell her you stopped by."

I was hoping to see Caroline and ask her about Christmas. I wanted to tell her that I'm getting a Shirley Temple doll. Guess I'll just have to wait till summer and show Shirley to her.

"Just a minute." Mrs. Simmons disappears and comes back with an unopened box of candy. "Chocolate-Covered-Cherries" is pictured brightly on the cover. My favorite!

"Mr. Simmons' company gives boxes of candy at Christmas, so here's an extra one for your family. Candy just makes me too fat and puts holes in the kids' teeth, but you enjoy them anyway."

I put the candy in the cookie box, thinking, instead of seeing Caroline, I'm getting a box of candy. You never know what to expect when you knock on a door.

"Be careful on the steps. We have to hire someone to come shovel the place out. Mr. Simmons fell yesterday in the snow and hurt his back."

"My dad, he could come and shovel for you. He's good at shoveling, and our place is all done," I quickly say.

"Wonderful! You tell your dad to come on over, soon as he can. And we'll pay him for doing the job."

Wow, a box of candy and a job for Daddy, all from the same house. Before Mrs. Simmons closes the door, I turn around and shout, "Merry Christmas!" loud as I can. I want everyone to hear.

Next stop is Miss Birch, the "old maid." The sidewalk in front of her house isn't shoveled. No footprints up to her porch either. After knocking for a while on the front door, I decide to go around back. No footprints there, either. I bang real hard on the back door. No answer. I go around to the front and bang again. Maybe she went away for Christmas. Maybe she's sick inside. Maybe, like Nine O'clock Mamie, she never comes out of her house anymore. I would have liked to say "Merry Christmas" to her and her dolls.

I walk away a bit sad. I like to know answers, and there were none at this house today.

The last stop is the new family that just moved in at the end of the block. Mama decided we should take cookies to them. I'm not happy about that. The kids go to public school and yell names at us when we walk by. Hardly anyone plays with them since they moved in.

Mama says, "Well, you just have to get to know them. And one way to get to know your neighbors is by sharing things with them. I'm sure they'd welcome some cookies, with all the kids they've got."

Fearfully, I go up the steps. The snow isn't shoveled here either. Everything looks crumbly and unpainted. I knock on the door, hoping no one will answer. A lady comes to the door and opens it only a crack. I can hear kids yelling inside. Lots of screaming, too.

"I'm sorry, we can't buy anything from you today," she says.

"I'm not selling anything," I say before she can close the door. "Mama sent a package of cookies for your family."

The lady is thin and scrawny. Some young children come near the door, looking hungry and dirty. One cute little one is crying, sobbing her heart out. Right then, I decide they need more than one package of cookies. I'll give them the one Miss Birch didn't get.

"Here's two packages of cookies for you," I say quickly. I want to get away before the bigger kids come to the door.

"You tell your Mama thank you. These will help make our Christmas just a little bit happier." She seems so nice. How could she have such bad kids?

"Merry Christmas," I say.

"Merry Christmas to you, too. And God bless you and your family."

I walk away, thinking that even if those kids go to public school, their family believes in God. Maybe there's a girl my age living there—she might be nice to play with.

I get home with lots of news to tell, about Miss Birch, and the new family. I hand over the box of chocolate covered cherries.

"And Mrs. Simmons says they need someone to shovel their

snow, because Mr. Simmons hurt his back. I told her Daddy could do it, and she said to send him right over. She'll pay him too."

Mama is all smiles. "I'll send him right over. Maybe we can buy fruit salad ingredients after all. And I'll tell Buddy to go check Miss Birch's place. And it's okay that you gave her cookies to the new family. We'll put this nice box of candy away and open it up on Christmas Day."

I almost wish there were more cookies to deliver so I could have more adventures on this Saturday that didn't start out so good.

~ SUNDAY ~

It's Sunday. One day closer.

We're back from church and playing in the snow. Daddy's scraping ice off our sidewalk. Later, he'll sprinkle stove ashes over it.

A big shiny car comes down the street. It's Dr. Mack's car, stopping in front of our house.

Why? Nobody's sick. Maybe he's mad Mama didn't come and clean their house on Friday. What if he fires her?

"Hello, Felix," he calls, getting out of his car. "You children having fun in the snow?"

He doesn't hear our answers, because he's already opening his car trunk, taking out a big crate filled with grapefruit and oranges. Then I remember, every year Dr. Mack gives us fruit for Christmas, which he orders from Florida. I'd rather get regular presents, but oranges are good, only his grapefruit is sometimes mouth-puckering sour.

Daddy carries the crate into the house, with Dr. Mack following.

"Thought I'd deliver my gifts today, before another snow storm blows in. The Mrs. and I will be off to Florida tomorrow. No snow there."

Why would anyone want to go to Florida for Christmas? Not want to see snow on Christmas day?

I'd like to follow them into the house and hear what he talks about with Mama, but she'd only tell us to get back outside. We know better than to butt in when grown-ups talk.

Pretty soon, Dr. Mack comes out. "Have a merry Christmas, children, and stay well." He gets in his car and drives away.

What happens if someone gets sick while he's in Florida?

We quickly go inside, pretending we're cold. Mama seems happier. Because of the grapefruit? We play in the spare room, but I sit near the door so I can hear Mama and Daddy talking.

"I told him he shouldn't give me the money, that I didn't work for it. But he said to just make it up another time. And it didn't matter that I didn't clean Friday—they cancelled their holiday party because of the snow."

I go in the kitchen to get a drink of water. Mama is holding up a sealed white envelope. "And this is the other envelope he left. But I'm not opening it till Christmas, otherwise I might just go out and buy more things."

We help Mama separate oranges and grapefruits into smaller boxes to store in the cool back hall.

"Now we can have oranges for Christmas, too, without going on Relief," Mama says. "All I had to do was go out and work for them."

Today is the day I'm going to see the play *Hansel and Gretel*. It's being put on by the Junior League at a real theater at 2 o'clock. Last week, everyone in class was given two free tickets. I was kind of excited about my first chance to see a play acted by grown-ups. Now I'm not so sure I want to go. Maybe that's why I kinda forgot till Mama reminded me. Geraldine's still sick, and no one in our family wants to go with me.

"See *Hansel and Gretel*? Nah, that's for babies," Buddy says.

When I tell Mama I don't want to go, she tells me I have to.

"Since you did so well on stage at school, you're going to take this opportunity to go see a real play. Free tickets don't come round every day."

"But I don't even know how to get there."

She explains where the theater is and how to get there.

"You know, it used to be the old opera house till the Junior League took it over and fancied it up. Now they perform plays there. At Christmas time, they put on special shows for poor children. So get going, or you're gonna be late."

Nobody said anything about getting free tickets because we were poor children. I don't want to be known as "poor children." We may not have lots of money, but we're certainly not poor, not like those families in stories wearing rags, starving, sleeping in gutters.

"Do I have to go?" I ask. "My stomach doesn't feel so good."

"Then seeing this show will help you forget about your no-good stomach. And since you have two tickets, you can take Sonny with you."

Taking Sonny is better than going by myself. I'll make the sacrifice, so at least Sonny can have a good time.

"I don't want to go, I'm too tired," he whines, rubbing his eyes.

"It's okay if you fall asleep during the play, Sonny. They don't care." I take his hand, pleading, "But I need you to go with me, so I don't have to walk home alone."

"Okay," he sighs, and off we go.

The Old Opera House is at the edge of downtown. High up on the wooden building, there's still faded letters reading "OPERA HOUSE." Down below, there's a sign with lights blinking all around it: "JUNIOR LEAGUE THEATRE."

Lots of children are waiting outside. They don't look poor. Mama must have been wrong about free shows for poor kids.

I hand my tickets to someone dressed up like an elf and enter a place I've never been in before. I'm not sure what's going to happen, or what I'm going to see.

It's big, with lots of seats, like a movie theater. There's a red velvet curtain across the front, and all kinds of strange lights hanging from the black ceiling. Balconies are around the sides and back of the theater. Nobody's allowed up there today, but I'd sure like to go up there to watch the play, and watch the people below too.

The children inside are really noisy, but they quiet down when a lady walks out in front of the curtain.

"Welcome, children, to the Junior League's Christmas present to you—our stage production of *Hansel and Gretel*. Now you know, plays are different than movies. There's real live people on this stage. So remember, you must be quiet during the show, no getting out of your seats or running in the aisles. So, sit back, take yourselves into fairy tale land, and enjoy the show!"

Lights dim. The red curtain parts slowly. There, right upon the stage, appearing like magic, is a thick woods, and the rickety cottage where Hansel and Gretel live. It's as if everything grew right up out of that floor.

I know the story by heart, but watching the words come alive before my eyes is much different than reading them. Hansel and Gretel walk in, looking as if they stepped out of the pages of a picture book. I'm entranced, and doubly glad Mama made me come.

It begins. The parents are so poor they can't feed Hansel and Gretel, so they decide to take them into the woods and lose them.

Do poor parents really do that? Try to lose their children, so they won't have to feed them? Is that why the Junior League did this show for poor kids—to warn them that such things could happen?

I shut these worrisome thoughts off, anxious to get back to the show and escape into the make-believe world.

Hansel and Gretel drop pebbles on their way into the woods, and use them to find their way home. The parents try to lose them again. This time, they drop bread crumbs, which the birds eat. Now they're really lost in the woods. Just as I'm all worried about what's going to happen next, the curtain closes.

What? It can't be over already. Then quickly, the curtains open again.

Now there's a big fancy gingerbread house up there. It's covered with delicious candy and dripping frosting. I just want to go up there and take a big bite. How could they build something like that so quick, get it on that stage so fast?

Hansel and Gretel are so hungry they start breaking off and eating pieces of the house.

Someone inside cries out in a squeaky voice, "Nibble nibble, little mouse—Who is nibbling at my house?"

An old lady hobbles out. At first, she seems pretty nice, till we find out she's going to cook and bake the children. Kids scream when they hear that. Then, when she tries to put Gretel in the big oven to bake her into gingerbread, everybody yells to warn Gretel. I'm feeling scared, even if I know how it ends.

What if they make a different ending on this stage today?

They don't. Hansel and Gretel put the witch into the oven, then go home with lots of pearls and precious stones. Everyone's happy.

The curtain closes.

We clap real loud. Happy endings are best. But you always have to wait till the very end to make sure it does end happy. Just like my Shirley Temple doll—I have to wait till my own happy ending.

I enjoyed the play so much I want to stay and see it over again, which I sometimes do at the movies. But, when a play's over, it's over. That's all folks!

We walk up the aisle, into the brightly lit lobby decorated for Christmas. Ladies in long ball gowns are standing there, smiling, handing out white bags of candy tied with red and green ribbon.

"Merry Christmas," the pretty lady says to me and gives me a bag. She doesn't even ask me if I'm a poor child or not, everybody gets a bag.

I just saw a good play and got candy too! I can't wait to tell Mama and everybody else all about it.

On the way home, Sonny repeats how much he liked the show and the candy. "And I didn't even fall asleep, it was so good."

That night, I go to bed thinking about all the things I saw in

Hansel and Gretel. It takes me away from thinking about Christmas and Shirley Temple, as I usually do each night before going to sleep. It also makes me consider that magic exists in so many places.

Magic doesn't only happen in books or movies—it can mysteriously appear almost anywhere, like it did on that stage today. But mostly it begins in your head, where everything you believe in is stored—a whole library of thoughts you can check out any time you want.

~ MONDAY ~

*O*n Monday morning there's no school, but everyone's still up early. No snow. That means I can go downtown and buy Mama's present!

Singing bursts from me as I jump out of bed. "Jingle bells, jingle bells—Jingle all the way!"

Catherine joins in, and pretty soon we're all singing as we get our clothes on. Mama, who ate much earlier, sits at the breakfast table with us.

"Today, we're getting the house cleaned spic and span. Then, before bed tonight, each of you gets a bath, and gets your hair washed, because tomorrow night—well, you all know what tomorrow night is—"

"Christmas Eve!" we shout together, banging our spoons against our cereal bowls. We start cleaning the house quick as we can.

"Anybody want to go up in the attic with me and help get wrappings and decorations down?"

Eagerly, we follow Mama up the hall stairs. She uses her key to unlock the small attic door, and shines the flashlight inside, because there's no lights in the attic. It's scary looking. Mama's flashlight shines on stacks of piled-up things. She goes to the corner, digging out boxes and handing them to us to take downstairs.

"Here's the box of wrappings...This one's the manger...A box with window wreaths...More decorations...Honeycomb bells...Tinsel stuff from Ida...No, don't come into this corner, just stay over there."

I want to go in, yet don't want to. The floor boards in the attic are far apart and bendy. I'm always afraid I could slip through those wide cracks and fall right into the room below.

Finally, Mama has everything she wants out. I still see other things in another corner that weren't there during summer. They're all covered with a white sheet.

While Mama's locking up, Frank opens his door, which is across from our attic door, and peers out. "Just getting Christmas things from the attic," Mama tells him. "Lots more to do before the big day." He closes his door without saying a word.

Maybe he thought we were going to break into his flat? He likes to think the second floor belongs only to him.

"Yes, you and Sonny can go downtown this morning," Mama says when I ask. "I don't know what you two do there all the time. And don't forget, presents have to be wrapped today so everything's cleaned up by tomorrow."

Off we go, both happy to be going downtown, running and sliding on the slippery icy parts of the sidewalk. Lots of people are shopping, carrying packages. The shelves in the toy department look a bit bare. The Shirley Temple dolls are all gone. There's just a big empty space. I hope Santa has enough. Long lines of kids are still waiting before his throne.

It might be too late to tell Santa what they want, especially if he still has to make those requested gifts. Why don't they just write him letters like we do, and do it early?

On to the dish department. I wait and wait until the store lady gets to me. "Please, I'd like to buy that ruby red wine glass." I point at it, handing her my dime.

She hurriedly wraps it in newspaper, puts it in a bag, wishes me "Merry Christmas" and goes on to the next customer before I can say "Merry Christmas" back.

Then I see it—a shiny penny, right on the store floor. I quick pick it up. No way to turn in a penny and find the owner, so it's okay to go to the candy counter, which was too tempting before to even look at. There they hang—candy cherries on a wire. Two bright red cherries connected by a thin wire, so you can put them over your Christmas tree branches. I spend the penny—a gift to myself today. I break one cherry off for Sonny and soon we're each sucking on a sweet cherry ball.

Sonny wants to stay downtown longer, but I tell him, "There's too much to do at home today. We have to get everything ready for Santa, who's coming tomorrow night. Tell you what, I'll read you, 'The Night Before Christmas' again."

"Okay." He smiles his big grin. He asks me to read that poem lots. He also asks me questions about Christmas and Santa, like I used to ask Catherine. Hope I give him the right answers. It's not so easy being the older sister.

When we get home, the sitting room is open, but not heated. Boxes from the attic are scattered about. The manger, made of cardboard, has been put together and placed on the bottom shelf of the big library table with small plaster figures of Mary and Joseph. Baby Jesus isn't put in till Christmas Eve, when we sing "Happy Birthday" to him.

Catherine and Betty Jane are hanging tinsel and garlands all around the room, using the stepladder. A big red paper honeycomb bell hangs from the center ceiling light fixture, air moving it about slowly. Wreaths with electric candles have been put up in the windows, but they won't be lit, not this year. Daddy already told us that.

The box of used wrapping paper is in the corner. Mama irons out each sheet after gifts are opened and saves them for the next year. We can use what we need, but have to be careful not to tear any. Little holiday stickers that we lick and stick hold the paper shut.

I like fingering the different sheets, remembering the gifts from last year.

Santa doesn't wrap our gifts. "Too much work," Mama says. So his presents are always on a chair with our name on it, near the Christmas tree. That way, we can see what we got right away.

"There'd be too much commotion if everybody unwrapped everything all at once," Mama says. "Santa's decision, not mine."

Other houses get their presents wrapped, how come he decided our house shouldn't?

We always wrap gifts to one another, though. With six children, Mama and Daddy, well, that gets to be a pretty big pile of wrapped presents.

I find some old soft paper, cut it into long hay-like shreds, carefully nest Mama's wine glass in it, then place it in a box and cover it with the prettiest paper. Mama won't ever guess what it is. Just hope she unwraps it carefully, and doesn't drop it.

Then I go about wrapping my other gifts. Hankies I made for Daddy. Two sock dolls for Mitzy. A jumping jack I made out of cardboard and string for Sonny. A ring I found at the beach for Betty Jane, making my own wish on it before wrapping it up. Toy flour-paste soldiers for Buddy I made in his soldier molds. They turned out pretty good. I just hope he doesn't shoot them apart right away. In an old macaroni box, I place cloth roses for Catherine, for her hair. I hand sewed them from leftover lavender chiffon material. I found the directions in a sewing book from the library.

We write names on stickers and pile wrapped gifts near the manger. It's still cold in the room, but we're in sweaters and long stockings and no one complains.

"Tomorrow night, we'll turn the heat on in here so it'll be nice and cozy for Santa while he puts up the tree and decorates it," Mama comes in to check on the decorating, wearing her old thick brown sweater. She lets us do everything by ourselves.

"Do what you want," she says, "I have plenty else to take care of."

I always wonder though—why are there the same ornaments on the tree each year? Does Santa keep them at the North Pole? Are there special boxes for each family? He sure is some magic person. Christmas is packed with so many magical and mysterious things, it's hard to keep track of them all. Even when I ask Mama, she sometimes says, "I just don't really know." And if she doesn't, who would?

By the end of the day, we're all pretty tired, from wrapping, decorating, and cleaning up after. Before supper, we have our baths, wash our hair, then sit down in pajamas, nice and clean, to eat our potato soup, which seems tastier tonight.

Mama's been baking stollen bread today, with red and green dried

267

fruit in it. We each get a piece with our supper. Tomorrow's a fast day, a church day, where you can only eat one full meal, no meat—and no stollen, just soup and bread.

It's hard to get to sleep tonight, so I talk with Catherine about Christmas and Santa. I always worry that because we don't have a fireplace he might not be able to get into our house.

"I've told you before, every time you ask, Mama and Daddy leave the door unlocked so he can get in through the door," Catherine tells me.

We leave our door unlocked anyway. I'll just triple check tomorrow night to make sure.

I go to sleep dreaming of Shirley Temple. She floats all around, talks to me, tells me how she can't wait to come to my house and be my favorite doll. She moves so fast I can't keep up with her. Then my dream mixes up with Mama's Christmas story. Mean people march in and grab my Shirley Temple doll away. I try to hang onto her, but can't. They're tearing off her dress. I run after them, screaming, "Give me back my doll! Give her back to me!"

My screaming wakes everybody up. "Why are you screaming?"

"Bad dream" is all I tell them. I don't want to share this one. I don't even want to think about it anymore.

I just hope bad dreams don't come true. I say extra prayers, fall asleep again and don't wake up till morning.

~ CHRISTMAS EVE ~

It's here—the day before Christmas! How can I wait 24 more hours?

The door to the sitting room's still shut. I wish I could keep looking at that Christmasy room all day, but I'm not even allowed to peek in now.

Mama went shopping early to buy fruit salad fixings and other holiday food. The big ham's already baking. Now she's making her yummy yeast rolls with poppy seeds sprinkled on top. The house smells sooo good.

Tomorrow morning, after opening presents, then going to church, we'll have our deluxe Christmas breakfast/lunch. Sliced ham, yeast rolls, Dr. Mack's grapefruit, and for dessert—fruit salad! The rest of the day, we won't eat meals, just snacks.

Mama says, "I'm just too tired to make anything else besides our big lunch/breakfast on Christmas day. Besides, you kids fill up on candy, nuts, cookies, root beer, and popcorn all day long anyway."

It's a day that never stops giving out good things.

While helping Mama make the fruit salad, we hear a noise outside. There are people coming up on the front porch.

"Now who can that be?" Mama wonders aloud, then looks out the kitchen window. "What on earth are those people doing here?"

There's knocking on the door. Mama opens it and steps outside. I peer through the curtain and see people wearing blue uniforms, carrying big bushel baskets with red bows on them.

I can't hear what they're saying. Pretty soon, the people are leaving. Mama calls after them, "Like I told you, we don't need those things here. You take them to someone who does."

She slams the door really hard when she comes back in.

Daddy comes up from the basement and asks who was at the door, and what did they want.

"Do you believe it? That was the Salvation Army bringing us Christmas baskets! To help make our Christmas a little merrier." Mama doesn't sound like it made her merrier at all. "I just wonder where they got our name from? Who gave them the information that we needed help—that we wouldn't have anything for Christmas? What gives others the right to decide who's poor and who's not poor? When I need handouts, I'll go ask for them myself." She pauses, "What will the neighbors think, seeing them bring all that stuff here."

"Didn't you tell them we were Catholic?" Daddy asks.

"No, I didn't. And why should I? They weren't trying to convert us. They don't care what we are—just that we have six kids, and you're not working, and—"

"What was in the baskets?" Catherine asks.

"I don't know, and I don't care. They brought two baskets—two!

That group must have been given too much money in their big black kettles."

"But Mama," Buddy interrupts, "They use that kettle money to give nice dinners on Christmas Day for all the poor people who want to come—"

"Well then, you go, you go to their nice dinner, if what we serve here isn't good enough for you."

"But Mama—" Catherine gets cut off.

"I don't want to hear anything more about it. If anybody asks, you just tell them they got the wrong house. And they most certainly did."

I don't know why Mama's so mad, just because people brought us baskets of food and other things for Christmas. It's what people do at Christmas time, give gifts—like those cookies I delivered. Well, anyway, I'm glad it wasn't the firemen bringing us used painted-over toys. If that had happened, it would really squash my hopes. I still have hopes, and I'm keeping them—at least till tomorrow morning.

After lunch, Ida comes downstairs and gives Mama a wrapped package. Mama gives her a wrapped fruit cake.

"Lizzie, I have to tell you—I won't be here for Christmas. I'm leaving this afternoon on the bus. Little Ginny's worse. Mrs. Yaeger got the phone call and let me call Dorothy back. I told Dorothy I'd be there as soon as I could. She needs family at a time like this."

"You just go and be with her. We'll keep an eye on Frank."

"Oh, Frank's going with me. You know, he's there if I need him. What would I do without Frank—" she thinks a bit. "Be alone I guess, and that's not good, not good for anybody. So, just keep an eye on our place while we're gone."

"Make sure you let us know everything when you get back."

271

"Oh, I will." She hesitates, then asks, "Was that the Salvation Army at your door, just a bit ago?"

"Oh, they had the wrong house—and we don't need their baskets, not this year."

"You're lucky you don't, cause there's so many that do."

"Ida," I pipe up, "Tell little Ginny we hope she gets better." I want to say more, but not sure what.

"I will, Lulu. You know, I'm gonna miss you kids on Christmas day. Nothing like a house full of children on Christmas. Hope Santa's good to you all." Ida gives each of us a big hug. "You're such a nice family. Just the kind of kids I would have liked if—" She gives a faint smile, hugs Mama real tight and she's out the door and up the stairs to her flat.

Later, I watch her and Frank going down the porch steps, both carrying small suitcases.

"You kids say extra prayers for little Ginny tonight," Mama reminds us. Then she adds, "You can put in some prayers for those Salvation Army people too. They're probably good people, and the world can sure use lots more good people. Somebody just sent them to the wrong place, that's all."

Finally, it's time for "Billie the Brownie," the best part of the day. All six of us children, already in pajamas, sit around the Philco radio that stands on the floor in our sitting room hallway. We soon hear "Jingle Bells" as Billie calls out, "Have you been good boys and girls this year?" We nod our heads, uttering "Yes" together.

It's only fifteen minutes long, but so much happens in those minutes.

Billie is one of Santa's helpers, and his squeaky voice tells us all what's going on at the North Pole each and every day. He reveals secret things too, otherwise we might never get to know what happens at Santa's workshop. We hear elves hammering and chattering in the background, bells ringing, and Christmas music.

Near the end of the program, Santa reads aloud letters from boys and girls, laughing heartily as he does. We keep our ears glued, in case he reads one of our letters.

There's lots of requests from girls wanting Shirley Temple dolls, boys wanting new bikes. Most end their letters with, "and please give gifts to the poor children" and "we'll leave cookies and milk out for you."

Just listening to the program reinforces my belief in Santa. Here he is, talking right on the radio, and radio is real.

Tonight's show is extra special, because tonight's when they pack the sleigh and get all set for Santa to leave on his trip to deliver gifts. There's so much excitement going on there—seeing that the reindeer are ready, getting presents packed, checking on the weather.

Mrs. Claus gives Santa his food bag and tells him, "Goodbye, Santa. Have a good trip!"

Billie is going to ride along with Santa and help him, like he always does.

We hear sleigh bells ringing. Pretty soon Santa's shouting, "Now Dasher! Now Dancer! Now Prancer and Vixen! On Comet! On Cupid! On Donner and Blitzen! Now dash away! Dash away! Dash away all!"

Next, we hear Santa shouting, "Merrrrrry Christmas!" His voice and laughter get fainter and fainter.

He's on his way. Yippee! He made it! Then I start thinking—sometimes things can go wrong. I stop immediately, no thinking anything like that.

Right after, we brush our teeth quick, sing "Happy Birthday" to Jesus outside the sitting room door and hop into bed. Catherine, who stays up later, says she'll put out the milk and cookies for Santa. Mama and Daddy come in shortly to kiss us good night. They tell us they'll be going to Midnight Mass later, like they do every year.

"Oh no, that's way too late for you kids to stay up. You'll be going to Children's Mass in the morning. So don't any of you get up during the night. You could scare Santa away. Wouldn't want that to happen, would we?"

"No!" we answer back.

I feel warm and cozy tucked in my bed, even hoping I see sugar plums dance in my head. Catherine put rag curls in my hair, so my head feels pokey. My stomach's jingly too.

Too much excitement bouncing around everywhere. I say my prayers and try real hard to stay awake so I can hear Santa's reindeer's hooves on the roof. It's very important that I hear them this time.

All too soon, I fall asleep into Christmas-filled dreams.

~ CHRISTMAS ~

It's Christmas morning, or am I still dreaming? Whispers sprinkle the air. Already awake, the other children are tiptoeing about with giddy excitement.

"It's Christmas, it's Christmas," they sing-song to one another in hushed voices. Within seconds I'm out of bed, into my bunny slippers, joining in the merriment.

How long before Mama comes in to tell us we can go into the sitting room? How long can I hold all this excitement within me?

So much anticipation ripples—it's as if we're all one wriggling ribbon tied around an unopened gift.

"I can't wait to see what Santa brought—"

"Did you hear him come last night?"

"I couldn't sleep all night."

"What if Mama forgot about us?"

"I think we should—"

We're interrupted by Mama cheerily calling through the door curtain. "Kids, it's time. You can come out now."

We scoot from the room like whirlwinds took hold of us. "Merry Christmas!" we shout, racing to the sitting room.

There it is—the beautiful, glorious, magical decorated Christmas tree! It's lit up as if covered with twinkling jewels. Glistening ornaments, shimmering tinsel, and the glowing star at the top. I stop for a moment and breathe it all in—this wondrous scene I've been waiting for all year. I want to make it last, not let it slip away too quickly, rapidly clicking pictures to store in my mind.

The room is wonderfully warm and shimmers in wavering dimness. Ceiling decorations move about in slow motion, casting a not-quite-real feeling, as if the room were no longer part of our house, but some imaginary other world we stepped into.

I keep the glowing tree in view while looking for my present chair. There it is! How can I tell? "LULU" is printed on a big sign. There's a red and white ruffled dress, just like the one Shirley Temple wears, spread across the chair. But where's the doll?

Quickly, I look under the dress. There's only another dress, a plaid jumper Catherine sewed for me. And other gifts.

Where is it? Where is my Shirley Temple doll? It can't be possible that I didn't get one!

Panic and disappointment take over. My stomach churns with pulsing waves. How could this happen—it wasn't supposed to happen. I wished. I prayed. I can't hold back the tears.

Then I see it, on the floor behind the chair, a huge box with a sparkling cellophane cover. Inside, smiling back at me, is Shirley Temple!

Tears continue, but only because I'm so happy now. I grab the box, hold it, gaze at it, make sure it's real. My fingers want to tear it open, but instead, I slowly take off the cellophane and open the box reverently. I carefully lift out the lifelike doll.

She's beautiful. Wonderful. The dimples, curls—just as they should be. Her eyes open and close, her arms and legs move. She's wearing the same dress I just saw on my chair. Shirley and I can be twins now. We'll go everywhere and do everything together.

After a bit, I look at my other presents. There's a blue glass tea set. A soft furry kitten, same as the one Mama made for my school gift. Some games. A Shirley Temple coloring book. Shirley Temple cutout dolls. They're all nice, but nothing could be better than my treasured doll.

Still, I can't keep myself separated from the excitement going on around me. Holding Shirley tightly in my arms, I look at the gifts others have received and listen to their delighted exclamations.

Buddy has a new two-wheel shiny red Schwinn bike.

"Wow! Just what I need for my new paper route. Yippee!" If he could, he'd ride it around the room right now.

Catherine received a new movie machine. "Two movies came with it. Now I can show movies, right here, in our own house," she exclaims. I sure want to see them.

Betty Jane has the whole series of Nancy Drew books. "Just what I wanted. But nobody can read them till I'm all done." Betty likes to read, only she takes much more time than I do, so it'll be awhile before I get to read them.

Sonny is already playing with his big toy dump truck that has headlights which turn off and on. He's zooming it across the linoleum floor. Mitzy cuddles her new Raggedy Ann doll. It's like we're in the midst of Toyland. All because Santa came.

Mama and Daddy, still in their night clothes, sit in their big chairs, watching and smiling. When we're done looking at all our gifts, Mama says, "I think Santa was very good to you children this year, don't you?"

"He sure was," we answer in unison. No one is unhappy. Other years, there were maybe a few complaints, but not this time.

"Okay, time for the wrapped gifts," Mama announces.

We go get the presents we've piled up for each other. This unwrapping takes a bit longer. But it's fun watching gifts get opened, each with a separate story.

Mama holds up new cotton stockings Buddy gave her. "Because your old ones have so many holes in the knees, from all that scrubbing you do," he tells her. Sometimes Buddy can be really nice. Mama gives him an extra big smile.

Mama's unwrapping my present now.

"I wonder what this could be?" She takes her time unfolding the extra wrappings.

Soon she's holding up the ruby red wine glass. It glitters even more in this room than at the store. Christmas tree lights reflect all over and through it.

"It's beautiful, Lulu," Mama says, running her fingers all around the rim.

"You can put it on the kitchen window sill, let the sun sparkle right through."

"Yes, that will be a perfect spot. It'll add some red color to my Irish green things."

Mama opens the package with the small bottle of Blue Waltz perfume Daddy gives her every Christmas from the Woolworth's dime store. She passes it around so we can each smell it. Daddy keeps smiling the whole time.

There's lots of gift opening, and everyone's happy and surprised about each of them. There are too many to remember. But I know I'll always remember my dream-come-true gift. You never forget a present like that.

"Time to get dressed now," Mama says after the last package is opened.

Mitzy stands before the Christmas tree with new wonder, then quickly grabs at a shiny ornament.

"Hot!" Mama says, the word she uses for anything she doesn't want Mitzy to touch. Right away Mitzy withdraws her tiny hand, repeating, "Hot!" We all repeat it with her.

I take down my rag curls and ask Mama if I can wear the Shirley Temple dress she made me.

"Wear what you want—it's Christmas," she says. I can tell it's a happy day for Mama too.

I put on the dress and look and feel just like Shirley, my tight curls bouncing, ruffles shaking. I even try a little tap dance and smile as if I have dimples.

Soon it's time to go to Children's Mass. We don't mind leaving our gifts, knowing they'll be there when we return, except I want to take Shirley with me.

Mama says, "No, dolls don't belong in church."

"But I want her to see the manger. I want others to see her too."

"Well, you can tell her all about it after."

I sit Shirley on my gift chair. "You can watch the tree while I'm gone," I tell her, then kiss her goodbye.

The church has big Christmas trees all over with bright lights on them. The manger at the front is surrounded by real evergreen branches. It's even better than store decorations, because these are holier. Today I can pray real hard without having to ask for anything.

We sing Christmas carols and the priest gives a nice sermon just for the children. Shirley would've liked hearing it.

This happy feeling about Baby Jesus being born fills the church. Still, I'm anxious to get back home, knowing Shirley's there waiting for me.

We rush home and sit down to our waiting ham and rolls breakfast/lunch. Mama decides to save the fruit salad till later. We don't protest. It's always nicer having something to look forward to, especially if it's fruit salad.

The rest of the day, the celebration continues. We play new games and watch the short films from Catherine's movie projector flicker onto a bed sheet tacked on the wall. Buddy goes outside in the snow to try his new bike. My dolls and I have tea parties using my new tea set, with Shirley, too. When I pour my root beer into the tiny cups, Sonny and Mitzy come to join us. Later, we each get a delicious piece of chocolate-covered cherry candy. I save the little pleated cups they come in so I can smell them again later. There's more root beer, caramel corn, candy canes, and fruit salad for supper.

The house has never seemed more joyful—as if it were lifted up, turned over, and shaking out joy all over us. I don't want it to end. Even if everything's still here tomorrow, it won't be the same as Christmas day. It's a day that can happen only once a year. Then it's gone. Going to sleep stops it all.

"It's way past bedtime," Mama calls out to everybody. "You'll have all day tomorrow to play some more."

The others start getting ready for bed. I'm sitting in the rocking chair near the tree, with Shirley in my arms. I want to take her to bed with me, only we're so squashed in that bed, I don't want Shirley squashed up too.

Mama comes in. "Time for bed, Lulu."

"Can't I sleep here in the rocking chair with Shirley? Just for tonight? The other bed's too tight, it will squish her."

"Well, I guess it's okay. But just for tonight. The tree lights have to be turned off, though." Mama pulls the plug, but I can still smell the tree, a Christmasy scent that fills every inch of the room.

Mama kisses me goodnight, leaves, then comes back with a green knit blanket and covers Shirley and me, then tiptoes out.

I'm warm. I'm happy. Slowly I rock back and forth and begin singing to Shirley. "Silent night—Holy night—All is calm—All is bright..."

I fall asleep in the dark with Christmas lights glowing in my head, arms overflowing with love.

~ THE WEEK AFTER ~

Following that dream-come-true Christmas, questions about Santa still linger. Where did all those gifts come from, if not Santa? I quickly set the questions aside. There's another whole year to think about that subject again.

It's Christmas vacation week. Games have all been played, books read. I'm ready to do something new, which leads me to search in Mama's bottom dresser drawer, where she keeps her papers and letters. I make sure Mama's in the basement doing the wash before opening the drawer.

I'm looking for those writings she sold to the movies that were made into shorts. I want to find out how it's done, because I think I could write some movie shorts. I'm anxious to try writing something new. I want to show them to Mama, but only after they're done.

Then I see it. Tucked away in the drawer corner is a small green book. I pick it up. I've never seen this book before. On the cover, printed in gold letters, is "Christmas Club Savings Account," Underneath, it says "Manitowoc Savings Bank."

Slowly, I open the book. There, neatly printed in Mama's handwriting, are $3 deposits for each week, beginning in January 1935, ending in December 1935, when all the money was taken out.

Suddenly it becomes clear, as if the last piece of the jigsaw puzzle was just put into place. Mama—her working every Friday, depositing her money—that's where it went—into "The Christmas Club Savings Account"!

No one told me, no one had to—the evidence is right here in front of me.

I quickly return the book to its hiding place and discontinue my search for the movie shorts. However, during that short span of time, something altered within me. I stepped over a line, and I can no longer return to where I was before I opened that drawer.

The next Friday, as I watch Mama come in the kitchen door, wearing her shabby coat and stockings with holes in the knees, she appears different to me. It's as if I can see past her outer appearance, view deeper inside.

In the same moment, I recall the day I went cleaning with Mama, the day she told me her sad Christmas story, saying afterward, "I made up my mind then, if ever I had children, I'd make sure they had a wonderful Christmas—no matter what. To make up for the ones I never had."

A huge surge of love comes over me. I run to Mama and give her a big hug. Surprised, she hugs me back real hard. I want to stay there, have her keep holding me as long as possible.

My heart's so happy.

Our Christmases have been wonderful because of Mama, not Santa. Mama works each Friday to put money into the Christmas Club—for us!

From then on, the house is still cold on Fridays, and the meals just as scanty, but the resentment's no longer there.

I feel a secret joy when Mama walks in the door, because I know now why she leaves us and goes to her cleaning job. Sometimes, just knowing the ending can make you happy in an extraordinary way.

AUTHOR'S NOTES
January 2014

Snow is gently falling outside my office window. Falling snowflakes stir Christmas memories as if a snow globe were being shaken, and tiny scenes emerge from within the clouded mists.

While writing this memoir, a gentle shake of words and the past came alive, with remembered scenes, forgotten events—and Mama.

I felt the need to write about this historic era that is gradually disappearing. Few writers are left to personally recall what it was like to be a young girl during the Great Depression. I chose to write about one year which remains especially fresh in my memory.

Progressing from childhood to girlhood, and learning to read and write, deeply affected my daily life and views of the outside world. Diligently, I wrote down numerous thoughts, certain happenings, and how I felt about them to preserve them in pencil for some future use. Maybe that's why the words transferred so easily from my mind to my computer, as if those penciled writings were lying in wait, ready to re-surface once more.

Thoughts from today kept intermingling with episodes of the past. So I'm including a few in this epilogue.

GYPSIES: That indelible encounter with a real live Gypsy still remains a colorful event. Every time I see a brightly feathered parrot, I recall that meeting—and the stories never told. If only I had stayed in that room a bit longer.

There are only so many doors opened to us in our lifetime. If we resist the invitation because we're not sure what might be on the other side, we lose those one-time opportunities to add to life's unexpected adventures. Age sometimes makes one more daring, knowing there aren't that many more doors to open.

MAMA'S CHRISTMAS STORY: This story never leaves my heart, returning each Christmas. I did have children, and their Christmases have always been special, even when times were poor, continuing my mother's tradition of making Christmases wonderful for her children, to make up for the ones she never had.

GUITARS and FLOWERS: After that memorable operetta, I never became a flower again. But giant orange poppies overflow in my summer garden these days. Watching them sway in the breeze, a magic feeling sometimes overtakes me, and I see fairy dust sprinkling about them.

I recall my daughter taking ballet lessons. I made sure she kept her ballet dress. That summer, watching her dance with her friends, she looked like a fairy princess in her frayed pink ballet costume. Tears fell freely as the past resurged.

MAY PROCESSIONS: Churches no longer hold May processions. But I still have a Mary altar in my home—a small statue of the Blessed Virgin, and I place fresh flowers there in May. Throughout the month, May hymns subtly surface as I do my housework or drive along in my car. Sometimes, I find myself singing them silently while wandering the aisles of the supermarket, a warm smile spreading across my face.

I especially chose a day in May for my wedding, asking the St. Boniface children's choir to sing the May hymns I remembered. As I proceeded down the aisle in my lovely dream gown, carrying a bouquet of fragrant sweet peas, in the very same church of my childhood, ethereal joy surrounded me and the whole building. The two May events, one past, one present, merged into a double exposure of time, both recorded in my picture album of life.

EASTER: Easter observances have vastly changed. Few businesses commemorate Good Friday or honor the solemnity of the other Holy Week days any more. But churches still do. I go to services during Holy Week, following a ritual established in my heart many years ago. It's not easy to break traditions that have been embedded, molded into one's life from your very beginnings.

I still color eggs, set out Easter baskets, bake the traditional ham, and have family gather around the decorated table. As we celebrate, connections to past Easter mornings impose their faint presence in fading colors and remembrances.

HOUSECLEANING: I don't follow the spring house cleaning ritual anymore. A vacuum cleaner accomplishes the tedious tasks once tackled during each year's house cleaning. A washer and dryer make it unnecessary to hang clothing or furnishings outside on clotheslines. But I never get that glorious feeling of a house that is completely clean all at one time.

MEMORIAL DAY: Many more soldiers have died since that long ago Memorial Day. Also many more wars have been fought—World War II, The Korean War, Vietnam, The Cold War, Persian Gulf, Iraq, Afghanistan. Who knows how many more will follow.

I remember each of these wars on Memorial Day, mostly because I lived through each. Though far away from the fighting, newspapers, radio, movie news, filled in the horrific accounts. Now, TV and the internet show all that is happening in those war-torn places in detail. I still keep soldiers in an honored place in my heart, remembering them as brave men and women who have sacrificed so much for others.

All wars are sad and nobody really wants them. I remember World War II, which was hailed as "the war to end all wars." Maybe there really is no such war, as it seems there's always war going on someplace in the world. Peace is never guaranteed, which makes the intervals in between times to truly treasure.

LAST DAY OF SCHOOL: Children coming home from school on the last day, whether from kindergarten, grade school, high school or college, denotes the end of a certain segment of their lives, and ours. Once school doors close, worlds of opportunities open, with new choices of which door to enter next. Home still maintains an Open Door Policy for entrance or exit.

SUMMER: Summers seem to go by much faster today, when they used to stretch out into long paths of endless episodes of overlapping sunshine and play. Time is elusive—it never stands still.

Temperature forecasts now tell us what to expect, even before the days happen. Before, it didn't matter whether it was going to be hot or cold, there was no way to change it anyhow. Now if one feels uncomfortable, turn on the heat or air conditioner. On really hot days, I sometimes keep the air conditioning off and wallow in the heat, trying to remember how it was during those long hot summers, with no escape. We just lived through it. Changes in weather and shifts in temperature were all part of accepted daily living.

Yes, everything is different today. Except when you look up into the night skies, the same stars are shining, and the moon still beams brightly. An awesome wonder overtakes me when looking up into the endless eternity that has been there forever.

Yet, somewhere within that captivating view, seeps the tarnish of knowing that space rockets have invaded this formerly pristine landscape. Satellites now circle invisibly within that expansive night sky. The moon has lost its ancient mystery, because man has been up there, marring its gleaming terrain with earthly footprints. Nothing, not even the skies, remains unaltered.

How can we retain our memories of long ago nights? It is possible. Some nights I look up into the sky and visually transport myself back in time, recapture a short glimpse of the past that never changes. It's still there, if you can let loose what holds you to the earth, and let yourself soar upward past human visibility into the vast unknown.

SUMMER STORMS: I'm still afraid of storms. This feeling of helplessness still takes over. To me, the worst is being on a plane during a storm. The other—telling children with mock certainty, "Oh, there's nothing to be afraid of."

We each have our own response to storms. I still pray, during storms. I will not use the computer, and can't concentrate on TV programs, so I turn them off. I stay clear of windows. All the while, I tell myself: "this too shall end." That's my present mantra, one I can use for any terrifying moments. "Yes, this too shall pass."

FOURTH OF JULY: This holiday is wholly different today. Firecrackers have mostly been outlawed. Cities provide their own fireworks, with gala extravaganzas exploding into the night skies. It's become traditional to go with family to "ooh" and "aah" as we watch the spectacular showcases in the heavens, sitting on blankets in the grass.

There's something about fireworks that instills awe from one generation to the next. My own tremors still quiver in an undertow of remembrance, but since my children always looked forward to all events of the day, including the loud and colorful closure, I tried not to pass on my fears, instead joining in their fun.

Kids still decorate bikes and buggies, and march in parades. Flags still fly from homes. It's a grand day for family and neighborhood get-togethers.

It's also the one day that cannot change, or be moved to a more convenient Monday—because it always has to be on the Fourth! Hooray for the traditionalists, those who hang onto certain days for holidays and continue celebrating them year after year.

PICNICS and FISHING: There are no Ten Cent places anymore. They've disappeared, gone the way of the Depression. Ten Cent dime stores have also vanished. These things cost so little, but gave back so much.

I still enjoy picnics. We no longer sit around on a blanket on the grass, but instead have an array of picnic furniture. I miss that touch with the earth, the grassroots approach, eating simple food with those we love, as we did on the grounds of the Ten Cent place, overlooking the river.

UNCLE STEVEN'S FARM: Visits back home with my own children generally included a trip to Uncle Steven's farm. My children looked forward to those visits, and I relived parts of the past as we walked down the same cow paths and fished in the same river as we did when I was a kid. Uncle Steven still wore a straw hat, still smoked his corncob pipe, and laughed even more, if a bit slower. It was like everything at the farm had gone into slow motion.

My dad retired from the factory job he later got and mellowed in many ways. But even retired, he couldn't stop working. He was always puttering with something. He and Mama kept a weedless garden, working on it daily. Mama still canned, out of habit, for a family that was no longer there. They're both gone now...

Uncle Steven and Auntie Ellen are gone, too. They didn't lose their farm like Mama and Daddy predicted. They sold it for quite a profit, as farmland became more valuable, even "weedy, worthless" farmland. After, they spent their days in a small nearby town, in a modern house with indoor plumbing, watching TV, playing cards, fishing. Their numerous grandchildren visited them. I got a Christmas card and birthday card from them every year, the handwriting progressively getting shakier.

Sometimes, on a summery day, when I'm sitting outside doing nothing, I half-expect my father to interrupt my non-productive solitude. Then other feelings surface, from days on Uncle Steven's farm, which were tempered with peaceful pauses. I'm grateful for those summer vacations, and the opportunity to view how another family made use of their time.

THE WORST VACATION: Mama never made me go back to that farm again. But many letters traveled back and forth. Sometimes I saw the Senator's picture in the local paper, and quickly turned the page, not wanting to remember his hollering or those frightening experiences at the farm.

I buried those memories as deep as possible, along with memories of other troubling times. Still, they rise briefly, kindling forgotten fears.

Years later, I did go to the old lady's funeral, with Mama and others in our family. I quickly looked at the old lady in her casket. She didn't look mean anymore. She even appeared rather peaceful. Yet, she still wasn't smiling.

BEAN PICKING: Periodically, I go back to my hometown and drive past the house where I once lived, noting the backyard, how small it seems. So bare. Lifeless. The flowering lilacs, plants, bushes, and sand box are gone. It looks as if no one lives there but I can readily visualize each room, as if I'm still living there.

Within moments, the yard fills up with images of all the children who once gathered there, who made the place vibrate all summer long. The activities that took place in that backyard quickly flash by. Even sounds and forgotten voices are resurrected.

I drive the roads on the outskirts of the city, where rows of green beans once flourished. They are no longer there. All the fields around Manitowoc have been subdivided into smaller lots, now filled with houses, garages, sidewalks, and curbs. There's no evidence at all that farms were ever there.

I've heard no one goes bean picking anymore, not since the bean-picking machine was invented. Canneries have moved elsewhere also.

When going out to dinner, even now, if green beans arrive on my plate unannounced, I leave them untouched. I don't even care to taste them, possibly still harboring a subconscious overfill of green beans from those days in the bean fields.

THE CHILDREN OF SIN: There are no more freaks at the carnivals anymore. They've been outlawed, and rightly so. Still, people remain curious about "freaks of nature." The only way to view them now is by seeing them in movies, or in photos in books. It's not the same as the slap-in-the-face shock of seeing them in person, catching the indiscernible looks in their eyes, observing their deformities up close.

What happened to the "Children of Sin"? That question flickers through my mind briefly each time I go to a carnival or fair and walk past the colorful canvases displaying oversized, exaggerated paintings of sideshow features. It's then that *"See them alive!—The Children of Sin!"* echoes in my mind, and the torment of that brief encounter so many years ago tugs at my memory. The pleading voice saying *"Help me"* still haunts me.

The question remains: Did the "Children of Sin" really have six-year-old mentalities in adult bodies, or were they adults deliberately maintained as six year olds? And—whatever happened to them?

NINE O'CLOCK MAMIE: It wasn't till I was an adult that all the emotional pieces of Nine O'Clock Mamie's life fit together, leaving many empty spaces, too late to fill them in. The house was re-sided with brownish fake slate. Her jungle was uprooted, and grass planted instead. But when I pass by, the house remains locked in the past, and I recall the scary image of how it was when Mamie lived there, when my childhood imagination made me believe there were all kinds of horrors crowded inside.

Maybe there were horrors within, but not the kind witches kept, only those which anguished, emotionally disturbed people lock up within themselves, trying to shield their lives from further disquieting encounters, which lay in wait in that frightening world outside.

POEMS and POOR HOUSES: I wasn't aware at the time why the poem "Over the Hill to the Poor House" affected so many in the show's audience, making them cry. I didn't realize many were on the verge of going to the poor house themselves. It was a time when most families were just a few steps away from that possibility, with nowhere else to turn.

Since then, I've learned that a popular silent movie was made about the poem, and later a talking movie. Will Carleton, the author, who wrote the piece after the Civil War, became quite famous, as did the phrase "Over the hill to the poor house," resounding over and over in many places. The poem also became a catalyst for promoting Social Security, which was put into effect in 1935. The group that opposed Social Security, The Townsend Plan, sent out 30 million postcards to promote their own pension agenda. Two photos were side by side on the card. One showed an old couple trudging up the road in a winter storm, with the caption: "Over the Hill to the Poor House."

The other, titled "Comfort in Old Age" pictured the same couple in front of a cozy fire. Ironically, when the public saw these two choices for old age, this contrasting depiction helped pass the New Deal Social Security Act.

Of course, the average life span in 1935 was about 55 years of age, so the age for Social Security to begin payments was set at 65. People figured there might not be too many left by that age to collect.

They don't have poor houses anymore. But we still have the poor.

THANKSGIVING: That year was the only Thanksgiving I spent away from home for a long, long time. Even after I moved to another city, I always tried as hard as I could to get back home to be with family for that one special day. Our family has continued the Thanksgiving tradition of gathering around the dining table with relatives, and also strangers who have nowhere else to go that day.

My children brought boyfriends and girlfriends to our abundant table. When they went off to college, they'd bring back students who were far away from home. Foreign students at the medical college my son attended later were always invited to an American Thanksgiving. We learned much in the exchange. I invited colleagues from work who didn't have families, not wanting anyone to be alone on that day. And somehow, there was always enough turkey to go around.

After the event at Grandma's, Mama continued making her fruit salad, passing on the recipe to Catherine, who also guarded it, but continued bringing the salad each year. Finally, she gave each of us a copy of the recipe. But it never tasted right. I think she deliberately left out some key ingredients.

After my marriage, our dining table, with expanding boards and inherited Havilland china, standing under the heirloom crystal chandelier, became the Thanksgiving center for close and distant relatives, though no one came from the farm anymore.

Catherine passed on, and her husband, Ralph, continued as a guest at our dining table. Then it was grandchildren, with cameras flashing, taking photos and videos.

Each year, my children made decorated place cards to help ease seating congestion. The cards were kept in a sterling silver box, with new cards added each year and old ones falling to the bottom, but never thrown away.

Reminders of faces around our dining table years ago reside in that box. Just reading their names revives images of previous gatherings. All are remembered, as we say our Thanksgiving prayer—for our family, our country, and the blessings the good Lord has bestowed on each of us.

It's still a special holiday. There's no decorating, no gifts, only the expectation of meeting dear ones again and giving thanks as a group. And eating turkey. What better reason to gather?

But I relive that one Thanksgiving at Grandma's each year. As I view the bare bones on the family platter at the end of the evening, that day returns, reviving the pain of being at Grandma's table on a day I was never thankful for.

296

WINTER: I never did learn how Mama and Daddy made the mortgage payment that month; yet somehow, they did. Catherine later said Grandpa finally came to the rescue, lending money from savings he miserly hoarded. Another time, she said Dr. Mack was the one who advanced Mama the money.

I never asked Mama about the mortgage; she was never very open about money matters. At the time, no one wanted others to know their financial status. Money and wages were guarded secrets.

Till both of their deaths, I never knew the amount in Mama or Daddy's bank accounts, only that they remained frugal even after the Depression, when it was no longer demanded. Debt was to be avoided. Paying cash was the only way to purchase something. They never even moved on to using credit cards. Their final net worth however, was proof that they accumulated much more money than they ever spent.

I still carry the Depression mantra of "saving for a rainy day," making sure you don't spend everything, always keeping something in reserve for the uncertain future. I also inherited the tradition (an exception to the rainy day rule) that one should always make sure to spend enough—whatever it takes—to make Christmas a grand and glorious day, even if it means struggling to pay the bills later.

One-time celebrations, be it weddings, graduations, or Christmas, somehow crystallize into the highlights of life, and are always worth the extra cost in time and money. Each is rewarded with priceless memories—luxuries that enrich the spirit.

SANTA: I'm not sure exactly when I did stop believing in Santa, but it wasn't that year. When the time did come, I was most reluctant to part with a belief that was so ingrained and looked forward to each year. To admit that a person who made magical dreams come true was just made up, and not real, was most difficult and heart-wrenching. The only compensation was that now I could be part of passing on this wonderful myth to the younger children. Being in on the secret helped ease my reluctance to move over to the other side.

But in my heart, I never stopped believing.

Even today, Santa brings special joy whenever I see him. He still spreads a magical mist over the whole Christmas season. It doesn't matter whether he's real or not, it's what he stands for that lives on. That's what I believe, and always will.

THE WEEK BEFORE: The "week" before Christmas? Well, these days it has morphed into the "months" before Christmas, pouncing about at a hectic pace. Generally the hubbub begins pre-Thanksgiving, spreading outward till after the New Year.

Decorations that used to be put up the week before are now hurriedly displayed weeks ahead, and extinguished shortly thereafter. In previous years, decorations were generally harbored within homes, their brightness shining out—a welcoming in. Today, so much ornamentation has moved outside. Yards overflow with Christmas displays, as if to exhibit publicly each home's contribution to the event, a community sharing of individual expression.

Despite debates about what the season should be called, it's rightly a "Holiday Season." A season that encompasses all the celebrations and family interchanges that take place within that expansive and inclusive time frame, with Christmas serving as the centerpiece, the gathering wreath for all.

CHRISTMAS: Occasionally I flip through old photos, viewing captured Christmas mornings of the past, the decorated tree glittering in the backgrounds. It makes a cameo each year, from the birth of our first child to the present. Christmas memories embossed in each photo.

Thinking back, I still wonder how my parents could have set out numerous toys, put up the natural tree in its wiggly wooden stand, strung all the lights, hung ornaments and tinsel, gone to Midnight Mass, then been cheerfully awake the next morning. Another one of the miracles of Christmas?

Midnight Mass (not always held at midnight anymore) is still a spirit-filled observance for me, flooding my heart with the significance of the birth of Jesus, amidst surroundings that mirror the message. The heavenly carols never lose their luster no matter how many times I've heard them before.

Sometimes it seems as if mass hysteria hits the country during Christmas time. One last hurrah before the year fades into anonymity. But there's never been another celebration like it—a season that sings out joyously, "God bless us, everyone!" And it does.

My Shirley Temple doll still resides on a shelf in my home. She's somewhat worn, with a few cracks in her face, and matted blond curls—but the dimples remain, and the smile never left.

I didn't realize upon opening the box that she wasn't a real Shirley Temple doll, only one of the imitations sold at that time. It didn't matter—she was real to me then, and still is. When I look at her now, and touch the threads in the dress Mama made for her, Mama's love reaches out, preserved in every tiny stitch. Mama's presence lingers in so many things.

ACKNOWLEDGMENTS

There are many to thank for their help in creating this memoir. My dear author friend, Sara Rath, read and critiqued the first final. And thanks to Margot Atwell for her valuable editing finesse. Elizabeth Ridley, Michelle Cozzens, and members of the Byliners writers group were also most helpful. My daughters, Suzanne Helgesen and Linda Bollow, son-in-law Gary Park, son Frederic, and my husband Bill, added unique comments, special encouragement, and help whenever needed. There are also family members, living and not living, who shared their special memories via various means. And to Mama, who instilled a love for Christmases that still glows and continues today.